# MASTER
# SERMONS
# THROUGH THE AGES

# MASTER
# SERMONS
# through the ages

*selected*
*and edited by*

WILLIAM ALAN SADLER, JR.

HARPER & ROW, PUBLISHERS
*New York, Evanston, and London*

FIRST EDITION

A—N

LIBRARY OF CONGRESS CATALOG CARD NUMBER: 63-7608

*To my parents*

# Contents

# Introduction

THE SERMONS OF THIS COLLECTION are representative of great Christian preaching through the ages. The historical reach extends from the fourth century into the twentieth; the geographical area ranges from Asia Minor to the United States. Several of the preachers enjoyed the privilege of living in a Church that was more visibly and fully one than we know today; the majority of them, however, represent traditions as diverse as the backgrounds against which the sermons were preached and the languages in which they were delivered. There are in these sermons vast differences of style and approach; furthermore, the interests and emphases manifested by these sermons indicate genuine individuality as well as divergence of traditions. Undoubtedly some of these preachers would find it embarrassing to be housed together with certain of the others. Yet, in spite of the extensive range and the patent differences, it is all the more remarkable that there is an underlying similarity, which gives notable witness to a shared faith. To find a unity of this kind is in itself encouraging in our fragmented world that is ministered to by a broken and disjointed Church. These sermons are indisputably Christian, not only because the preachers shared a common membership in the Church of Christ, no matter how divided visibly, but also because they give a common witness to the present and active reality of God, who has made himself known decisively in Jesus Christ. Not all of these sermons are great in the sense of being historically significant or stylistically elegant; but they were all preached by distinguished and dedicated Christians, who were lights to their generations and bearers of the living truth of Christ as this was known to them. In our generation, which has shown new interest in preaching and is recovering a sense of the importance of it, this collection of sermons may by example help throw some light on what constitutes authentic Christian preaching.

As the diversity of styles and subject matter of these sermons would indicate, it is neither the form nor the content which is decisive for a Christian sermon. There is something deeper, something which goes beyond definite words and a way of putting them together. These sermons do not suggest that a genuinely Christian sermon is primarily a retelling of the same old story. The sermon differs with the man. This does not mean that the essential factors are subjective, at least not in the pejorative sense in which that term is often used. What strikes us about these sermons is the way in which they communicate truth to the hearers, and this implies an understanding of the character of the truth to be imparted. The task of the preacher, after all, is to set forth the truth in a convincing way; and it is the truthfulness of a sermon which makes it outstanding and memorable. Phillips Brooks said that preaching is the communication of truth through personality; this states succinctly an insight that applies to true preaching and hence to these sermons. They show a definite understanding by each preacher of the character of truth, the Truth, and exhibit a distinct way of telling it.

What is perhaps most notable about the large majority of these sermons (it is less pronounced but still there in a few of them) is the firm conviction on the part of the preacher that he has seen a great light, has caught hold of the truth—and he desires passionately to share it with his hearers. Without conviction, these sermons would have been essays in religion which might or might not have been of interest to the listener. Sermons are not talks about religion; they are attestations of religious men. As Prof. John Knox has pointed out, what makes a sermon good is the man*; these sermons are expressions of conviction by men who were dedicated in worship and service to the God who had laid personal claim to their lives. They issued from men of personal stature; and their preaching testified to the fact that the indispensable ingredient in their own spiritual growth was not fortune nor individual capacity but grace. These were men who, in the words of Newman,

* *The Integrity of Preaching* (Nashville: Abingdon Press, 1957), pp. 59–63.

had responded to the "calls of grace." The element of conviction points to the inclusive reality of the man's commitment and of the "object" of that commitment. The truth which these men have endeavored to impart and which has inspired their conviction is one which has grasped the lives of each of them and compelled them to attest it. As an earlier master of preaching put it, "Woe to me if I do not preach the gospel!"*

Another striking feature in preaching which also suggests something about the nature of the truth to be imparted is an awareness of the hearers. One of the remarkable characteristics of these sermons is relevance, not only to the generations which first heard them but to our own as well. These men knew that they had something important to say. They had a message for a congregation as a community, for the individual as a whole person, for human beings who were thirsty for the truth that is the "water of life." Such truth, they knew, is not something about which one can be indifferent, once it has grasped one. It is of deep concern, vitally important both to the man who preaches and to his listeners, even if the latter do not consciously recognize it. The preacher's task is to help the hearer recognize his need and the divine answer to that need. The truth these men sought to impart was relevant truth, relevant to the hearer as a person and not conceived of abstractly as a mind or soul. If the Word of God is really the Word of Life, then it must be relevant. These sermons are that, and consequently are not dull. A dull sermon is one which misrepresents the truth and which stifles the human spirit rather than stimulating it; in that sense it is a betrayal of the Word of Life who has commissioned the preacher to represent him.

In that they impart truth, these sermons are obviously forms of instruction. Some are more didactic than others, but there is not one of them which lacks a teaching element. It would be confusing to try to isolate abstractly proclamation from teaching, or evangelical sermons from doctrinal and ethical ones, as has been suggested by some theories about Christian homiletics. As expressions of conviction, these sermons are truly proclamations and incite commitment. They are undeniably

* St. Paul, I Cor. 9:16.

teaching as well. Yet they teach truth which is relevant to human life as essentially personal. There is a difference between academic instruction and the instruction of genuine preaching as indicated by these sermons, a difference which these preachers, many of whom were academic teachers as well, appreciated even if they did not articulate their awareness of it. Their instruction does not have the character of a catechism, of drumming home facts to be memorized for occasional repetition at appropriate times, nor is it merely the telling or retelling of a story about a remote event. The truth of these sermons stems from, participates in, and extends the revelatory event in which Christianity has its origin. What is imparted is not truth which is primarily conceptual, something reasonably verifiable by controlled experimentation; these sermons show that the truth which matters to the recovery of humanity and the fullness of human living is existential truth. The preachers of these sermons were not concerned in the pulpit mainly to convince their hearers that certain propositions about the nature of some specified part of reality were in conformity with the respective facts. Nor did they use the methods of deduction or induction to persuade. There is yet another mode of truth, one which is used in these sermons and in all genuine preaching, and that is the mode of witness which attests to the living truth, the truth which is spirit.

To grasp better the nature of such truth, the image of light is helpful. These men have "seen" something; that something has been illumined for them. Others have either lived and persisted in darkness, or they have forgotten and ignored what they, too, had seen. The sermon is a lantern, a beacon of truth, which shines in the darkness, revealing what is present but unrecognized, within reach though hidden from sight. The main purpose of light is not to expose darkness. The truly great preachers are not accusers of men, who dwell upon the sinfulness of their hearers; they seek rather to show forth something wonderful to them and to encourage their congregations to participate in it through understanding, commitment, and fellowship, to respond to the gifts and the demands of the gospel. The preachers here have pointed to, in the hope of pointing out, the renewing power of the divine presence. For those who have ears to hear, such preaching is revelatory; the truth imparted in Christian preaching is in fact revelation. It is revelation of realities graceful, natural, and sinful; equally important, these sermons reveal, in addition to facts, grand possibilities and opportunities for the future made possible by the presence of grace. These men were gifted with an awareness of human beings that helped them interpret the perplexing and mysterious phenomenon of man in such a way as to behold and then to show to others a reality of a future of meaning and potential fulfillment. The basis of their vision and testimony is the light of God's loving and commanding presence that is obscured by finitude and sin.

The truth imparted by witness does not consist in abstract truths; it is existential, or better, personal truth. These preachers obviously knew that such truth could not be shown in the same way as a scientist might indicate a reaction-pattern by a formula. The light of truth cannot be captured and contained; it is not a thing which the preachers possessed as an object of their own. It is a reality in which they had been allowed to participate. They bore witness to that reality so that others might see it for themselves, might find the Truth to be their truth. Such witnessing thus molded the nature of their instruction, which was not to point out a detached object but to show by sharing.

Preaching cannot occur in a vacuum. It is communication of truth which is shared; in this sense it can be understood how genuine Christian preaching creates community or recreates it as the case may be. Thus it is a liturgical event, an action which achieves community participation in addition to expressing the meanings and purpose of that community. These preachers have let the divine light shine forth so as to illumine, penetrate, and bind together in unity those who have listened responsively. It is clear also from these sermons that they have built windows into themselves. There is an element of self-exposure in these sermons, though admittedly it is more obvious in some than in others. That is not to say that a preacher is an exhibitionist; but to communicate the living truth of the gospel he has necessarily been a personal participant in it. This truth is shown by sharing, and it is a sharing of what is deeply and personally true for the man who bears good witness. Surely it is because the preacher shares his intimate and most personal experiences with his hearers, revealing his own relationship with God, that his hearers are brought to a decision or commitment, which is an indication that the Word was truly preached and truly received.

These sermons are at once doctrinal, evangelical, and liturgical in the broad senses of these terms; such is the nature of their testimonies. There is another aspect to the truth imparted, which is to be understood primarily in terms of its effects. In this collection of sermons there is an implicit if not explicit understanding of a sermon as a sacrament. That is, it is not only something said and done but something "worked." In the medieval view of preaching, the sermon was primarily a preparation for the traditional sacraments of the Church; it was the genius of the Reformers to realize that preaching, too, imparted the Bread of Life. As they expressed it, "the preaching of the Word of God is the Word of God." Even those preachers in this collection who would not have consciously so expressed their understanding of preaching, nevertheless, by the character of their witness, have shown by implication the sacramental nature of preaching; the sermons show their appreciation of the importance and mystery of preaching. Those familiar with the major themes and thoughts which came from the pens of these preachers in their other writings will recognize, also, that their sermon preparations involved not just a few hours but their whole lives. Their intelligence, insight, scholarship, and existential learning were dedicated toward the goal of being faithful and persuasive witnesses to that reality which had claimed their total allegiance. It is of course impossible to judge the effect of these or any sermons, yet one intuitively senses the sacramental character of the original event, whereby these outward and visible signs communicated to the respective congregations inward and spiritual grace. Certainly one of the effects of great preaching is that we who have been privileged to receive it have sensed deeply that the preacher has "shown us things we never saw before" or has revealed to us dimensions and powers of which we have been negligent and has done so in a way that has enabled them to touch the core of our lives and to restore and renew us for the real adventure of living that is made possible by the redeeming action of Christ and the recreating power of his Spirit. Genuine Christian preaching changes us, for it is the sacrament of truth.

Another characteristic of Christian preaching is also to be noted in this collection. One of the striking features of the majority of these sermons is the profound appreciation the preacher shows for some aspect of God's handiwork or his Being. There are parts of these sermons which aim not to proclaim or instruct but which are basically expressions of praise. Almost the entire sermon by St. Thomas Aquinas is a paean; a similar type of literature is to be found throughout this collection, ranging from the exceptionally eloquent rejoicing over the mystery of the created order as by Morrison and Brooks to the exulting over the person of Christ by Hopkins, from Donne's appraisal of the joy of heaven to Schleiermacher's expressed appreciation of the new character of Christian life, to mention but a few of the outstanding examples. The laudatory element is not restricted to denomination, century, or culture. It seems, in fact, to be a natural and integral part of a great Christian sermon. In imparting the truth a sermon is not only revelatory, relevant, liturgical, personal, and sacramental; there is the added fact that preaching is praise.

One of the lessons that a collection such as this teaches is that great Christian preaching for our day and age will not be achieved by copying the great preachers of another time. These sermons show indisputably that the preachers were men of their respective generations, sharing both the privileges and advantages as well as the limitations and biases of the cultures in which they took their origin and to which they directed their messages. They preached with relevance not only because they were enabled by grace to perceive and then to reveal the Word of Life, but because they were also aware of, and sensitive to, the particular needs, problems, and aspirations of their generations. Thus they became grand interpreters of the gospel truth to their people. If preachers today will perform a similar service, they cannot copy the masters, though they should certainly imitate their ways in terms of full response to the calls of grace and the procuring of knowledge about their world and fellow men.

The biblical image of a true preacher, one which eminently suits the men represented in this collection, is that of a watchman. "Son of man, I have made you a watchman for the house of Israel" (Ezek. 3:17). He is commissioned to assume a vantage point which gives him a perspective that others frequently have not the time nor the opportunity to acquire. The watchman lives part of his time on the top of the city wall or in a tower, overlooking the total situation, using his powers to scan the horizon, to perceive the structures and dynamics of the present so as to understand and interpret it and also to discern, if possible, what seems to be coming. In this sense his role is the opposite of an applied scientist who presses near to his material to analyze it upon closer inspection. The watchman must for a time isolate himself and achieve distance, which is for the purpose of seeing beyond the complexities of the immediate present, to discover the determinative forces at work in the crowd whose members are too close to those forces for accurate interpretation and evaluation. The preacher's studies, prayers, and reflections give him the perspective of the man in the watchtower. However, if the man in the tower does not come down and speak to the people intelligibly and persuasively, he will be of no use to them. He must help them understand and share in his vision, and thereby to direct their actions accordingly.

Consequently the man of the tower who is to be a true witness must also be close to his people; if not, he may do more harm than good, for the people may, by ignoring him, forget that there is another perspective and more to reality than that which is only immediately recognizable in the active ways of life. The other danger to the watchman's task is that he will become so immersed in the people's activities as to forget to climb into his tower. Neither way can he perform the function set for him. These great preachers of the past were notable examples of watchmen, both in the sense of having an acute vision of reality and also in being close to their people so as to communicate effectively the relevance and intimate meaning of their visions of true life. As in their generations, so in ours the people cry: "Watchman, what of the night?" (Isa. 21:11.) And it is still the duty of a good and faithful servant to tell of the morning and of the night, that the people in the lanes, fields, and towns may be comforted or alarmed, as the situation demands, so that they may direct their ways according to the Lord.

Something remains to be said about this collection itself. This is best done by explaining how it started. In the fall of 1960 an experiment was begun at St. Thomas' Church, Manhattan. Each Monday noon for the regular service, sermons from past masters of the pulpit were read. It was felt that the worshipers should have an opportunity to discover some of the homiletic treasures which are usually reserved for theological libraries and the clergyman's bookshelf. Furthermore, it was realized that sermons are not primarily things which are *written*. Basically they are *events;* they *happen,* and should be *heard*. The services were advertised as occasions in which great sermons would be recreated. Because of the limitation of time, the sermons had to be carefully edited. In some cases this meant that what was presented was only about one-third or one-half of the original. Yet it was discovered that a definite unity could be retained; often the original structure of the sermon became more apparent through a reduction in length. In a few cases, however, the only recourse was to give a rather complete segment of a whole. Nine of the sermons in this collection were used in those services. I have continued to use the criteria of relevance and of time limitation in completing the selection.

Each sermon has been edited, though the words and order remain those of the preacher's. I have tried to imagine how these men themselves might have edited their sermons had they been able to accept the invitation to preach them within a twenty-minute service in the contemporary setting such as is provided by a large Episcopal church on Fifth Avenue in New York City. It should be emphasized that the list of preachers is in no way intended to be inclusive; this selection is merely representative of a vast history of great preaching. That history continues to impart light in our generation; the selection here is but a sample from great lights in former generations. The threefold arrangement of the sermons is a result of three general types into which the sermons naturally fall, and it also indicates the practical relevance these sermons have in a contemporary church year.

The first group has a more general subject matter than the others, which I have chosen to call "The Gifts and Demands of the Gospel."

The next group speaks specifically about Christian nurture in piety and sacramental living. The third group is appropriate to major traditional Christian festivals and seasons. Advent is placed at the end of the year, because the two sermons deal with the traditional theme of "last things" rather than the more popular Advent theme of preparing for Christmas. Most of the sermons from the last group were not preached on or for such occasions, though they are quite appropriate for them; often because they were not prepared specifically for such occasions they provide interesting and unusual approaches and themes for moments which have often, regrettably, witnessed unimaginative and monotonous sermons. If any erroneous impressions of these great men and their sermons have been fostered through the manner of editing, the guilt lies firmly upon me. I hope, however, that these sermons do bear faithful witness to the originals as well as to the men who preached them, and most of all that they will help provide light for our generation as they did in their own.

Full citation of the work in which a sermon first appeared is given in the footnote accompanying each selection. I wish to express my appreciation to the publishers who have kindly given me permission to use sermons from books still protected by copyright.

I want to express my appreciation for the help and encouragement given to me by many people; though I cannot now name them all, there are a few who were especially helpful. I am particularly grateful for the support of the Rev. Sidney Lanier, who shared the responsibility of conducting the experimental preaching services at St. Thomas' Church, and for the suggestions and criticisms so kindly offered by the Revs. Norman Pittenger, Duncan Porteous, and Charles Scott. Dr. Charles L. Wallis has also given me invaluable suggestions. Finally I wish to thank my wife, in print, for typing the manuscript and for giving me her constant support and womanly, practical suggestions to make a more readable, helpful book.

WILLIAM ALAN SADLER, JR.

# MASTER
# SERMONS
# THROUGH THE AGES

# PART ONE

# The

# Gifts

# and

# Demands

# of the

# Gospel

**JOHN WESLEY** (1703–1791) The fifteenth son of an Anglican clergyman and his wife, John was educated at home before going to Oxford, where he resided as a classics scholar until 1735. In 1725, he was made a deacon of the Church of England and the following year, ordained priest. While at Oxford he became leader of the "Holy Club," founded by his brother Charles; the methodical piety and asceticism of the members earned them the derogatory nickname of "methodists." After three frustrating years as a missionary in Georgia, John returned to England in 1738. That same year in London during a prayer meeting of Moravians, whose piety and evangelical fervor had deeply impressed him, he felt his "heart strangely warmed." Shortly after this conversion experience, the evangelical preacher, George Whitefield, who was preaching to the poor and neglected masses, invited Wesley to share this preaching. Wesley began preaching to these people, who often gathered in the field to hear him, with amazing results; the responses were extremely enthusiastic. Unlike Whitefield, Wesley avoided histrionics; he preached in a quiet manner with the style of an Oxford don. Emphasizing conversion, he nevertheless stressed that it should consist of daily growth in God's love rather than be identified with an instantaneous, highly emotional experience. He soon broke with Whitefield—the cause of the break being John Wesley's insistence that the life of conversion and the newly organized Methodist movement had to remain within the Church of England, which it did until shortly after his death.

Wesley remained a high churchman, even though many in his church were suspicious and hostile; if the churches refused to open their doors to him, he preached in the open, and frequently he celebrated the Holy Communion after preaching. Wesley led an unusually active life, which was partially responsible for his unhappy marriage. He was an itinerant preacher averaging annually eight thousand miles on horseback. He organized and directed in detail the flourishing Methodist movement. He wrote and edited many books as well as countless tracts and sermons. His sermon included in this collection was preached to the university in St. Mary's, Oxford, on July 25, 1741, and raised some controversy; John emphasized the need to become a new creature in Christ through personal faith, telling his hearers to be, not almost but altogether Christians.

# The Almost Christian*

*Almost thou persuadest me to be a Christian.* Acts 26:28

And many there are who go thus far: ever since the Christian religion was in the world there have been many in every age and nation who were "almost persuaded to be Christians." But seeing it avails nothing before God to go only thus far, it highly imports us to consider: first, what is implied in being almost; secondly, what, in being altogether a Christian.

Now, in the being almost a Christian is implied first, heathen honesty. No one, I suppose, will make any question of this; especially, since by heathen honesty here I mean not that which is recommended in the writings of their philosophers only, but such as the common heathens expected one of another, and many of them actually practiced. By the rules of this they were taught that they ought not to be unjust; not to take away their neighbor's goods either by robbery or theft; not to oppress the poor, neither to use extortion towards any; not to cheat or overreach either the poor or rich in whatsoever commerce they had with them; to defraud no man of his right; and, if it were possible, to owe no man any thing.

Again, the common heathens allowed that some regard was to be

* From *Sermons on Several Occasions*, Vol. I (New York: Lane and Scott, 1850).

3

paid to truth as well as to justice. Yet again there was a sort of love
and assistance which they expected one from another. They expected
whatever assistance any one could give another without prejudice to
himself.

A second thing implied in the being almost a Christian is the having
a form of godliness, of that godliness which is prescribed in the gospel
of Christ; the having the outside of a real Christian. Accordingly the
almost Christian does nothing which the gospel forbids. He taketh not
the name of God in vain: he blesseth and curseth not: he sweareth not
at all, but his communication is yea, yea; nay, nay. He profanes not
the day of the Lord, nor suffers it to be profaned even by the stranger
that is within his gates. He not only avoids all actual adultery, fornica-
tion, and uncleanness, but every word or look that either directly or
indirectly tends thereto.

He does not willingly wrong, hurt, or grieve any man; but in all
things acts and speaks by that plain rule, "Whatsoever thou wouldest
not he should do unto thee, that do not thou to another." And in doing
good he does not confine himself to cheap and easy offices of kindness,
but labors and suffers for the profit of many, that by all means he may
help some.

He that hath the form of godliness uses also the means of grace;
yea, all of them, and at all opportunities. He constantly frequents the
house of God. More especially when he approaches the table of the
Lord it is not with a light or careless behaviour, but with an air, ges-
ture, and deportment which speak nothing else but "God be merciful
to me a sinner."

To this, if we add the constant use of family prayer by those who
are masters of families, and the setting times apart for private addresses
to God, with a daily seriousness of behaviour; he who uniformly practices this outward religion has the form of godliness. There needs but
one thing more in order to his being almost a Christian, and that is
sincerity.

By sincerity I mean a real, inward principle of religion from whence
these outward actions flow. And, indeed, if we have not this, we have

not heathen honesty. If any man to avoid punishment, to avoid the loss of his friends, or his gain, or his reputation, should not only abstain from doing evil, but also do ever so much good, yea, and use all the means of grace, yet we could not with any propriety say, This man is even almost a Christian. If he has no better principle in his heart, he is only a hypocrite altogether. Sincerity, therefore, is necessarily implied in the being almost a Christian. This is the moving principle, both in his doing good, his abstaining from evil, and his using the ordinances of God.

But here it will probably be inquired, Is it possible, that any man living should go so far as this and nevertheless be only almost a Christian? What more than this can be implied in the being a Christian altogether? I answer, first, that it is possible to go thus far and yet be but almost a Christian, I learn not only from the oracles of God, but also from the sure testimony of experience.

Brethren, great is "my boldness towards you in this behalf." And "forgive me this wrong," if I declare my own folly upon the housetop, for yours and the gospel's sake. Suffer me then to speak freely of myself even as of another man.

I did go thus far for many years, as many of this place can testify; using diligence to eschew all evil, and to have a conscience void of offence; redeeming the time; buying up every opportunity of doing all good to all men; constantly and carefully using all the public and all the private means of grace; endeavoring after a steady seriousness of behaviour, at all times, and in all places; and, God is my record, before whom I stand, doing all this in sincerity; having a real design to serve God; a hearty desire to do his will in all things; to please him, who had called me to "fight the good fight" and to "lay hold on eternal life." Yet my own conscience beareth me witness in the Holy Ghost that all this time I was but almost a Christian.

If it be inquired, What more than this is implied in the being altogether a Christian? I answer, first, the love of God. For thus saith his word, "Thou shalt love the Lord thy God with all thy heart, and with all thy soul, and with all thy mind, and with all thy strength." Such a love of God is this, as engrosses the whole heart, as takes up all the affections, as fills the entire capacity of the soul, and employs the utmost extent of all its faculties. He that thus loves the Lord his God, his spirit continually "rejoiceth in God his Saviour." His delight is in the Lord, his Lord and his All, to whom "in every thing he giveth thanks." "All his desire is unto God and to the remembrance of his name." His heart is ever crying out, "Whom have I in heaven but thee, and there is none upon earth that I desire beside thee." Indeed, what can he desire beside God? Not the world, or the things of the world. For he is "crucified to the world, and the world crucified to him."

The second thing implied in the being altogether a Christian is the love of our neighbor. For thus said our Lord in the following words, "Thou shalt love thy neighbor as thyself." If any man ask, Who is my neighbor? we reply, every man in the world; every child of his, who is the Father of the spirits of all flesh. Nor may we in any wise except our enemies, or the enemies of God and their own souls. But every Christian loveth these also as himself, yea, "as Christ loved us."

There is yet one thing more that may be separately considered, though it cannot actually be separate from the preceding, which is implied in the being altogether a Christian, and that is the ground of all, even faith. Very excellent things are spoken of this throughout the oracles of God. "Every one," saith the beloved disciple, "that believeth is born of God." "To as many as received him, gave he power to become the sons of God, even to them that believe in his name." And "this is the victory that overcometh the world, even our faith." Yea, our Lord himself declares, "He that believeth in the Son hath everlasting life; and cometh not into condemnation, but is passed from death unto life."

But here let no man deceive his own soul. It is diligently to be noted, the faith which bringeth not forth repentance and love and all good works is not that right living faith which is here spoken of, but a dead and devilish one. For, even the devils believe, and yet, for all this faith they be but devils.

"The right and true Christian faith is," to go on in the words of our own church, "not only to believe that Holy Scripture and the articles of our faith are true, but also to have a sure trust and confidence to be saved from everlasting damnation by Christ. It is a sure trust and confidence which a man hath in God, that by the merits of Christ his sins are forgiven, and he reconciled to the favor of God; whereof doth follow a loving heart to obey his commandments."

Now whosoever has this faith which purifies the heart (by the power of God, who dwelleth therein) from pride, anger, desire, from all unrighteousness, from "all filthiness of flesh and spirit"; which fills it with love stronger than death, both to God and to all mankind; love that doth the works of God, glorying to spend and to be spent for all men, and that endureth with joy not only the reproach of Christ, the being mocked, despised, and hated of all men, but whatsoever the wisdom of God permits the malice of men or devils to inflict; whosoever has this faith, thus working by love, is not almost only, but altogether a Christian.

But who are the living witnesses of these things? I beseech you, brethren, as in the presence of that God, before whom "hell and destruction are without a covering," that each of you would ask his own heart, "Am I of that number? Do I so far practice justice, mercy, and truth, as even the rules of heathen honesty require? If so, have I the very outside of a Christian? Do I seriously use all the ordinances of God at all opportunities? And is all this done with a sincere design and desire to please God in all things?"

Are not many of you conscious that you never came thus far; that you have not been even almost a Christian; that you have not come up to the standard of heathen honesty; at least, not to the form of Christian godliness?—much less hath God seen sincerity in you, a real design of pleasing him in all things. You never so much as intended to devote all your words and works, your business, studies, diversions, to his glory. You never even designed or desired that whatsoever you did should be done "in the name of the Lord Jesus," and as such should be a "spiritual sacrifice, acceptable to God through Christ."

But supposing you had, do good designs and good desires make a

Christian? By no means, unless they are brought to good effect. "Hell is paved," saith one, "with good intentions." The great question of all, then, still remains. Is the love of God shed abroad in your heart? Can you cry out, "My God and my All?" Do you desire nothing but him? Are you happy in God? Is he your glory, your delight, your crown of rejoicing? And is this commandment written in your heart, That he who loveth God love his brother also? Do you then love your neighbor as yourself? Do you love every man, even your enemies, even the enemies of God, as your own soul? As Christ loved you? Yea, dost thou believe that Christ loved thee, and gave himself for thee? Hast thou faith in his blood? Believest thou the Lamb of God hath taken away thy sins and cast them as a stone into the depth of the sea? That he hath blotted out the handwriting that was against thee, taking it out of the way, nailing it to his cross? Hast thou indeed redemption through his blood, even the remission of thy sins? And doth his Spirit bear witness with thy spirit that thou art a child of God?

The God and Father of our Lord Jesus Christ, who now standeth in the midst of us, knoweth that if any man die without this faith and this love, good it were for him that he had never been born. "Awake, then, thou that sleepest, and call upon thy God: call in the day when he may be found. Let him not rest till he make his goodness to pass before thee," till he proclaim unto thee the name of the Lord; "the Lord, the Lord God, merciful and gracious, long suffering, and abundant in goodness and truth, keeping mercy for thousands, forgiving iniquity, and transgression, and sin." Let no man persuade thee by vain words to rest short of this prize of thy high calling. But cry unto him day and night, who, "while we were without strength, died for the ungodly," until thou knowest in whom thou hast believed and canst say, "My Lord, and my God!" Remember "always to pray, and not to faint," till thou also canst lift up thy hand unto heaven and declare to him that liveth for ever and ever, "Lord, thou knowest all things, thou knowest that I love thee."

May we all thus experience what it is to be not almost only, but altogether Christians; being justified freely by his grace through the redemption that is in Jesus; knowing we have peace with God through Jesus Christ; rejoicing in hope of the glory of God; and having the love of God shed abroad in our hearts by the Holy Ghost given unto us!

# THOMAS CHALMERS (1780–1847)

After Thomas Chalmers graduated from St. Andrew's University he was ordained to the ministry of the Established Church of Scotland; however, he remained at the university to teach mathematics and chemistry. In 1808, he published his *Inquiry into National Resources*. These facts merely suggest his vast range of interests and competence. He became famous not only as a scientist, but also as an outstanding intellectual defender of Christianity, a pioneer of popular education and of modern methods of poor relief, a remarkable teacher of theology and moral philosophy, and the unrivaled religious orator of Scotland in his day. After seven years of a fruitless ministry, he underwent a change of heart and began to speak out with blazing force. When he went to Tron parish in Glasgow in 1815, his pulpit oratory took the city by storm.

In 1823, after three tiring years in another parish, one that was large but poor, Chalmers took the chair of moral philosophy at St. Andrew's, and in 1828 he became professor of theology at Edinburgh University. Four years later he published an important book on political economy. He was prominent in the movement which led to the disruption of the Established Church; in 1843, he led the formation of the Free Church of Scotland and was elected its first moderator. That same year Chalmers became principal and professor of divinity at this church's New College at Edinburgh, and it was there that he wrote his *Institutes of Theology*.

Not least of his talents was his amazing capacity for sharp, psychological insight; this he used to best advantage in his sermons. Though he was bound to his manuscript and used long sentences, he emphasized one idea in each sermon in brilliant fashion and spoke with such passion that his hearers could not miss his message. Even today his "The Expulsive Power of a New Affection" is one of the most memorable sermons in print. The edited sermon here presented is also one of his best.

# The Restlessness of Human Ambition*

*How say ye to my soul, Flee as a bird to your mountain? . . . O that I had the wings of a dove, that I may fly away and be at rest.* PSALMS 11:1; 55:6

To all those who are conversant in the scenery of external nature, it is evident that an object, to be seen to the greatest advantage, must be placed at a certain distance from the eye of the observer. The poor man's hut, though all within be raggedness and disorder, and all around it be full of the most nauseous and disgusting spectacles—yet if seen at a sufficient distance, may appear a sweet and interesting cottage. That field where the thistle grows, and the face of which is deformed by the wild exuberance of a rank and pernicious vegetation, may delight the eye of a distant spectator by the loveliness of its verdure. All is the effect of distance. It softens the harsh and disgusting features of every object. What is gross and ordinary, it can dress in the most romantic attractions. The country hamlet it can transform into a paradise of beauty, in spite of the abominations that are at every door, and the angry brawlings of the men and the women who occupy it. All that is loathsome or offensive is softened down by the power of distance.

This principle may serve to explain a feeling which some of us may

* From *Sermons and Discourses,* Vol. II (New York: Robert Carter and Brothers, 1854).

have experienced. On a fine day, when the sun threw its unclouded splendors over a whole neighborhood, did we never form a wish that our place could be transferred to some distant and more beautiful part of the landscape? Did the idea never rise in our fancy, that the people who sport on yon sunny bank are happier than ourselves—that we should like to be buried in that distant grove, and forget, for a while, in silence and in solitude, the distractions of the world? In a word, was there no secret aspiration of the soul for another place than what we actually occupied? Instead of resting in a quiet enjoyment of our present situation, did not our wishes wander abroad and around us—and were not we ready to exclaim, with the Psalmist in the text, "O that I had the wings of a dove; for I would fly to yonder mountain, and be at rest"?

But what is of most importance to be observed is, that even when we have reached the mountains, rest is far from us as ever. As we get nearer the wished for spot, the fairy enchantments in which distance had arrayed it, gradually disappear; when we at last arrive at our object, the illusion is entirely dissipated; and we are grieved to find that we have carried the same principle of restlessness and discontent along with us.

Now, what is true of a natural landscape, is also true of that moral landscape, which is presented to the eye of the mind when it contemplates human life, and casts a wide survey over the face of human society. The position which I myself occupy is seen and felt with all its disadvantages. Its vexations come home to my feelings with all the certainty of experience. I see it before mine eyes with a vision so near and intimate as to admit of no coloring, and to preclude the exercise of fancy. It is only in those situations which are without me, where the principle of deception operates, and where the vacancies of an imperfect experience are filled up by the power of imagination, ever ready to summon the fairest forms of pure and unmingled enjoyment.

Am I unlearned? I feel the disgrace of ignorance, and sigh for the name and distinctions of philosophy. Do I stand upon a literary eminence? I feel the vexations of rivalship, and could almost renounce the splendors of my dear-bought reputation for the peace and shelter which insignificance bestows. Am I poor? I riot in fancy upon the gratification of luxury, and think how great I would be, if invested with all the consequence of wealth and of patronage. Am I rich? I sicken at the deceitful splendor which surrounds me, and am at times tempted to think that I would have been happier far if born to a humbler station, had I been trained to the peace and innocence of poverty. Am I immersed in business? I repine at the fatigues of employment; and envy the lot of those who have every hour at their disposal, and can spend all their time in the sweet relaxations of amusement and society.

This, in fact, is the grand principle of human ambition; and it serves to explain both its restlessness and vanity. What is present is seen in all its minuteness; and we overlook not a single article in the train of little drawbacks, and difficulties, and disappointments. What is distant is seen under a broad and general aspect; and the illusions of fancy are substituted in those places which we cannot fill up with the details of actual observation. What is present fills me with disgust. What is distant allures me to enterprise. The perpetual tendency is not to enjoy our actual position, but to get away from it—and not an individual amongst us who does not every day of his life join in the aspiration of the Psalmist, "O that I had the wings of a dove, that I may fly to yonder mountain, and be at rest."

This restless ambition is not peculiar to any one class of society. A court only offers to one's notice a more exalted theater for the play of rivalship and political enterprise. In the bosom of a cottage, we may witness the operation of the same principle, only directed to objects of greater insignificance—and though a place for my girl, or an apprenticeship for my boy, be all that I aspire after, yet an enlightened observer of the human character will perceive in it the same eagerness of competition, the same jealousy, the same malicious attempts to undermine the success of a more likely pretender, the same busy train of passions and anxieties which animate the exertions of him who struggles for precedency in the cabinet, and lifts his ambitious eye to the management of an empire.

This is the universal property of our nature. In the whole circle of our experience, did we ever see a man sit down to the full enjoyment of the present, without a hope or a wish unsatisfied? Did he carry in his mind no reference to futurity—no longing of the soul after some remote or inaccessible object—no day-dream which played its enchantments around him, and which, even when accomplished, left him nothing more than the delirium of a momentary triumph?

This is the true, though the curious, and we had almost said, the farcical picture of human life. Look into the heart which is the seat of feeling, and we there perceive a perpetual tendency to enjoyment, but not enjoyment itself—the cheerfulness of hope, but not the happiness of actual possession. The present is but an instant of time. The moment when we call it our own, it abandons us. It is not the actual sensation which occupies the mind. It is what is to come next. Man lives in futurity. The pleasurable feelings of the moment form almost no part of his happiness. It is not the reality of today which interests his heart. It is the vision of tomorrow. It is the distant object on which fancy has thrown its deceitful splendor. When tomorrow comes, the animating hope is transformed into the dull and insipid reality. As the distant object draws near, it becomes cold, and tasteless, and uninteresting. The only way in which the mind can support itself, is by recurring to some new anticipation. This may give buoyancy for a time—but it will share the fate of all its predecessors, and be the addition of another folly to the wretched train of disappointments that have gone before it.

Where then is that resting place which the Psalmist aspired after? What are we to mean by that mountain, that wilderness, to which he prayed the wings of a dove may convey him, afar from the noise and distractions of the world, and hasten his escape from the windy storm and the tempest? Is there no object in the whole round of human enjoyment, which can give rest to the agitated spirit of man—where he might sit down in the fulness of contentment, after he has reached it, and bid a final adieu to the cares and fatigues of ambition? Is this longing of the mind a principle of his nature, which no gratification can extinguish? Must it condemn him to perpetual agitation, and to the wild impulses of an ambition which is never satisfied?

Man must have an object to look forward to. Without this incitement the mind languishes. It is thrown out of its element; and, in the unnatural suspension of its powers, it feels a dreariness and a discomfort far more insufferable than it ever experienced from the visitations of a real or positive calamity. If such an object is not offered, he will create one for himself. The mere possession of wealth, and of all its enjoyments, will not satisfy him. Possession carries along with it the dullness of certainty; and to escape from this dullness, he will transform it into an uncertainty—he will embark it in a hazardous speculation, or he will stake it at the gaming table; and from no other principle, than that he may exchange the listlessness of possession for the animating sensations of hope and enterprise. It is a paradox in the moral constitution of man; but the experience of every day confirms it —that man follows what he knows to be a delusion, with as much eagerness as if he were assured of its reality.

Now to find fault with man for the pleasure which he derives from the mere excitement of a distant object, would be to find fault with the constitution of his nature. It is not the general principle of his activity which we condemn. It is the direction of that activity to a useless and unprofitable object. The mere happiness of the pursuit does not supersede the choice of the object. The mere pleasure of exertion is not enough to justify every kind of it: we must look forward to the object and the termination, and it is the judicious choice of the object which, even in the estimation of worldly wisdom, forms the great point of distinction betwixt prudence and folly. Now all that we ask of you is, to extend the application of the same principle to a life of religion. Compare the wisdom of the children of light with the wisdom of a blind and worldly generation—the prudence of the Christian who labors for immortality, with the prudence of him who labors for the objects of a vain and perishable ambition. Contrast the littleness of time with the greatness of eternity—and tell us which plays the higher game—he, all whose anxiety is frittered away on the pursuits of a scene that is ever shifting and ever transitory; or he who contemplates the life of man in all its magnitude, who acts upon the wide and comprehensive survey of its interests, and takes into his estimate the mighty roll of innumerable ages.

There is no resting place to be found on this side of death. It is the doctrine of the Bible, and all experience loudly proclaims it.

What meaneth the restlessness of our nature? What meaneth this unceasing activity which longs for exercise and employment, even after every object is gained which first roused it to enterprise? What mean those unmeasurable longings, which no gratification can extinguish, and which still continue to agitate the heart of man even in the fulness of plenty and of enjoyment. If they mean anything at all, they mean that all which this world can offer is not enough to fill up his capacity for happiness—that time is too small for him, and he is born for something beyond it—that the scene of his earthly existence is too limited, and he is formed to expatiate in a wider and grander theater —that nobler destiny is reserved for him—and that to accomplish the purpose of his being he must soar above the littleness of the world, and aim at a loftier prize. It forms the peculiar honor and excellence of religion, that it accommodates to this property of our nature—that it holds out a prize suited to our high calling—that there is a grandeur in its objects which can fill and surpass the imagination—that it dignifies the present scene by connecting it with eternity—that it reveals to the eye of faith the glories of an imperishable world—and how, from the high eminences of heaven, a cloud of witnesses is looking down upon earth, not as a scene for the petty anxieties of time, but as a splendid theater for the ambition of immortal spirits.

# JOHN HENRY NEWMAN (1809–1890)

On board a ship bound for Marseilles, suffering from the effects of a severe illness contracted while spending the winter in Italy and Greece, and longing for home, John Henry Newman was moved to write a poem which has become a hymn known to millions, "Lead, Kindly Light." That was in June, 1833, when he was thirty-two years old and an extremely pious, self-disciplined priest of the Anglican church. He was returning to England with new determination to be of greater service to his God and his church. Shortly after his return to Oxford, the turning point in his life was reached which was also to influence the whole of the Church of England and many persons outside it. In July, John Keble preached his Assize Sermon in the university pulpit on "National Apostasy"; this led Newman and others to assert the rights and privileges of the church as a divine institution. A movement began, producing tracts attempting to demonstrate the Catholic and Apostolic nature of the Church of England. Newman was an articulate leader of the Tractarian movement; the scholarship and zeal displayed in his tracts brought him a growing following of young churchmen. When in 1841 he published Tract 90 he stimulated violent controversy; he had attempted to demonstrate that the Thirty-nine Articles were congruous with post-Reformation Catholicism, that they had attacked merely the supremacy of the Pope and certain abuses. Newman's thesis was repudiated by episcopal authority; this, in addition to growing doubts about the nature of the Church of England, brought him to the conviction several years later that he should become a Roman Catholic. When in 1845 he was received into the Roman church, that church acquired an able scholar, a brilliant writer of prose and poetry, a scrupulously disciplined and dedicated priest, and one of the finest preachers in nineteenth century England.

Prior to his conversion to Roman Catholicism, Newman served as Vicar of St. Mary the Virgin, the university church at Oxford (1828–1843). He became famous among the students for his Sunday four o'clock sermons. He at first revealed his strong evangelical background, but gradually his interest in early church doctrine became apparent; this frail man with his eyes glued to his lengthy manuscript would certainly not appeal today as he did then. As a Roman priest, however, his preaching style changed. After a year and a half in Rome, Newman returned to England in 1848 as a Roman priest and preached in the style of that church, using only a few notes.

The sermon included here was one of the first he preached to a Roman Catholic congregation, and it shows marked simplicity and definite awareness of his hearers; yet it does not lack his amazing command of language and it is not without rhetoric. As a Roman Catholic, Newman continued to engage in the academic life, being Rector of Dublin University from 1854 until 1858. He was also a seminary teacher and wrote numerous books and articles which are still read and admired. Although for years little appreciated by his new church, in 1879 he received the cardinal's hat, which he wore until his death eleven years later.

# The Calls of Grace*

In the parable of the Sower, we have set before us four descriptions of men, all of whom receive the word of God. The sower sows first on the hard ground or road, then on the shallow earth or rock, then on a ground where other seeds were sown, and lastly on really good, rich, well-prepared soil. By the sower is meant the preacher; and by the seed the word preached; and by the rock, the road, the preoccupied ground, and the good soil are meant four different states of mind of those who hear the word. Now here we have a picture laid out before us which will, through God's mercy, provide us with a fitting subject of thought.

First let us consider the case of the hard ground and the seed that was sown there—"some fell by the road and was trodden down and the birds of the air ate it up." Such is the power of the divine word, spoken by its appointed preacher; so blessed and prospered is it by divine grace, that it goes forth like a dart or an arrow. The word goeth forth, as the prophet Isaiah says, and does not return unto him void, but prospers in the thing whereto he sends it. Nothing can stop it but a closed heart. Nothing can resist it but a deliberately worldly, carnal, and godless will—and such a will can. But where the heart is ever so little softened, the divine word enters it; where it is not softened, it lies on the surface. It lies on the surface, and we learn from the parable the immediate consequence—"the birds of the air stole it away." It did not lie there long—there was but the alternative—it was admitted within, or the wind or the birds or the foot of the passer-by, as it might be, destroyed it.

* From *Catholic Sermons of Cardinal Newman,* edited at Birmingham Oratory (London: Burns and Oates, 1957). Used by permission of the publisher.

Now, I can fancy some of those who hear me thinking that this is an extreme case—when perhaps it is their own. When they read or hear this picture of the seed falling on the hard wayside, they may hear it in an unconcerned way, as if they had no interest in it, when they may have a great concern in the description. There are a very great many persons whose hearts are like the hard wayside. Now I will explain what I mean. I suppose it occurs to all of us to hear names of persons mentioned, or to hear of events, or occurrences, which we hear one moment and forget the next: they simply pass through our minds and make no impression. Why? Because we never heard of them before; we take no interest in them, and so they don't take hold of us. They are like an unknown language, and go as they came. But now supposing the person mentioned is one whose history we know. Supposing it is a public man, whom we have heard about or read of for years— Why, did we hear of anything happening to him, did we hear he had left the country, or fallen into misfortune, or fallen ill, or been promoted, or had died, his name kindles up a whole history, and we take great interest in the news brought us. We connect what we now hear with what we already know. And so you often may find, coming into a party of men, and saying this or that of a certain person, that the news produces a great effect on one, and is simply unmeaning to another. The latter turns off to some other subject at once, and is not struck, but the former expresses surprise, or pleasure, or grief, and says: "Is it possible?" "I remember such a man twenty years ago—how he is changed, or how great a rise, or what a sad end."

You see the difference between one whose heart is hard and one whose heart is softened. One man has often thought about religion, another never. The latter will be interested enough if you speak to him of things connected with this world; if you talk to him of how to raise crops, or how to make money in any way, or of any worldly amusement or pleasure, his attention is arrested at once. But if you speak to him about the four last things, about heaven or hell, death or judgment, he stares or laughs out. If you speak good and holy words to him, he hears and forgets. On the contrary, some sacred place or sacred name is like a magic spell to those whose hearts are accustomed to the thought of religion, or are in any way disposed and prepared by God's grace. Take a person who has been tried by misfortune, or who has suffered the loss of some dear relative, or who has fallen into sin and is under compunctions, then when he hears the words "What shall I do to be saved?" or "After death, the judgment," or "Believe and be saved," or "Comfort ye, comfort ye, my people," or "Christ died for sinners"—such few words fit into this habitual state of mind, and at once kindle him—he cannot help listening—he seizes the word and devours it. Nay, we know that to holy people the very name of Jesus is a name to feed upon, a name to transport. These are the words which can raise the dead and transfigure and beautify the living.

You will observe that, in the parable, not only did the fowls carry off the word of life, but the foot of the passer-by trampled it. I have hitherto spoken of those who were ignorant, careless, and heartless— and from whom the devil stole the divine treasure while they let it lie on the surface of their minds. But there are others who are worse than this; who, as it were, trample on the divine words. It is an awful thing to say, but we see it before our eyes how many people there are who hate the doctrine which Christ revealed and the Church teaches. Of course many do so in mere ignorance, and would feel and act otherwise if they had the opportunity. But there are those, and not a few, who scorn and are irritated at the preaching of the word of life, and spurn it from them. It has been so from the beginning. Our Lord "came unto his own and his own received him not." And as he was abominated and cast out by a sinful generation, so since he has departed, his word is abominated by the world still. Sometimes it is for want of love. You hear people revile the Church, ridicule the most sacred things, and spread from a deep prejudice the most untrue stories. Sometimes from want of faith: they think it quite wonderful, beyond expression strange and marvellous, that men can be found to believe this or that doctrine; and sometimes it arises from a bad conscience and impatience at being told their duty. Carnal, sensual people wish to live their own way; they do not like to be warned of hell and judgment, and when the warning voice comes to them, they rise up against it, and think it a personal offence to themselves that it declares the truth of God. They put their foot upon it, and tread out the heavenly flame.

But I will now go on to mention a third case of hardness of heart, which not infrequently occurs, and that is the case of those who get familiar with the word of life and then are not moved by it. When persons who are living in sin hear for the first time the sound of Catholic truth they are affected by it; it is something new, and the novelty of the doctrine is God's instrument. It is blest by God to make an effect upon them. It moves and draws them. And then the worship of the Church is so overcoming. They, as it were, give up, they surrender themselves to God, they feel themselves in the hands of their Savior. They are led to cry out: "Take me, make what thou wilt of me." This lasts for some time, and in a number of cases, praised be God, it ends happily; this excitement and transport of mind leads on to a lasting conversion. But in other cases it does not. A person is moved for a while, and then the excitement goes off. I have seen cases of this kind—many people may know them. A man is on the point of taking up religion seriously. He is on the point of putting one and one object alone before him as the end of his being and the aim of his life—to please God and save his soul. But all of a sudden a change comes over him. Almost while we turn our head and look another way, it has taken place. We look back to him and he is quite another man—or rather he is the same, the same as he was. No, for he is worse. The latter state of that man is worse than the first. He was hard before, and now is he ten times as hard. Not only the good seed has been trampled on, but his heart has been trodden down; it is as hard as the pavement, and nothing will move him again. This, alas, is often the case in places where truth has been preached for many years, compared with new places. In the new place you find the word prospers; but there is coldness, deadness, languor, tepidity, backwardness, insincerity in the old.

"Today if ye shall hear his voice, harden not your hearts. . . . Exhort one another every day, lest any be hardened by the deceitfulness of sin" (Hebrews 3:13). When the heart is hard, the birds take away the divine seed. They do not bring it back; it goes for ever. Make the most of the precious time. Delay not—many a soul has been damned by delay. God's opportunities do not wait; they come and they go. The word of life waits not—if it is not appropriated by you, the devil will appropriate.

And if you are conscious that your hearts are hard and are desirous that they should be softened, do not despair. All things are possible to you through God's grace. Come to him for the will and the power to do that to which he calls you. He never puts any trial on a man but he gives him grace to overcome it. Do not despair then; nay, do not despond, even though you do come to him, yet are not at once exalted to overcome yourselves. He gives grace by little and little. It is by coming daily into his presence that by degrees we find ourselves awed by that presence and able to believe and obey him. Therefore if anyone desires illumination to know God's will, as well as strength to do it, let him daily offer his heart to his Incarnate Savior, to be influenced, changed, and sanctified under the eye and by the grace of the Eternal Son. And let him every now and then through the day make some short prayer to the Lord. Let him now and then collect his mind and place himself, as if in heaven, in the presence of God; as if before God's throne, let him fancy he sees the All-Holy Lamb of God, which taketh away the sin of the world. These are the means by which, with God's grace, he will be able in course of time to soften his heart—not all at once, but by degrees. Thus it is that saints have begun. They have begun by these little things; they were not saints all at once, but by little and little. So we must still proceed by the same road; by lowliness, patience, trust in God, recollection that we are in his presence, and thankfulness for his mercies.

And now, my brethren, though I have said but a little on a large subject, I have said enough, not enough for the subject, but enough for you to get a lesson from. May you lay it to heart, as I am sure you do and will, and may you gain a blessing from it.

**JOSEPH PARKER** (1830–1902) It was said that when the architect for the projected City Temple, of London, asked Joseph Parker what style of architecture he would like used, he replied: "Of the style, I do not care. Only, build it so, that when Queen Victoria passes by, she will stop and ask: 'Why, what building is that?' and will be told, 'That is where Dr. Parker preaches.'" This famous English Congregational minister had a long ministry, and for much of it he was noted for his strong, highly original, evangelical sermons. He was an individualist and has been accused of gross egotism; a close follower of his has stated that his honest self-estimation was balanced and spiced by a great sense of humor. It was this humor, when it became caustic and satirical, that could frighten Parker's hearers toward the kingdom of heaven. Yet his preaching usually did not consist of solemn exhortations to repentance, but of expressions of a warm, human sentiment, of the wondering love of Jesus Christ.

In addition to preaching and his pastoral ministry, Parker was also a controversialist, fighting in his own dramatic way for such things as temperance and fundamentalistic adherence to Scripture. By the end of his ministry he had become a legend, and often people visiting London would include the City Temple at service time on their itineraries; this lion of the pulpit did not let them go away disappointed. Whatever the subject, the manner was unique; the personality of the preacher and his theatrical presentations were things to treasure in the mind. In spite of obvious techniques, he was sincere in his message, and sought to help people appreciate it and be grasped by it with his own unique methods. His sermons do not read well: so much depended upon his tone and expression. He talked very slowly, and then would suddenly burst into rapid eloquence; however, with imagination, the reader will sense some of Parker's power and surely profit from his message.

# A Word to the Weary[*]

*The Lord God hath given me the tongue of the learned, that I should know
how to speak a word in season to him that is weary.*  ISAIAH 50:4

It is a common notion that anybody can sing. Why can you sing?
Why, because I have been taught. That is your mistake. You can sing
mechanically, exactly, properly, with right time, right tune, but really
and truly you can not sing. Here is a man with his music and with the
words; he sings every note, pronounces every word, goes through his
lesson, finishes his task, and nobody wants to hear him any more.
Another man takes up the same music, the same words, and the same
hearers exclaim, "Oh, that he would go on for ever!" How is that?—
the words exactly the same, the notes identical—how? Soul, fire, ever-
burning, never consuming, making a bush like a planet. The great
difficulty in all such cases is the difficulty of transferring to paper a
proper or adequate conception of the power of the men who thus
sway the human heart. There are some men whose biographies simply
belie them, and yet every sentence in the biography is true in the letter;
but the biography is little else than a travesty and a caricature, because
the power was personal, it was in the face, in the voice, in the presence,
in the gait, in the touch—in incommunicable power; the hem of the
garment trembled under it, but no biographer could catch it in his
scholarly ink.

* From Grenville Kleiser (ed.), *The World's Great Sermons*, Vol. VII (New York:
Funk & Wagnalls Co., 1908). Copyright 1908 by Funk & Wagnalls Co. Used by permission of the publisher.

Very few ministers can enter a sick chamber with any probability of doing real and lasting good. They can read the Bible, and they can pray, and yet, when they have gone, the room seems as if they had never been there. There is no sense of emptiness or desolation. Other men, probably not so much gifted in some other directions, will enter the sick room, and there will be a light upon the wall, summer will gleam upon the windowpane, and angels will rustle in the air, and it will be a scene of gladness and a vision of triumph. How is that? The Lord God hath given me the tongue of the learned that I might know how—how to speak a word in season to him that is weary. The Lord God hath not only given me a word to say, but hath given me learning to teach me how to speak it. Place the emphasis upon the how, and then you develop all the mystery, all the tender music, all the infinite capacity of manner.

We may say the right word in the wrong tone; we may preach the gospel as if it were a curse. The common notion is that anybody can go into the Sunday school and teach the young. We sometimes think that it would be well if a great many persons left the Sunday school all over the world. Teach the young—would God I had that great gift, to break the bread for the children, and to be able to lure and captivate opening minds, and to enter into the spirit of the words—

> Delightful task! to rear the tender thought,
> To teach the young idea how to shoot.

It requires to be father and mother and sister and nurse and genius to speak to the young. They may hear you and not care for you: they may understand your words, and be repelled by your spirit. You require the tongue of the learned to know how to speak, and that tongue of the learned is not to be had at school, college, university—it is not included in any curriculum of learning—it is a gift divine, breathing an afflatus, an inspiration—the direct and distinct creation of God, as is the star, the sun. The speaker, then, is Jesus Christ, the Son of God, the representative of the Father, the incarnate Deity—he it is who is charged with the subtle learning.

Though the gift itself is divine, we must remember that it is to be exercised seasonably. The text is, "That I should know how to speak a word in season." There is a time for everything. It is not enough to speak the right word, it must be spoken at the right moment. Who can know when that is! We can not be taught. We must feel it, see it hours beyond: nay, must know when to be silent for the whole twenty-four hours and to say, "Tomorrow, at such and such a time, we will drop that sentence upon the listening ear." "The day after tomorrow, he will probably be in circumstances to admit of this communication being delivered with sympathy and effect." How few persons know the right time—the right time in conversation. Some people are never heard in conversation though they are talking all the time. They talk so unseasonably, they talk when other people are talking; they can not wait; they do not know how to come in along the fine line of silence: they do not understand the German expression, "Now an angel has passed," and they do not quickly enough follow in his wake. Consequently, though chattering much they are saying nothing —though their words be multitudinous, the impression they make is a blank.

As a nurse, I will attend to my patient (perhaps I will over attend to him—some patients are killed by over nursing), and I will give the patient this medicine—it is the right medicine. So it is, but you are going to give it at the wrong time, and if you give the medicine at the wrong time, though itself be right, the hour being wrong you will bring suffering upon the patient, and you yourself will be involved in pains and penalties. Thus we touch that very subtle and sensitive line in human life, the line of refined discrimination. You may say, "I am sure I told him." You are right—you did tell him and he did not hear you. You may reply, "I am perfectly confident I delivered the message —I preached the exact words of the gospel." So you did, but you never got the hearing heart, your manner was so unsympathetic, so ungentle, so cruel (not meant to be—unconsciously so), that the man never understood it to be a gospel. You spoiled the music in the delivery, in the giving of the message. The Lord God giveth the tongue of the learned, that he to whom it is given may know how to speak the right word at the right point of time. You want divine teaching in all things, in speech not least.

This is a curious word to find in the Bible. Does the Bible care about

weary people? We have next to no sympathy with them. If a man be
weary, we give him notice to quit: if he ask us to what place he can
retire, we tell him that it is his business not ours. Now the tenderness
of this Book is one of the most telling, convincing arguments on behalf
of its inspiration, and its divine authority. This Book means to help
us, wants to help us; it says, "I will try to help you, never hinder you:
I will wait for you, I will soften the wind into a whisper, I will order
the thunder to be silent, I will quiet the raging sea; I will wait upon
you at home, in solitude, at midnight, anywhere—fix the place, the
time, yourself, and when your heart most needs me I will be most to
your heart." Any book found in den, in gutter, that wants to do this,
should be received with respect. The purpose is good: if it fail, it fails
in a noble spirit.

Everywhere in this Book of God we find a supreme wish to help
man. When we most need help the words are sweeter than the honey-
comb. When other books are dumb, this Book speaks most sweetly. It
is like a star, it shines in the darkness, it waits the going down of the
superficial sun of our transient prosperity, and then it breaks upon us
as the shadows thicken. This is the real greatness of God: he will not
break the bruised reed. Because the reed is bruised, therefore the rude
man says he may break it. His argument in brief is this: "If the reed
were strong, I should not touch it, but seeing that it is bruised what
harm can there be in completing the wound under which it is already
suffering? I will even snap it and throw the sundered parts away."
That is the reasoning of the rude man—that is the vulgar view of the
case. The idea of the healing is the idea of the creator. He who creates
also heals. Herein we see God's estimate of human nature: if he cared
only for the great, the splendid, the magnificent, the robust, and the
everlasting, then he would indeed be too like ourselves. The greatness
of God and the estimate which he places upon human nature are most
seen in all these ministrations in reference to the weak and the weary
and the young and the feeble and the sad. Made originally in the image
of God, man is dear to his Maker, though ever so broken.

When we are weary, even in weariness, God sees the possibility of
greatness that may yet take place and be developed and supervene in

immortality. How do we talk? Thus: "The survival of the fittest." It is amazing with what patience and magnanimity and majestic disregard of circumstances we allow people to die off. When we hear that thousands have perished, we write this epitaph on their white slate tombstones: "The survival of the fittest required the decay of the weakest and the poorest." We pick off the fruit which we think will not come to perfection. The gardener lays his finger and thumb upon the tree, and he says, "This will not come to much"—he wrenches the poor unpromising piece of fruit off the twig and throws it down as useless. In our march we leave the sick and wounded behind. That is the great little, the majestic insignificant, the human contradiction. We go in for things that are fittest, strongest, most promising, healthy, self-complete, and therein we think we are wise. God says, "Not a lamb must be left out—bring it up: not a sick man must be omitted: not a poor publican sobbing his 'God be merciful to me a sinner' must be omitted from the great host. Bring them all in, sick, weary, wounded, feeble, young, illiterate, poor, insignificant, without name, fame, station, force —all in: gather up the fragments that nothing be lost." Let us go to that Shepherd—he will spare us and love us. When our poor strength gives out, he will not set his cruel heel upon us and kill us, he will gather us in his arms and make the whole flock stand still till he has saved the weakest one.

Did we but know the name for our pain we should call it sin. Some of us know how dark it is when the full shadow of our sin falls upon our life, and how all the help of earth and time and man does but mock the pain it can not reach. Let no man say that Christ will not go so low down as to find one so base and vile as he. Christ is calling for thee; I heard his sweet voice lift itself up in the wild wind and ask whither thou hadst fled, that he might save thee from death and bring thee home. There is no wrath in his face or voice, no sword is swung by his hand as if in cruel joy, saying, "Now at last I have my chance with you." His eyes gleam with love: his voice melts in pity: his words are gospels, every one. Let him but see thee sad for sin, full of grief because of the wrong thou hast done, and he will raise thee out of the deep pit and set thy feet upon the rock.

## ALEXANDER MACLAREN

**ALEXANDER MACLAREN** (1826 – 1910) Though born and schooled in Glasgow, Alexander Maclaren is best known as a great English preacher and Baptist leader. He was a quiet, tall, slender man who was interested in scholarship, happily involved in his family, and who outwardly led a simple, undramatic life. Yet his forty-five years in the pulpit of Union Chapel in Manchester brought him world-wide renown. Though he was fully dedicated to his pastoral ministry, it is said that he lived between his study and the pulpit. His sermons were not, however, written out; he wrote a few things to begin with and something to finish up on, besides a few notes. His sermons were written down by someone while being preached, indicating his amazing gift of "spoken composition."

Maclaren's preaching is definitely biblical preaching, making use of text, topic, and exposition together; he read both Testaments in the original languages and contributed to expository commentaries. His sermons are marked, as is "Ittai of Gath" which follows, by a lucid profundity; they speak directly and with power. It is a sermon on love, love for both God and man, which includes insight into the nature of man that is reminiscent of St. Augustine. Though he lived for his preaching and pastoral duties, Maclaren did not escape being president of the Baptist Union twice, and toward the end of his life he was honored to preside over the first Congress of the Baptist World Alliance in 1905. He died five years later in Manchester.

# Ittai of Gath*

*And Ittai answered the king, and said, As the Lord liveth, and as my lord the king liveth, surely in what place my lord the king shall be, whether in death or life, even there also will thy servant be.* II SAMUEL 15:21

It was the darkest hour in David's life. No more pathetic page is found in the Old Testament than that which tells the story of his flight before Absalom. He is crushed by the consciousness that his punishment is deserved—the bitter fruit of the sin that filled all his later life with darkness. His courage and his buoyancy have left him. He has no spirit to make a stand or strike a blow. If Shimei runs along the hillside abreast of him, shrieking curses as he goes, all he says is: "Let him curse; for the Lord hath bidden him."

So, heartbroken and spiritless, he leaves Jerusalem. And as soon as he has got clear of the city he calls a halt, in order that he may muster his followers and see on whom he may depend. Foremost among the little band come six hundred men from Gath—Philistines—from Goliath's city. These men, singularly enough, the king had chosen as his bodyguard; perhaps he was not altogether sure of the loyalty of his own subjects, and possibly felt safer with foreign mercenaries, who could have no secret leanings to the deposed house of Saul. Be that as it may, the narrative tells us that these men had "come after him from Gath." He had been there twice in the old days in his flight from Saul, and the second visit had extended over something more than a year.

* From Gaius Glenn Atkins (ed.), *The Best of Alexander Maclaren* (London: Hodder & Stoughton, Ltd., 1950). Used by permission of the publisher.

Probably during that period his personal attraction, and his reputation as a brilliant leader, had led these rough soldiers to attach themselves to his service, and to be ready to forsake home and kindred in order to fight beside him.

At all events here they are, "faithful among the faithless" as foreign soldiers surrounding a king often are—notably, for instance, the Swiss guard in the French Revolution. Their strong arms might have been of great use to David, but his generosity cannot think of involving them in his fall, and so he says to them: "I am not going to fight; I have no plan. I am going where I can. You go back and 'worship the rising sun.' Absalom will take you and be glad of your help. And as for me, I thank you for your past loyalty. Mercy and peace be with you!"

It is a beautiful nature that in the depth of sorrow shrinks from dragging other people down with itself. Generosity breeds generosity, and the Philistine captain breaks out into a burst of passionate devotion, garnished, in soldier fashion, with an unnecessary oath or two, but ringing very sincere and meaning a great deal. As for himself and his men, they have chosen their side. Whoever goes, they stay. Whatever befalls, they stick by David; and if the worst comes to the worst they can all die together, and their corpses lie in firm ranks round about their dead king. David's heart is touched and warmed by their outspoken loyalty; he yields and accepts their service. Ittai and his noble six hundred tramp on, out of our sight, and all their household behind them. Now what is there, in all that, to make a sermon out of?

1. First, look at the picture of that Philistine soldier as teaching us what grand passionate self-sacrifice may be evolved out of the roughest natures.

Analyse his words, and do you not hear, ringing in them, these three things, which are the seed of all nobility and splendor in human character? First, a passionate personal attachment; then, that love, issuing as such love always does, in willing sacrifice that recks not for a moment of personal consequences; that is ready to accept anything for itself if it can serve the object of its devotion, and will count life well expended if it is flung away in such a service. And we see, lastly, in these words a supreme restful delight in the presence of him whom the heart loves. For Ittai and his men, the one thing needful was to be beside him in whose eye they had lived, from whose presence they had caught inspiration; their trusted leader, before whom their souls bowed down. So then his vehement speech is the pure language of love.

Now these three things—a passionate personal attachment issuing in spontaneous heroism of self-abandonment, and in supreme satisfaction in the beloved presence—may spring up in the rudest, roughest nature. A Philistine soldier was not a very likely man in whom to find refined and lofty emotion. He was hard by nature, hardened by his rough trade, and unconscious that he was doing anything at all heroic or great. Something had smitten this rock, and out of it there came the pure refreshing stream. And so I say to you, the weakest and the lowest, the roughest and the hardest, the most selfishly absorbed man and woman among us, has lying in him and her dormant capacities for flaming up into such a splendor of devotion and magnificence of heroic self-sacrifice as is represented in these words of my text.

And lastly, this capacity which lies dormant in all of us, if once it is roused to action, will make a man blessed and dignified as nothing else will. The joy of unselfish love is the purest joy that man can taste; the joy of perfect self-sacrifice is the highest joy that humanity can possess; and they lie open for us all.

And wherever, in some humble measure, these emotions of which I have been speaking are realized, there you get weakness springing up into strength, and the ignoble into loftiness. Astronomers tell us that, sometimes, a star that has shone inconspicuous, and stood low down in their catalogues as of fifth or sixth magnitude, will all at once flame out, having kindled and caught fire somehow, and will blaze in the heavens, outshining Jupiter and Venus. And so some poor, vulgar, narrow nature, touched by the Promethean fire of pure love that leads to perfect sacrifice, will "flame in the forehead of the morning sky," an undying splendor, and a light for evermore.

Brethren! My appeal to you is a very plain and simple one, founded

on these facts: You have all that capacity in you, and you are all responsible for the use of it. What have you done with it? Is there any
person or thing in this world that has ever been able to lift you up
out of your miserable selves? Is there any magnet that has proved
strong enough to raise you from the low levels along which your life
creeps? Have you ever known the thrill of resolving to become the
bondservant and the slave of some great cause not your own? Or are
you, as so many of you are, like spiders living in the midst of your web,
mainly intent upon what you can catch in it? You have these capacities
slumbering in you. Have you ever set a light to that inert mass of
enthusiasm that lies in you? Have you ever waked up the sleeper?
Look at this rough soldier of my text, and learn from him the lesson
that there is nothing that so ennobles and dignifies a commonplace
nature as enthusiasm for a great cause, or self-sacrificing love for a
worthy heart.

2. The second remark which I make is this: These possibilities of
love and sacrifice point plainly to God in Christ as their true object.
"Whose image and superscription hath it?" said Christ, looking at the
Roman denarius that they brought and laid on his palm. If the emperor's head is on it, why, then, he has a right to it as tribute. And
then he went on to say, "Render therefore unto Caesar the things
which are Caesar's; and unto God the things that are God's." So there
are things that have God's image and superscription stamped on them,
and such are our hearts, our whole constitution and nature. As plainly
as the penny had the head of Augustus on it, and therefore proclaimed
that he was emperor where it was current, so plainly does every soul
carry in the image of God the witness that he is its owner and that it
should be rendered in tribute to him.

We are made with hearts that need to rest upon an absolute love;
we are made with understandings that need to grasp a pure, a perfect,
and as I believe, paradoxical though it may sound, a personal truth.
We are made with wills that crave for an absolute authoritative command, and we are made with a moral nature that needs a perfect holiness. And we need all that love, truth, authority, purity, to be gathered

into one, for the misery of the world is that when we set out to look for treasures we have to go into many lands and to many merchants to buy many goodly pearls. But we need one of great price, in which all our wealth may be invested. We need that one to be an undying and perpetual possession. There is one to whom our love can ever cleave, and fear none of the sorrows or imperfections that make earthward-turned love a rose with many a thorn, one for whom it is pure gain to lose ourselves, one who is plainly the only worthy recipient of the whole love and self-surrender of the heart.

That one is God, revealed and brought near to us in Jesus Christ. In that great Savior we have a love at once divine and human, we have the great transcendent instance of love leading to sacrifice. On that love and sacrifice for us Christ builds his claim on us for our hearts, and our all. Life alone can communicate life; it is only light that can diffuse light. It is only love that can kindle love; it is only sacrifice that can inspire sacrifice. And so he comes to us, and asks that we should just love him back again as he has loved us. He first gives himself utterly for and to us, and then asks us to give ourselves wholly to him. He first yields up his own life, and then he says: "He that loseth his life for my sake shall find it." The object, the true object for all this depth of love which lies slumbering in our hearts, is God in Christ, the Christ that died for us.

3. And now, lastly, observe that the terrible misdirection of these capacities is the sin and the misery of the world.

I will not say that such emotions, even when expended on creatures, are ever wasted. For however unworthy may be the objects on which they are lavished, the man himself is the better and the higher for having cherished them. The mother, when she forgets self in her child, though her love and self-forgetfulness and self-sacrifice may, in some respects, be called but an animal instinct, is elevated and ennobled by the exercise of them.

And so I am not going to say that when men love each other passionately and deeply, and sacrifice themselves for one another, or for some cause or purpose affecting only temporal matters, the precious elixir of love is wasted. God forbid! But I do say that all these objects, sweet and gracious as some of them are, ennobling and elevating as some of them are, if they are taken apart from God, are insufficient to fill your hearts; and that if they are slipped in between you and God, as they often are, then they bring sin and sorrow. There is nothing more tragic in the world than the misdirection of man's capacity for love and sacrifice.

Ah! brethren, we should be our own rebukes in this matter, and the heroism of the world should put to shame the cowardice and the self-ishness of the Church. Contrast the depth of your affection for your household with the tepidity of your love for your Savior. Contrast the willingness with which you sacrifice yourself for some dear one with the grudgingness with which you yield yourselves to him. Contrast the rest and the sense of satisfaction in the presence of those you love, and your desolation when they are absent, with the indifference whether you have Christ beside you or not. And remember that the measure of your power of loving is the measure of your obligation to love your Lord; and that if you are all frost to him and fervor to them, then in a very solemn sense "a man's foes shall be they of his own household." "He that loveth father or mother more than me is not worthy of me!"

And so let me gather all that I have been saying into the one earnest beseeching of you that you would bring that power of uncalculating love and self-sacrificing affection which is in you, and would fasten it where it ought to fix—on Christ who died on the Cross for you. Such a love will bring blessedness to you. Such a love will ennoble and dignify your whole nature, and make you a far greater and fairer man or woman than you otherwise ever could be. Like some little bit of black carbon put into an electric current, my poor nature will flame into beauty and radiance when that spark touches it. So love him and be at peace; give yourselves to him and he will give you back your-selves, ennobled and transfigured by the surrender. Lay yourselves on his altar, and that altar will sanctify both the giver and the gift. If you can take this rough Philistine soldier's words in their spirit, and in a higher sense, say, "Whether I live, I live unto the Lord, or whether I die, I die unto the Lord; living or dying, I am the Lord's," he will let you enlist in his army; and give you for your marching orders this command and this hope, "If any man serve me, let him follow me; and where I am, there shall also my servant be."

# CHARLES HADDON SPURGEON (1834-1892)

Born in the southeast section of England and having little formal schooling, Charles Haddon Spurgeon became a self-made Baptist preacher at an early age. He first preached in a cottage at the age of sixteen, and soon thereafter he began to preach with regularity, although sometimes he had to go from house to house to gather a congregation. Within four years he was called to London to be the pastor of a Baptist Church. His preaching drew such crowds that by the time he was thirty his congregation had to build for him the Metropolitan Tabernacle, which seated six thousand persons. In addition to his activities as a pastor he started a pastor's college to teach theological students, founded an orphanage, and published inspirational literature. His own sermons amount to nearly forty volumes. He was an independent Baptist, who had formerly refused to attend college because he did not care to enter the halls of liberalism and unbelief; he persistently ridiculed formal theology and detested biblical criticism. When, in 1887, he was certain that the Baptist church tolerated liberal thinking, he withdrew from the Baptist Union to become officially independent.

As a preacher, Spurgeon communicated the reality of the atoning work of Christ to many people; his vivid imagination, his clear, strong voice, and his plain, direct English spoken with a definite sense of rhythm helped his sermons strike home. He was a short, stocky, and rather homely man, but he was good-natured and in the pulpit he was natural and serious. Not infrequently parts of his sermons were polemical, which served to strengthen his own position at the cost of distorting other points of view; he played on the psychology that a victory is more certain when the enemy is not only exposed but slain in clear view. The slaying of straw men has been edited out of the sermon printed here; nevertheless, it remains a powerful presentation of a gospel truth and a sample of first-rate evangelical preaching.

# Forgiveness and Fear[*]

*There is forgiveness with thee, that thou mayest be feared.* PSALM 130:4

This is good news; indeed, the best of news; and they will prize it most who are like the psalmist was when he wrote these words. And who are they?

First, they are those who are in soul-trouble: "Out of the depths have I cried unto thee, O Lord." Some of you may, perhaps, think this subject is a very commonplace one, but the soul that is in deep spiritual trouble will not think so. Bread is a very commonplace thing, but it is very precious to starving men. Liberty is an everyday enjoyment to us, but it would be a great boon to those who are in slavery. O you, who are in the depths of soul-trouble, like shipwrecked mariners who seem to be sinking in the trough of the sea, or being dragged down by a whirlpool, this text will bring sweet music to your ears! "There is forgiveness"; there is forgiveness with God.

This good news will also have a peculiar sweetness to those who have begun to pray. And if, to soul-trouble and earnest prayer, there should be added a very deep sense of sin, amounting even to utter self-condemnation, then I am quite certain that there is no carol that will have sweeter music in it than my text has. Do you feel that your iniquities condemn you? Are you compelled to plead guilty before God? Well, then, though you cannot claim acquittal on the ground

* From Charles T. Cook (ed.), *C. H. Spurgeon's Evangelistic Sermons,* Kelvedon Edition, Vol. VIII (London: Marshall, Morgan & Scott, 1959). Used by permission of the publisher.

that you have no sins, yet here is the blessed information that there is forgiveness for sinners. Stand in the dock, where the guilty ought to stand; and let the Judge condemn you. Nay, spare him the trouble, condemn yourself; and, when you have done so, and have also trusted the great Atonement made by his dear Son, he will say to you, "There is forgiveness; be of good cheer: thy sins, which are many, are all forgiven thee." I do not expect to say anything to delight deaf ears; but I do believe that the simple tidings I have to tell will have great weight with those who are in soul-trouble, with those who have begun to pray, and those who are self-condemned on account of sin.

First, here is a most cheering announcement: "There is forgiveness with thee."

This announcement has great force and value, because it is most certainly true. When a man hears some news which pleases him, he loses that pleasure if he has reason to suspect that it is not true. The first questions you ask, when someone tells you of some good fortune that concerns you, are of this sort, "Are you quite sure it is so? Can you give me good authority for your assertion?"

Well, this news is certainly true, for it is consistent with God's very nature. He is a gracious God. "He delighteth in mercy." Mercy was the last of his attributes that he was able to reveal. He could be great and good when the world was made, but he could not be merciful until sin had marred his perfect handiwork. There must be an offence committed before there can be mercy displayed towards the offender. Mercy, then, I may say, is God's Benjamin—his last-born, his favored one, the son of his right hand. I never read that he delighteth in power, or that he delighteth in justice; but I do read, "He delighteth in mercy."

We are even more sure that it is so when we remember that God has given us the best pledge of forgiveness by giving us his dear Son. He could not be merciful at the expense of his justice, for his throne is established in righteousness; and that righteousness requires that he should by no means spare the guilty. How, then, could he display his grace and mercy, and yet be the just God? He did it thus. The offended one took the nature and the place of the offenders; and here, on this earth, Jesus of Nazareth, who was "very God of very God," suffered all that we had brought upon ourselves, that the law might be honored by executing its full penalty, and yet that the free grace and mighty mercy of God might be equally manifest. If any of you doubt whether there is forgiveness with God, I pray you to stand on Calvary, in imagination, and to look into the wounds of Jesus, gaze upon his nail-pierced hands and feet, his thorn-crowned brow, and look right into his heart, where the soldier's spear was thrust, and blood and water flowed out, for the double cleansing of all who trust him. O Christ of God, it could not be that thou shouldst die, and yet that sinners cannot be forgiven! It would be a monstrous thing that thou shouldst have bled to death, and yet that no sinner should be saved by that death. It cannot be; there must be forgiveness, there is forgiveness, since Jesus died, "the Just for the unjust, that he might bring us to God."

We are certain, also, that there is forgiveness, because there is a Gospel, and the very essence of the Gospel lies in the proclamation of the pardon of sin. The Lord Jesus said to his disciples, "Go ye into all the world, and preach the Gospel to every creature. He that believeth and is baptized shall be saved"; but no one can be saved without sin being pardoned; therefore, there is pardon for the sin of everyone who believes and is baptized according to the Gospel command. Christ's ministers may all go home, for their office is useless, if there be no forgiveness of sins. We may shut up all our houses of prayer, for it is a mockery to God and man to keep them open if there be no forgiveness of sins. What value can there be in the means of grace—what can be the use or signification of any Gospel at all—if sin be not pardonable? But it can be pardoned; there is forgiveness. If you want evidence in confirmation of that declaration, there are hundreds of us who are prepared to prove that we have been forgiven, and there are hundreds of thousands, now alive, who know that their sins have been pardoned, and that they have been absolved from all their guilt for Christ's sake; and there are millions, beyond all count, before yon burning throne of God, who continually praise him who loved them, and washed them from their sins in his own blood. I bear my own personal testimony that I know there is forgiveness, for I have been forgiven.

This fact gathers additional sweetness from another source, namely, that the declaration is in the present tense: "There *is* forgiveness." When? Now—at this moment—there *is* forgiveness. Possibly, you are eighty years of age; but there is forgiveness. Or you may be very young —a little boy or girl, but there is forgiveness for the young as well as for the old. You tell me that you have already rejected many invitations; yes, but there is forgiveness. It is to be had now, blessed be God, for "behold, now is the accepted time; behold, now is the day of salvation." Believe thou now in Jesus Christ, God's Son, and thou hast forgiveness now—in a moment. It takes no appreciable period of time for God to forgive sin. Swifter than the lightning-flash is the glance from the eye of God that conveys peace and pardon to the soul that trusts in Jesus. You would need time to get a pardon signed and sealed by an earthly monarch; but time is out of the question with the God of everlasting love. A sigh, a groan, a genuine confession of sin, a believing glance in the eye to Christ on Calvary—and all is done, thy sin has passed away, there is forgiveness, and thou hast received it. Therefore, go and rejoice in it.

Notice next in the text the unlimited character of this forgiveness: "There is forgiveness with thee." You see, there is no word to limit it; it does not say that there is forgiveness only for a certain number; there is no such restriction as that. Nor does it say that there is forgiveness only for a certain sort of sin; there is no such limit as that. Nor is it said, "There is forgiveness up to a certain point, or forgiveness up to a certain date." No, but the declaration, "there is forgiveness with thee," stands out in all its glorious fulness and simplicity, with no abridging or qualifying words whatsoever. Do not thou, poor sinner, put a limit where God puts none; but build thy hope of pardon and salvation on this declaration, and go thou to God, through Jesus Christ, and thou shalt find that there is forgiveness for thee—even for thee, at this very hour.

Now I pass on to the second part of our subject, which is, a most admirable design: "There is forgiveness with thee, that thou mayest be feared." How does forgiveness cause men to fear God?

First, it is clear that God's design in proclaiming forgiveness is the opposite of what some men have said and thought. We have known many who have said, "There is forgiveness, so let us keep on sinning." Others, not quite so base, have said, "There is forgiveness, so we can have it whenever we please." Holding this idea, they have trifled with sin, and they have delayed to seek forgiveness, drawing—oh, I am ashamed to say it of my fellowmen!—drawing the infamous inference that, as God is merciful, they may live in sin as long as they like, and then find mercy at the last. I would like any man, who has adopted that strangely cruel and wicked way of dealing with God's mercy, to look straight at it for a minute. I do think that, if I had a friend whom I had grieved, and I knew that he was ready to forgive me, I should not, therefore, put off the reconciliation, and so grieve him still more; I should be very base indeed if I did act like that.

If there were no pardon, it is quite certain that nobody would fear God at all. There is no forgiveness for the devil and all his legions, and there is not a devil that has any reverence or love or adoration for God. No, they abide in sullen despair. They have a certain sort of dread; and, without pardon, there may be a dread and horror of God; but that is not what our text means, for the fear of God, in Scripture, does not signify dread; it signifies true religion, holy reverence and awe: "The fear of the Lord is the beginning of wisdom"; and, unless there is pardon of sin, it is clear that its absence drives the sinners to despair, and prevents them from worshipping God.

Again, if there were no pardon, there would be nobody to fear God; for, brethren, if God had not had mercy upon us, he would long ago have swept us away. It is mercy—even if it be not pardoning mercy, it is mercy—which permits us still to live. If God had no pardon for any of the whole human race, there would be no necessity for reprieving men at all, the tree of humanity would long since have been cut down as a cumberer of the ground.

Now turn to the positive side of this subject. When the Gospel is faithfully preached, and attentively heard, the very hearing of it, under the blessing of the Holy Spirit, breeds faith in the soul; for "faith cometh by hearing, and hearing by the Word of God." But, brethren, suppose we had no pardon to preach, would there be any faith then?

Could there be any faith then? Have you ever heard of a man who believed in an unpardoning god? Did anybody ever yet hear of a sinner believing in a god who manifests no mercy, and bestows no forgiveness? Only the heathen trust to such gods, which are no gods. The very fact that pardon is proclaimed, and carried to the heart by the power of the Holy Spirit, produces faith in the soul; and faith is the root and foundation of all true fear of God.

After faith, comes repentance; or, rather, repentance is faith's twin-brother, and is born at the same time. Nobody ever repented until he heard of pardon. Let a man be certain that he cannot be pardoned, and you may be quite sure that he will not repent. He may feel remorse; he may regret and lament his sin because of the penalty which follows it; but that gentle softening of the soul, which makes us hate sin because it is committed against such a good and gracious God, is not possible until, first of all, the heart has believed that there is forgiveness with God.

It is also the good news of pardon that inclines the heart of prayer. You would never have heard of a man praying for mercy if there had been no mercy to be obtained. If Jesus had never died, and the Gospel had never been sent into the world; if there had been no proclamation of pardon, it would never have been said of Saul of Tarsus, "Behold, he prayeth." No; prayer arises in the soul as a result of the telling of the glad tidings that pardon is to be had; and prayer, like faith and repentance, is a large part of "the fear of the Lord." The man, who truly prays, is certainly one who fears God.

When a man really receives the pardon of all his sins, he is the man who fears the Lord. This is clearly the case, for pardon breeds love in the soul; and the more a man is forgiven, the more he loves. Where great sin has been blotted out, there comes to be great love. Well, is not love the very core of the true fear of God? If a man really loves God, has he not discovered the very essence of true religion? But how could he love God if there was no pardon to be had?

And, oftentimes, this forgiving love of God breeds in the soul deep devotion and intense consecration to him. There have lived, and there are living now, men and women, who have given their whole selves to Jesus, many of whom are laboring for him even beyond their strength; and many such men and women have died, for his sake, the most cruel deaths, without shrinking back, or seeking to escape that terrible cross. Whence came such a fear of God as that? Why, it could never have come into their hearts if they had not received the forgiveness of their sins for Christ's sake; but, having been forgiven, they came to love and fear—not with a servile fear, but with a holy awe— the blessed one through whose precious blood they had been cleansed. Thus, forgiveness of sin is essential to true fear of God; and wherever it is enjoyed, it is the main motive which moves them to fear God, and brings them into that blessed condition.

As there is forgiveness to be had, why should not *you* have it? "But," says someone, "I am afraid of what I may do in the future. If I were forgiven, now, I am afraid I should again act just as I have done before." Well, then, take the text as a whole: "There is forgiveness with thee, that thou mayest be feared." If you receive the forgiveness of God, you will have the fear of God put into your heart at the same time, for this is a part of the ancient covenant: "I will put my fear in their hearts, that they shall not depart from me." "A new heart also will I give you, and a new spirit will I put within you." Poor sinner, here is a wonder of grace for you—the past forgiven, and the future guaranteed by a wondrous miracle of mercy wrought within your heart, making you a new creature in Christ Jesus.

# FREDERICK DENISON MAURICE (1805–1872)

The son of a Unitarian minister, Frederick Denison Maurice went to Cambridge with the intention of becoming a lawyer. After he had left Cambridge and was living in London he gradually accepted the Anglican faith; he then studied several years at Oxford and was ordained a priest in the Church of England in 1834. As a curate and then chaplain at Guy's Hospital he produced numerous writings, including a novel and his large and enduring book, *The Kingdom of Christ*. In 1840, he became Professor of English Literature at King's College, London. He was also a prominent lecturer on moral philosophy. Later he became Professor of Theology at King's College. His active interest in social reform, which he saw as the application of Christian principles to social and political life, led some to disapprove of him and others to suspect his orthodoxy. The controversy over his *Theological Essays* (1853) in which he attacked the literalist interpretation of eternity, led him to resign his position at King's College. He was always much concerned about improving the condition of the working classes and the poor, and in 1854 he founded Working Men's College in London; he was also one of the founders of Queen's College for Women. Throughout this time he lectured and wrote on biblical and ethical matters. In 1866, he became Professor of Moral Philosophy at Cambridge, where he remained until his death.

Maurice was one of the great thinkers in the field of Christian ethics, and furthermore he was one who applied his ethics to the whole of life. He was the mainspring of Christian socialism, and he showed undaunted courage to stand against what he knew to be wrong. He fought against religious and political selfishness, which often caused him to be out of favor with many; but he did exert influence upon a large circle of persons who sympathized with his opinions and aims. He impressed those who knew him as a holy and learned man. Though many of his sermons were over the heads of his working-class congregations, there are both clarity and force in the sermon that follows, preached in 1857, in which he states the gospel ideal for the good life as contrasted with Pharisaism, which frequently masquerades in its place.

# Be Ye
# Therefore Perfect . . . *

*Be ye therefore perfect, even as your Father which is in heaven is perfect.*
MATTHEW 5:48

I think, my brethren, that the command to be "perfect" must cause
despair to the man who has been aspiring to be a transcendent saint,
who has fancied that he is not as other men are. What our Lord tells
his disciples in this sermon is that their righteousness must exceed the
righteousness of the Scribes and Pharisees. They were men of this
class: they had raised themselves above the level of their fellows; from
the heights which they had reached they did look down with lofty
pity upon the crowd that they could just see at an immeasurable distance beneath. They were no doubt aiming at perfection; by this difference from others, they measured their approaches to it. He who began
with saying, "Blessed are the poor in spirit, for of them is the kingdom," was laying the ax to the root of this perfection. He was not
saying, "You are much further from the top of the ladder than you
have fancied." He was not saying, "You want aids to ascend which
you have not found, or which you are rejecting." He was declaring,
simply and broadly, "You are on a wrong road. You are proposing to
yourselves a false end. Every step in this direction does not take you

* From *Sermons by F. D. Maurice*, First Series, Vol. II (London: Smith, Elder, and
Co., 1860).

nearer perfection, but further from it." He tells his disciples why it must do so. The Pharisee does his works to be seen of men; yes! to be seen by those very men whom he is scorning, to be admired and worshiped by those whom it is his glory to trample upon. This is the inevitable condition of such aspirants. They live for observation. The world is to see how much they are above it. Thus the question with them is more and more, not what they shall be, but how they shall appear. With this terrible motive to become mere actors—in the strictest sense of the word, hypocrites—another conspired. God himself was necessarily regarded as one who demands an outside apparent service. He had given a law to his people. They were not to take his name in vain, not to kill, not to commit adultery. These were common precepts; the vulgarest men must be forced by actual penalties now, or threats of penalties hereafter, to observe them. The exalted man was to practice a different, a meritorious obedience. But though different in degree, it was to be the same in kind. He was not to eat with unwashen hands; not to eat at all at certain times; not to neglect the hours of prayer. Additional obligations were laid upon him that he might be perfect— obligations not deduced from the law, except by accident, but appended to it—obligations which, even if they interfered with the law according to the simple letter of it, were still to be recognized as means by which the select class might win God's favor. Our Lord dwells on one commandment which was treated with peculiar contempt by those who were aiming at peculiar holiness. It was a sign of devoutness not to honor the father and mother, not to contribute to the support of their weakness and age, if the money which would have been given to them was dedicated to the service of the Temple. No more characteristic sign can be found of the nature of this Pharisaic religion, of the results to which it was leading. Common duties—most of all, relative duties, those which had to do with the family—were trifled with and discarded. The holiness was altogether individual. It was to procure advantages and rewards for the individual man. And this, though in another sense it was altogether social, inasmuch as it demanded spectators, as a very great part of it would have been wasted, if there had not been bystanders to notice it and be affected by it.

To understand how entirely the perfection of which our Lord speaks was the reverse of this perfection, we must remember another quality of it, which is clearly implied in those I have spoken of already. The Pharisaical aspirant assumed evil as the ground from which he started. Evil was the condition of his race. Every step that raised him above evil, raised him above mankind. The nearer he approached to the Being he worshiped, the further he was from those among whom that Being had placed him. Godliness and humanity were direct and deadly opposites.

Now when our Lord said to his disciples, "Be perfect," he made it evident by all the rest of his discourse that he meant, "Be men. You cannot by any possibility be anything better than that which you are created to be. You must make yourselves worse by becoming anything else than that." Those to whom he said the kingdom of heaven belonged were those who did not lift themselves above their fellows— the meek, the merciful. Those who should obtain consolation were precisely those who were suffering as ordinary men suffer, who were suffering with them. Those were not rewarded who had righteousness, but who were hungering and thirsting after it, and would find the attainment of it their reward. Not those whom the world looked upon, but those whom no eye but God could see, the pure in heart, were to have that which they coveted, to see him as he saw them. Not those whom men thought well of, but those whom they thought ill of, whose names they cast out as evil, might claim fellowship with the prophets of old. All therefore in this perfection is social, not, like the Pharisaic, individual. And yet all is out of sight, not, like the Pharisaic perfection, apparent, cognizable by the eye.

Look again how this difference affects the relation of this Gospel of perfection to the Law which had been given in the old time. Evidently the difference is in kind and not in degree. It is not that a new code is appended to the old code. It is not that there is a code for a class of men which is different from the code for men generally. It is that the Gospel commandment belongs to the man himself, that the legal precept belongs to the acts of the man. It is therefore that the Gospel perfects, completes, fulfills the Law, without destroying one jot or tittle of it. Each stands out in its own distinctness. Each sustains and is necessary to the other. They do not clash, for they belong to different regions. They must be continually acting and reacting upon each other; the weakness of the one must be the weakness of the other; the strength of the one must be the strength of the other; because both equally apply to the same man, to the same human race. The Lawgiver, who deals with acts, says, "Thou shalt not kill"; the King, who speaks to the minds of his subjects, says, "Thou shalt not be angry with thy brother without a cause." The Lawgiver, who deals with acts, says, "Thou shalt not commit adultery." The King, who speaks to the heart, says, "Thou shalt not look upon a woman to lust after her." The Lawgiver says, "Thou shalt not forswear thyself, but shalt perform unto the Lord thine oaths"; so announcing that every overt act of perjury will be avenged by the all-seeing ruler. The King over the spirit says, "Swear not at all, for heaven is God's throne, earth is his footstool, Jerusalem is his city, the hairs of your head cannot be white or black without him"; so guarding the continual hourly reverence of him in whom we live and move and have our being.

But secondly, he says, "Be ye perfect even as your Father in Heaven is perfect." If the first clause is not fatal to all human endeavor, if it does not prescribe an absolutely impossible enterprise—what must we say of this addition to it? What I say is that we have in these words, "as your Father is perfect," that which removes any discouragement which the other, after all explanation, might have left on our minds; that we have a maxim of ethics set before us, which differs from the maxims of ordinary moral philosophers in being compassionate, practical, hopeful; that we have here the proof that our Lord's doctrine is higher in its demands than any other, and yet that "his yoke is easy and his burden is light."

A man may say, "I am quite convinced that the social, human morality is the highest morality, that this is what God seeks of us. I feel that to be a good father, a good son, a good husband, a good citizen, in the full sense of that word, may be, must be, to lead a more perfect life than to be practicing the most admired religious selfishness, than to be seeking after the highest selfish rewards which religious teachers have ever spoken of. But the more I wish for this perfection, commonplace as it is said to be, the more distant it appears to be from me. God may require nothing more of me than to do justice, to love mercy, and to walk humbly before him; but oh, how hard is doing justice! how the love of mercy vanishes when I have some personal injury to avenge! what pride springs up in me and enslaves me, when I fancy most that I have acquired humility! The best laws, the most admirable rules of conduct, cannot make me what St. Paul says I should be, to my children, to my servants. Suppose I love those who love me; suppose I yield to impulses of affection; does not my conscience tell me that I am partial, and therefore am doing injury to those whom I fondle, as well as to those whom I treat with coldness and indifference?"

Such thoughts arise in one who is aspiring after no fantastic excellence, who is simply caring to do his duty in that state in which he finds himself. He certainly does not scorn laws, not the most vulgar, earthly laws. The Ten Commandments he reverences as divine, but somehow they do not reach him; he wants help which they do not give. To act out any one relation, he must not only avoid transgression, but do right; he must not only do right, but be right. How can he be right? Our Lord tells him that he is actually, really a child, not only of an earthly parent, but of a Father in Heaven. These relationships on earth are grounded on that celestial relationship; they exist because it exists; they are formed in its likeness. The Eternal Father has constituted each family, because he has established one universal family in his Son. This is the state which Christ has revealed to us. The Pharisee would not honor father and mother, that he might reserve all his honor for God; therefore he could not honor God, because he did not believe in God as a father. Jesus Christ bids us not love father or mother more than him, because in him dwells the only love which we can show to father and mother; because it becomes a mere selfish affection, dependent on accident or circumstance, sure to dry up, if it is not derived from his love, not constantly renewed by it. Thus then the perfection which he enjoins, the true human perfection, is possible when we submit to the will which is governing the universe and governing us; when we cease to kick against the pricks; when we will permit the Spirit which is proceeding at every moment from the Father and the Son to take from us the conceit, vanity, restlessness which are making us miserable.

But as there lies in this name the power which may make us all that we can want to be, so there is in it also the infinite compassion and forgiveness for our failures, which we ask and ask in vain from all the doctors in the world, even those who seem most tolerant, even those who bid us content ourselves with acts and states of mind with which our consciences refuse to be content. I have a right to be like our Father in heaven. Likeness to him is my proper human condition. But I have also a right to go to him and say, "Father, I have not cared to be like thee, I have not believed that I could be like thee, I have not confessed myself to be thy child." I have a right to lay bare all my weakness before him, to speak to him as one who knows how great it is, as one who understands all my deflections from his ways, and cares for me more than I possibly can. "Be perfect according to this rule or that." "Yes, but may I confess to the rule? Will it understand me when I say I am sorry? Will it make me sorry?"—"Be perfect according to the standard of this holy man or that."—"Yes, but does he know what I am striving after?—Do his thoughts comprehend me? all my stupidity, all my selfishness? Can his life become mine?" "Be perfect as your Father in heaven is perfect." The wrestler who has had most falls, who has had most experience of the strength of the enemy, of his own feebleness; the man who is in deep mire where no ground is; he who is in fetters from which he only wishes to be free—hears this message and finds in it the assurance that he may yet rise up and walk; that there is a home for him, that there is one who will bring him to it. What anger, rage, inclination to hate, there is in him! How circumstances seem to conspire with it! What strong pleas seem to justify it! How it is banishing God from him! What a distance it is creating between him and his child! But he in whom is all mercy, forgiveness of enemies, patience, is not afar off. He bids me be what he is! He can convert me to be what he is! Who that has had a quiet, even pious education, can tell what infinite efforts it may be costing some poor or rich man, bred among people whose language was half made up of curses, to obey the precept "Swear not at all"? What would become of him if he might not throw himself on the pity and strength of the very Being whose name he is tempted continually to trifle with! When he does, how much more he may know of that Being than men do whose lot has been more fortunate!

This text, therefore, cuts through a number of webs in which casuists have entangled the human conscience. It does so by putting an end to those tricks of the deceitful heart into which we are all falling continually. "How oft," asks the Galilean—for he was just learning the first rudiments of his faith, under the divine teacher—"How oft shall my brother sin against me, and I forgive him?" What an opening for the refinements of a confessor or spiritual director! How accurately the degrees, qualities, occasions, times, objects, places of forgiveness, might be set down! What delicate distinctions, what hairbreadth evasions of difficulties! What torments to the memory and heart of the doubter, what practical indulgences to his worst inclinations! In our Lord's answer not a single subtlety. He replies by a simple parable which brings out the very meaning of our text. God forgives, thou art not unlike God, therefore thou art miserable if thou dost not forgive. There is no measure or limit in the command. God's mind is the standard. Try your mind by that. Be perfect as your Father in heaven is perfect.

**PHILLIPS BROOKS** (1835–1893) The writer of "O little town of Bethlehem" was one of the most prominent clergymen in the United States during the nineteenth century and certainly one of its greatest preachers. Phillips Brooks was raised in Boston and graduated from Harvard; after finishing his theological training at Virginia Seminary he was ordained to the priesthood in the Episcopal church. While rector of Holy Trinity Church, Philadelphia, he attracted attention because of his eloquent sermons, his keen intelligence, and his impressive personality. In 1869 he became rector of Trinity Church, Boston. Though baptized in the Unitarian church he had been reared as an Evangelical; he was subsequently influenced by the thought of two other men represented in this book, F. W. Robertson and F. D. Maurice. Their ideas contributed to Brooks's broad theological perspective. He became one of the leaders of liberal theological thought in his church; although his theology remained orthodox, he was opposed to biblical literalism and theological dogmatism. Nevertheless when he was elected Bishop of Massachusetts in 1891 there were loud voices in conservative ranks which protested his elevation. As he consistently maintained and as his famous Yale *Lectures on Preaching* made clear, the chief values in Christianity are personal not conceptual; as a preacher he sought to impart truth through personality, and his preaching contributed to the deepening and broadening of the Christian Faith for countless Americans. His untimely death was observed as a deep national loss.

Phillips Brooks brought a mature Christian faith into contact with a modern and changing world; this earned him much respect then and has been influential in theological thought and education into our own times. Brooks wrote out his sermons, and it has been said that he read from a manuscript at a rapid speed; if his words ever failed to gain the attention of his hearers, surely his massive frame would do so. He was six feet four inches tall and weighed three hundred pounds.

"The Light of the World" is one of Brooks's best known and most representative sermons.

# The Light
# of the World*

*Then spake Jesus again unto them, saying, I am the Light of the World: he that followeth me shall not walk in darkness, but shall have the Light of Life.*

JOHN 8:12

When the sun rose this morning it found the world here. It did not make the world. It did not fling forth on its earliest ray this solid globe, which was not and would not have been but for the sun's rising. What did it do? It found the world in darkness, torpid and heavy and asleep; with powers all wrapped up in sluggishness; with life that was hardly better or more alive than death. The sun found this great sleeping world and woke it. It bade it be itself. It quickened every slow and sluggish faculty. It called to the dull streams, and said, "Be quick"; to the dull birds and bade them sing; to the dull fields and bade them grow; to the dull men and bade them talk and think and work. It flashed electric invitation to the whole mass of sleeping power which really was the world, and summoned it to action. It did not make the world. It did not sweep a dead world off and set a live world in its place. It did not start another set of processes unlike those which had been sluggishly moving in the darkness. It poured strength into the essential processes which belonged to the very nature of the earth

* Condensed from the book *Phillips Brooks: Selected Sermons*, edited by Bishop William Scarlett. Copyright, 1949, by E. P. Dutton & Co., Inc. Reprinted by permission of the publisher.

which it illuminated. It glorified, intensified, fulfilled the earth; so that with the sun's work incomplete, with part of the earth illuminated and the rest lying in the darkness still, we can most easily conceive of the dark region looking in its half-life drowsily over to the region which was flooded with light, and saying, "There, there is the true earth! That is the real planet. In light and not in darkness the earth truly is itself."

That is the parable of the light. And now it seems to me to be of all importance to remember and assert all that to be distinctly a true parable of Christ. He says it is: "I am the Light of the world." A thousand things that means. A thousand subtle, mystic miracles of deep and intricate relationship between Christ and humanity must be enfolded in those words; but over and behind and within all other meanings, it means this—the essential richness and possibility of humanity and its essential belonging to Divinity.

Do you see what I mean? Christ rises on a soul. Christ rises on the world. I speak in crude and superficial language. For the moment I make no account of the deep and sacred truth—the truth which alone is finally and absolutely true—that Christ has always been with every soul and all the world. I talk in crude and superficial words, and say Christ comes to any soul or to the world. What is it that happens? If the figure of the Light is true, Christ when he comes finds the soul or the world really existent, really having within itself its holiest capabilities, really moving, though dimly and darkly, in spite of all its hindrances, in its true directions; and what he does for it is to quicken it through and through, to sound the bugle of its true life in its ears, to make it feel the nobleness of movements which have seemed to it ignoble, the hopefulness of impulses which have seemed hopeless, to bid it be itself.

The truth is that every higher life to which man comes, and especially the highest life in Christ, is in the true like of man's humanity; there is no transportation to a foreign region. There is the quickening and fulfilling of what man by the very essence of his nature is. The more man becomes irradiated with Divinity, the more, not the less, truly he is man. The fullest Christian experience is simply the fullest life. To enter into it therefore is no wise strange. The wonder and the unnaturalness is that any child of God should live outside of it, and so in all his life should never be himself.

When I repeat such truths they seem self-evident. No man, I think, denies them; and yet I feel the absence of their power all through men's struggles for the Christian life. A sense of foreignness and unnaturalness and strangeness lies like a fog across the entrance of the divine country; a certain wonder whether I, a man, have any business there; an unreality about it all; a break and gulf between what the world is and what we know it ought to be—all these are elements in the obscurity, the feebleness, the vague remoteness, of religion.

And yet how clear the Bible is about it all! How clear Christ is! It is redemption and fulfilment which he comes to bring to man. Those are his words. There is a true humanity which is to be restored, and all whose unattained possibilities are to be filled out. There is no human affection, of fatherhood, brotherhood, childhood, which is not capable of expressing divine relations. Man is a child of God, for whom his Father's house is waiting. The whole creation is groaning and travailing till man shall be complete. Christ comes not to destroy but to fulfil.

Let us see how all this is true in various applications. Apply it first to the standards of character. We talk of Christian character as if it were some separate and special thing unattempted, unsuggested by the human soul until it became aware of Christ. There would come a great flood of light and reality into it all if we knew thoroughly that the Christian character is nothing but the completed human character. The Christian is nothing but the true man. Nothing but the true man, do I say? As if that were a little thing! As if man, with any inflow of Divinity, could be, could wish to be anything more or different from man! But we imagine a certain vague array of qualities which are to belong to the Christian life which are not the intrinsic human qualities; and so our Christian type becomes unreal, and our human type loses its dignity and greatness. Human courage, human patience, human trustiness, human humility—these filled with the fire of God make the graces of the Christian life. We are still haunted by the false old distinction of the natural virtues and the Christian graces. The

Christian graces are nothing but the natural virtues held up into the light of Christ. They are made of the same stuff; they are lifted along the same lines; but they have found their pinnacle. They have caught the illumination which their souls desire. Manliness has not been changed into Godliness; it has fulfilled itself in Godliness.

As soon as we understand all this, then what a great, clear thing salvation becomes. Its one idea is health. Not rescue from suffering, not plucking out of fire, not deportation to some strange, beautiful region where the winds blow with other influences and the skies drop with other dews, not the enchanting of the spirit with some unreal celestial spell, but health—the cool, calm vigor of the normal human life; the making of the man to be himself; the calling up out of the depths of his being and the filling with vitality of that self which is truly he— this is salvation.

Of course it all assumes that in this mixture of good and evil which we call Man, this motley and medley which we call human character, it is the good and not the evil which is the foundation color of the whole. Man is a son of God on whom the Devil has laid his hand, not a child of the Devil whom God is trying to steal. That is the first truth of all religion. That is what Christ is teaching everywhere and always. "We called the chessboard white, we call it black"; but it is, this chessboard of our human life, white not black—black spotted on white, not white spotted upon black.

Does this make smaller or less important that great Power of God whereby the human life passes from the old condition to the new— the power of conversion? Certainly not! What task could be more worthy of the Father's power and love than this assertion and fulfilment of his child? All of our Christian thinking and talking has been and is haunted by a certain idea of failure and recommencement. Man is a failure, so there shall be a new attempt; and in place of the man we will make the Christian! There is nothing of that tone about what Jesus says. The Christian to Jesus is the man. The Christian, to all who think the thought of Jesus after him, is the perfected and completed man.

This makes the higher life intelligible, and so makes it real. This alone makes such a thing as Christian Manliness conceivable. Christian Unmanliness is what a great many of men's pious, earnest struggles have been seeking. If the saint on to all eternity is to be the ever-ripening man, never changing into any new and unknown thing which he was not before, never to all eternity unfolding one capacity which was not in the substance of his humanity from its creation, then it follows that the most celestial and transcendent goodnesses must still be one in kind with the familiar virtues which sometimes in their crude and earthly shapes seem low and commonplace. Courage in all the worlds is the same courage. Truth before the throne of God is the same thing as when neighbor talks with neighbor on the street. Mercy will grow tenderer and finer, but will be the old blessed balm of life in the fields of eternity that it was in your workshop and your home. Unselfishness will expand and richen till it enfolds the life like sunshine, but it will be the same self-denial, opening into a richer self-indulgence, which it was when it first stole in with one thin sunbeam on the startled soul. There is no new world of virtues in any heaven or in any heavenly experience of life. God is good and man is good; and as man becomes more good, he becomes not merely more like God, but more himself. As he becomes more godly, he becomes more manly too. It is so hard for us to believe in the Mystery of Man.

The Mystery of Man! How Christ believed in that! Oh, my dear friends, he who does not believe in that cannot enter into the full glory of the Incarnation, cannot really believe in Christ. Where the mysterious reach of manhood touches the divine, there Christ appears.

Men talk about the Christhood, and say, "How strange it is! Strange that Christ should have been—strange that Christ should have suffered for mankind." Once feel the mystery of man and is it strange? Once think with himself, once see humanity capable of being filled with God, and can you conceive of his not doing it? Must there not be an Incarnation? Do you not instantly begin to search earth for the holy steps? Once think it possible that Christ can, and are you not sure that Christ must give himself for our Redemption? So only, when it seems inevitable and natural, does the Christhood become our pattern. Then only does it shine on the mountaintop up toward which we can feel the low lines of our low life aspiring. The Son of God is also the Son of Man. Then in us, the sons of men, there is the key to the secret of his being and his work. Know Christ that you may know yourself. But, oh, also know yourself that you may know Christ.

I think to every Christian there come times when all the strangeness disappears from the divine humanity which stands radiant at the center of his faith. He finds it hard to believe in himself and in his brethren perhaps; but that Christ should be and should be Christ appears the one reasonable, natural, certain thing in all the universe. In him all broken lines unite; in him all scattered sounds are gathered into harmony; and out of the consummate certainty of him, the soul comes back to find the certainty of common things which the lower faith holds, which advancing faith loses, and then finds again in Christ.

How every truth attains to its enlargement and reality in this great truth—that the soul of man carries the highest possibilities within itself, and that what Christ does for it is to kindle and call forth these possibilities to actual existence. We do not understand the Church until we understand this truth. Seen in its light the Christian Church is nothing in the world except the promise and prophecy and picture of what the world in its idea is and always has been, and in its completion must visibly become. It is the primary crystallization of humanity. It is no favored, elect body caught from the ruin, given a salvation in which the rest can have no part. It is an attempt to realize the universal possibility. All men are its potential members. The strange thing for any man is not that he should be within it, but that he should be without it. Every good movement of any most secular sort is a struggle toward it, a part of its activity. All the world's history is ecclesiastical history, is the story of the success and failure, the advance and hindrance of the ideal humanity, the Church of the living God.

Great is the power of a life which knows that its highest experiences are its truest experiences, that it is most itself when it is at its best. For it each high achievement, each splendid vision, is a sign and token of the whole nature's possibility.

My dear friends, you never will know the horror and misery of sin till you know the glory and mystery of man. You never can estimate the disaster of an interruption till you know the worth of what it interrupts. You never will understand wickedness by dwelling on the innate depravity of man. You can understand wickedness only by knowing that the very word man means holiness and strength.

Here, too, lies the sublime and beautiful variety of human life. It is as beings come to their reality that they assert their individuality. In the gutter all the poor wretches lie huddled together, one indistinguishable mass of woe; but on the mountaintop each figure stands out separate and clear against the blueness of the sky. The intense variety of Light! The awful monotony of darkness! Men are various; Christians ought to be various a thousandfold. Strive for your best, that there you may find your most distinctive life. We cannot dream of what interest the world will have when every being in its human multitude shall shine with his own light and color, and be the child of God which it is possible for him to be—which he has ever been in the true homeland of this Father's thought.

Do I talk fancies? Do I paint visions upon unsubstantial clouds? If it seem to you that I do, I beg you to come back now, as I close, to those words which I quoted to you at the beginning. "I am the Light of the world," said Jesus. Do you not see now what I meant when I declared that it was in making the world know itself that Christ was primarily the Power of the world's redemption? The Revealer and the Redeemer are not two persons, but only one—one Saviour.

What then? If Christ can make you know yourself; if as you walk with him day by day, he can reveal to you your sonship to the Father; if, keeping daily company with him, you can come more and more to know how native is goodness and how unnatural sin is to the soul of man; if, dwelling with him who is both God and Man, you can come to believe both in God and in Man through him, then you are saved— saved from contempt, saved from despair, saved into courage and hope and charity and the power to resist temptation, and the passionate pursuit of perfectness.

It is as simple and as clear as that. Our religion is not a system of ideas about Christ. It is Christ. To believe in him is what? To say a creed? To join a church? No; but to have a great, strong, divine

Master, whom we perfectly love, whom we perfectly trust, whom we will follow anywhere, and who, as we follow him or walk by his side, is always drawing out in us our true nature and making us determined to be true to it through everything, is always compelling us to see through falsehood and find the deepest truth, which is, in one great utterance of it, that we are the sons of God, who is thus always "leading us to the Father."

The hope of the world is in the ever-richer naturalness of the highest life. "The earth shall be full of the knowledge of God as the waters cover the sea."

Your hope and mine is the same. The day of our salvation has not come till every voice brings us one message; till Christ, the Light of the world, everywhere reveals to us the divine secret of our life; till everything without joins with the consciousness all alive within, and "the Spirit itself beareth witness with our spirits that we are the children of God."

# HERBERT HENSLEY HENSON (1863–1947)

H. Hensley Henson was born in London and educated at Oxford; in 1884, he was elected a Fellow of All Souls, Oxford, and several years later he served as a Vicar and a Chaplain in the Church of England. From 1900 to 1912 he was Rector of St. Margaret's, which is beside Westminster Abbey; it was then that his quiet, incisive sermons began to attract attention and it was in the Abbey in 1901 that the sermon we include here was preached. Henson was a small man of feeble constitution and had a thin voice, but there was magnetism in his manner; and his keen mind, deep convictions, and acute observation of social and moral trends of the times combined to make his sermons both important and pertinent. As this sermon indicates, he was concerned to translate the basic principles of Christianity into contemporary terms and to see them affect current and changing situations; here the clarification of the essence of Christianity as discipleship in turn points to the recovery of Christian unity among the churches, a cause to which he devoted himself with characteristic fervor.

There were other important causes to which Henson gave himself. He was a leader of the broad Church movement and liberal theology; his views on the Virgin Birth and Christ's miracles caused no little disturbance among other clergy and conservative churchmen. He apparently retracted some of his opinions before being consecrated as Bishop of Hereford in 1918. In 1920 he became Bishop of Durham, where from 1912 to 1918 he had been Dean of the Cathedral. As a bishop he continued to be a controversial figure, causing some alarm in 1929, and thereafter fighting for the disestablishment of the Church of England. To him controversy was inevitable for a clergyman who was faithful to the truth of Christ. His was a formidable personality, but his diocesan clergy grew to know him as a warm person and a true friend and pastor. His sermons and addresses to those about to be ordained deacons and priests were deeply treasured by the ordinands, and they are still read throughout the Anglican communion as helpful, encouraging guides for pastoral care.

# Discipleship*

*Jesus Christ is the same yesterday, and today, yea, and for ever.*  HEBREWS 13:8

Essential Christianity must be original Christianity, Christianity as the Founder presented it, before the distorting, disintegrating influences of history had borne down upon it, before it had attracted to itself alien interests, and contracted compromising affinities, Christianity in the simplicity of its beginnings, in the unspotted purity of its new birth—in a word, the Christianity of Christ, and not the Christianity of Christendom. When we ask what original Christianity actually was, our appeal lies of necessity to the New Testament, and therein, primarily, to the Gospels. In those brief narratives, so brief that the whole of their contents would not fill a single file of the *Times,* we must find the answer to our question.

The answer is on the surface. Original Christianity was a discipleship to Jesus Christ. He claimed from men love, teachableness, self-surrender in obedience. He offered himself as their friend, their teacher, and their Lord, and he built his expectation of their acceptance on the impression he had made on them by his life and doctrine. Living frankly in their midst, no distant figure girt with a halo of romance, but a familiar object in their daily experience, "the Son of Man came eating and drinking," mingling without reserve in the ordinary intercourse of human society. He invited them to study his character at

* From *Godly Union and Concord* (London: John Murray, 1902). Used by permission of the publisher.

short range, to consider his conduct in detail, to weigh his habitual conversation as well as his formal teachings, and so to come to a decision on his claim when in due time he proposed it to them.

Discipleship implied the frank acceptance of Christ's personal claims, and the power which won that acceptance was the power of Christ's personal influence. Our Lord rarely argued about himself. His self-assertion was, for the most part, unmitigated by explanations. Men had to face it, so to say, in its natural difficulty. But this he did: he brought them into his own intimate society. He made them the companions of his daily life. He bade them know him thoroughly, observe him closely, criticize him anxiously; and to these ends he placed them in habitual contact with himself, and on the basis of their intimate and protracted knowledge of him, challenged their verdict of his personal claim: "Who say ye that I am?"

But what did discipleship practically involve? Obviously, at the time to those first disciples, peril, loss, temporal ruin. They did not see it. Probably if they had seen the future that lay before them, they would not have found the courage to respond to Christ's appeal. They did not see it; but he saw it, and, with frankness of perfect honesty, set it before them. Nothing could be sterner or more threatening than the prospect which he unfolded before his disciples. His own rejection, passion, death of ignominy would mean for them disappointment, opprobrium, danger. Yet, throughout, the note of divine authority prevails: "He that loveth father or mother more than me is not worthy of me, and he that loveth son or daughter more than me is not worthy of me. And he that doth not take up his cross and follow after me is not worthy of me."

Times would change: they did change. So far as the world is concerned, discipleship would not involve trouble. Would, then, the "offence of the cross" have ceased? Surely not, for, in truth, the least part of the difficulty lay in the external sphere where violence is possible. It is in our own time, out of the midst of an ostentatiously religious society, that the cry has been heard, so full of perplexity and anguish:

> How very hard it is to be
> A Christian! Hard for you and me.

Discipleship goes deeper than the external circumstances of life. "Jesus Christ is the same, yesterday, and today, yea, and for ever." The terms of his service reflect his changelessness. His standpoints, his standards of value, his judgments remain, amid all revolutions of society, unalterable; and in the honest acceptance of these lies the essence of discipleship.

Discipleship is the abiding aspect of Christianity. Look at the facts. Christianity, regarded from the standpoints of the ecclesiastic and the theologian, has a very unstable appearance. We are, indeed, very familiar with the claim that churches and creeds do not change. The human mind, pathetically conscious of its own infirmity, clings desperately to the delusion of changelessness. Persistently it claims for some ecclesiastical order or some theological system that it reproduces faithfully the institutions and doctrines of the Divine Founder. When the fact of novelty is too evident to be denied, refuge is taken in the notion of development. In this Church, or in that dogmatic system, alone must the founder's intention be recognized. Christendom is weary of the civil wars of Christians in which every banner bears the proud device, "The faith which was once for all delivered unto the saints." There has come on the scene the one impartial and authoritative arbiter. Institutions and beliefs, churches and creeds, are forced to plead before the judgment seat of historical science. One result has been an extensive destruction of controversial assumptions. The divine right of existing types of ecclesiastical order, and systems of theology—insofar as it rests on the claim to perpetuate the founder's original arrangements—cannot survive the criticism of historical students. We know now that the Church of Christ received from the divine Founder no rigid and articulated organization, that neither the faith, nor the government, nor the discipline of the Christian society was defined in advance; that the apostles, to whom the task of founding the Church was given, were assured the presence of the guiding "Spirit of Truth," and sent out into the world to learn by experiment and failure the right methods of organization. Apart from this appeal to the past, our own observations might well convince us of the futility of the claim to changelessness. Everything is in process of change. Churches and creeds, as such, have no immunity from the law of change: but if the essence of Christianity be not the membership of a church, nor yet the acceptance of a system of belief, but, rather, discipleship to a living Person, then it seems possible to hope that Christianity may possess an indestructible life. For its "life is hid with Christ in God."

The religion of Christ will last precisely so long as Christ is able to command the hearts, intellects, and wills of men. Discipleship, in the common experience of mankind, terminates in one of two ways. On the one hand, the disciple may outstrip his teacher, learn all he has to teach, and advance into regions where he has no message. On the other hand, the disciple may lose confidence in the teacher, shake off the spell of his personal influence, set himself free from his moral and intellectual control. Can either of these contingencies happen in the case of the Christian discipleship? Are there any signs that Christians have outgrown the teachings of the Master? Is the world growing weary of the ideal presented in the Gospel? As far as I can see, the evidence points in the opposite direction. Men are doubtful and sceptical about the Church; they suspect and dislike the clergy: they are impatient of theological systems; but for Jesus Christ, as he stands out to view in the sacred pages, as they dimly realize him in their own best selves, as they catch faint traces of him in the lives of his saints, they have no other sentiments than those of respect and affection. In the twentieth century he allures men as in the first, by the attraction of himself. "Jesus Christ is the same, yesterday, and today, yea, and for ever."

The changes of Christianity which, at first sight, perplex and distress us, are not only intelligible, but even necessary, when Christianity is conceived as a discipleship. For discipleship must always include the notion of advance. In truth, not to advance is to cease to be a disciple. That is the best discipleship which, as time passes, enters ever more deeply into the Master's mind, assimilates more of the Master's teaching, and moves onward into a closer agreement with the Master's character. This is certainly true of the individual Christian. He advances slowly in spiritual knowledge, surrenders himself more completely to the government of the divine Spirit, accepts more frankly the standpoints of Jesus, and so, by very gradual stages, and with many backslidings, grows into the likeness of his Lord. Not otherwise is the case of the Christian society, the Body of Christ, the visible Church. There is through the centuries an advance in Christianity. The resources of the gospel are drawn upon in the successive crises of Christian experience. The bearings of Christ's doctrine are slowly perceived. Every generation has its own problems; and in finding their own solution in the Christian revelation, every generation finds out something more of Christ's message, and hands on the great Christian tradition, enriched and extended. It is manifest that there can be no finality in the sphere of organization and formulated doctrine, for these have reference to conditions of life and thought, which are constantly changing. In these respects, the past cannot give law to the present, for the very obvious and sufficient reason that the needs of the present are not the same as the needs of the past, and the whole circumstances are different.

Certainly if, abandoning all formal notions of ecclesiastical continuity and all rigid theories of theological uniformity, we regard the history of Christianity as the long-drawn-out probation of discipleship, it seems to me that we gather comfort and confidence. Consider what amazing fortunes have been experienced by the religion of Jesus. I can find no parallel in the religious history of mankind. Christianity has mastered the two highest human civilizations. The "seed of God" was cast into the very midst of classical society in the heart of its golden age: it seemed predestined to rapid extinction or to an utter sterility. The gospel of a crucified Messiah revolted the Jews: the revelation of a suffering Deity scandalized the Greeks: the severity of its moral demand alienated the Orientals: the homage it paid to weakness —the woman and the child—moved the laughter of the imperial race. It seemed to have at the time no recommendations whatever. Looking back, with the commentary of many centuries to guide us, we can see what at the time was not seen, that, unknown to themselves, Jew and Greek, Oriental and Roman were blindly groping after that which Christianity was actually offering. At the time, however, so extreme seemed the aversion which the gospel provoked, that an inspired apostle could only describe it in the terms of an audacious paradox: "The foolishness of God is wiser than men; and the weakness of God is stronger than men." Then befell the mightiest ruin of all history, that downfall of the Roman Empire, which has been not excessively described as "the foundering of a world." Christianity faced the barbarians of the North in the flush of victory, in the exasperation of conflict.

Christ's personal influence was never more potent:

> And centuries came and ran their course,
> And unspent all that time
> Still, still went forth that Child's dear force
> And still was at its prime.

Under its spell our rude ancestors passed and became the artificers of a nobler civilization than that which they wrecked—the civilization of modern Christendom. Pass on to the sixteenth century, when the mediaeval church, overweighted with its corruptions, fell with a violence and suddenness which shook the very bases of society. All the time-honored securities of Christian faith and morals seemed to have been finally abandoned. Yet the ruin did not come. The New Testament, rising, as it were suddenly from centuries of neglect, took the place of the discredited Church tradition. The Founder came nearer to men again, and his personal influence refounded Christianity. The sixteenth century witnessed the downfall of exaggerated ecclesiasticism; the nineteenth witnessed the downfall of exaggerated dogmatism. The Founder stands out again in more marked prominence, and draws to himself a more ample homage. "Jesus Christ is the same, yesterday, and today, yea, and for ever."

Finally, it is in realizing our Christian profession as before all things a discipleship to Jesus Christ that we shall recover fraternity. The nearer we draw to our Master, the nearer we draw also to one another. The two relationships are inseparable. Perfect discipleship implies perfect fraternity. So he said, "One is your Teacher, and all ye are brethren." Discipleship is not destructive of church membership, only it discovers the link of union not in any external agreement or discipline, but in a common allegiance to a living Lord. It lies on the surface of the gospel that Christ contemplated the organization of his disciples; and the visible Church, with its ministry, sacraments and discipline, is unquestionably his creation; indeed, the visible Church is a practical necessity if the mission of Christ is to be perpetuated in the world: but with all this the primary truth remains, that the basis of union and the essence of religion does not lie in the social organization but in the personal relationship.

If, as disciples, we approach the matters that now divide us from one another, how extraordinarily petty they appear! The late Bishop Creighton,* in his primary charge, asserted his belief that we Anglicans are ready to co-operate with all other Christians for purposes which we have in common.

Wherever Christians are forced back on discipleship, they cannot refrain themselves from confessing their brotherhood in the Holy Communion. In front of the heathen, the intercommunion for which I have pleaded is already an accomplished fact, wherever the issue is directly raised. "Yesterday," wrote that illustrious missionary, Bishop French, "I turned my little sitting room here into a chapel and had ten worshippers—prayers, sermon, and Holy Communion, to which seven stayed, mostly Presbyterians, whom I could not possibly exclude. These dear, good American missionaries and professors will sit much nearer to the Lamb at his supper table, I believe, than I shall, and I should blush if admitted there, to think that I had warned them off the eucharistic table on earth."

I say with Bishop French, "It is the infinite concern which I have for Christ and his blessed truth and Church, which makes me eschew soft utterances at some moments of almost desperation at the way in which the regiments within the Christian army—those who have the same devotion to the King and his Bride—set to work fighting each other and riddling the allied ranks with grape-shot and worse, instead of charging with one heart and soul the common foe." And I make appeal with confidence to the consciences of all those in all the churches which bear Christ's honorable Name, who feel the shame and weakness of our present state, and are ready to make some effort and even some sacrifice, to recover the lost fraternity of Christ's disciples.

* Mandell Creighton (1843–1901) became Bishop of London in 1897 and was also a noted church historian.

# HENRY SLOANE COFFIN (1877–1954) A notable preacher recently remarked that almost all he could hope to teach students of homiletics he himself had learned from Dr. Coffin. Today many clergy of several denominations are profoundly indebted to the wisdom and advice which they have received from him. Henry Sloane Coffin was not only a great preacher, scholar, seminary president, and pastor, he was also a great man. Born in New York City, he later attended Yale University; upon graduating from Yale he then studied at New College, Edinburgh, at the University of Marburg, and at Union Theological Seminary in New York, from which he received his Bachelor of Divinity. He was a Presbyterian and ministered to the Bedford Park Presbyterian Church in New York from 1900 to 1905; from then to 1926 he was minister at the Madison Avenue Presbyterian Church, where he achieved a widespread reputation as one of the country's outstanding preachers. From 1926 until 1945 he was president of Union Theological Seminary during days in which important theological history was in the making.

Henry Sloane Coffin was no bystander toward the important events and movements in the Church during the first half of this century; he was active in the ecumenical movement, an advocate of social reform, an able apologist, a theologian in his own right, and a preacher and teacher of preachers as well. He also wrote numerous books. In the year 1943–44 he was Moderator of the Presbyterian Church in the United States. During his lifetime he was University Preacher at such universities as Yale, Princeton, Harvard, Columbia, and Chicago. Though liberal in outlook and contemporary in spirit, he nevertheless preached in bold fashion the faith once delivered unto the saints. Central to his faith and preaching was the cross and its meaning, as this sermon, "Christ as Suffering Savior," which came from his early days as a pastor, clearly shows.

# Christ as
# Suffering Savior*

*The Son of man must suffer.* MARK 8:31

How came Jesus to be so confident? Was it that from childhood he had been aware of a clash between his ideals and those of everyone he met, making him feel misunderstood at home, lonely among his companions, isolated in the midst of the group of men who came closest to him, and out of sympathy with the hopes and plans of the most earnest in Israel; so that in all the thoughts and aspirations of his day he had no where to lay his head? Was it through his familiarity with the fate of God's messengers before him—a destiny brought home to him most keenly in the murder of his friend, John the Baptist? Certainly their martyrdoms were often in his mind—"O Jerusalem, Jerusalem, which killeth the prophets and stoneth them that are sent unto her!" Was it from his penetration into the profoundest principles of the universe, and his discovery that suffering enters into the divine law of the whole creation, where all life is born of pain and death—golden harvest fields of grains of wheat which die in lonely darkness, and man of woman in travail? Was it a deeper insight than that of his contemporaries into certain messages of the Hebrew Scriptures which convinced him that God's Messiah must be a sufferer for his people

* From *The Creed of Jesus and Other Sermons* (New York: Charles Scribner's Sons, 1907). Copyright 1907 by Charles Scribner's Sons. Used by permission of the publisher.

"wounded for their transgressions and bruised for their iniquities?" Perhaps through one of these, or through all of them together, he became certain that the Son of man to save must suffer.

And how? First, in sympathy. Jesus was himself spared many of the ills and woes that pain his brethren. So far as the records go, he never knew a day of sickness. He touched the leper without the slightest fear of contagion. Matthew applies to him the saying, "Himself took our infirmities and bare our diseases," but he did so only in his compassion for the sufferers. Nor are we shown him sorrowing in intense loneliness at the death of those he loved. If one evangelist pictures him as shedding tears for his friend Lazarus, it is with the consciousness that in a very few minutes he can awake him from his sleep. He never laid wife or child of his own in a grave.

To be sure he had his personal griefs—unbelieving brothers, fierce temptations to be faced in solitary struggle, constant misunderstandings and misrepresentations from those he was eager to do most for, faithless friends—one a traitor, a mother to be parted from in death, life itself to be given up in excruciating agony—life which meant more to him than to any other human being because he could do so much more with it; "Greater love hath no man than this that a man lay down his *life.*" "A Man of Sorrows and acquainted with grief!"

But as one reads the Gospels one is seldom aware of Jesus' personal sadness. He had lost himself too completely to let his own griefs cast any shadow on the scenes through which he moved. His figure throws no shadow because it is itself so shaded by the shadows of others.

His sensitive nature throbbed in response to every mute appeal of wretchedness. The poor and illiterate, upon whom the scribes looked down as of no account in things religious, he spoke of affectionately as "the little ones," and as babes who see things hidden from the wise and learned. The tedious infirmity of chronic sufferers, like that of the woman bent in body for eighteen years, the injustice endured by the victims of long-praying Pharisees who devoured widows' houses, the ostracism of publicans and harlots by those who should have embodied the loving forgiveness of their God touched his heart. He pitied others until he had no pity left for himself. "Daughters of Jerusalem, weep not for me, but weep for yourselves and for your children!"

Such an intensely sensitive soul was foredoomed in a world like ours to be a constant sufferer.

> For he who lives more lives than one,
> More deaths than one must die.

Jesus lived as many lives as he had brothers. He was ill in their sicknesses, slighted in their neglect, burdened in their oppression, disgraced in their wrong-doing and sad in their sorrows. "The Son of man must suffer."

Secondly, he suffered as a martyr for a cause. His convictions of God and of the Kingdom God purposed for his children compelled him to say and do many things that brought him into conflict with the principles and prejudices of the best people of his day. He felt bound to associate in the most friendly fashion with publicans and disreputable women; and that scandalized the Jewish Church. He felt compelled to disregard the Sabbath Law in the interests of humanity, and to treat the distinction between things clean and unclean as of no value, because it took the emphasis off cleanness of motive. He felt it necessary to criticize and disagree with parts of their inspired Scriptures, such as Moses' Law of Divorce, because it did not do justice to the woman as a child of the Father in heaven, and with other Scripture sayings because they tended to obscure the love of God for everybody: "Ye have heard that it was said by them of old time, but I say unto you."

To the respectable and devout who took him seriously he seemed an anarchist, a socialist, a heretic, a revolutionary; and to others a fanatic and a visionary. In Galilee, where religious thought was freer, he had conflicts here and there with local scribes, and with committees from the more earnest men at the capital, who took the trouble to come down and see what he was doing. And when at length he felt called to go up to orthodox and conservative Jerusalem, and to enter it openly as the Messiah, amid the Hosannas of the crowds of provincial pilgrims attending the Passover, the leaders felt that some action must be taken.

Then came the cleansing of the Temple—a direct attack in public upon the vested rights of the wealthy priestly families—and his name was on every man's tongue. Religious Pharisees and indifferent Sadducees agreed that this Man was dangerous and must be got rid of. Between these men of average, or more than average, goodness, in what was probably the most morally religious land in the world of that day, and the character and purpose of God represented by Jesus there came an inevitable collision. "The Son of man must suffer."

Thirdly, he suffered as a sin-bearer. We are surprised at the way in which Jesus, usually so fearless, confronts death. He does not speak of it beforehand with the tone of triumph we should have expected. "I have a baptism to be baptized with, and how am I straitened till it be accomplished." As the dreaded event comes nearer, he shrinks from it with abhorrence and loathing, as from a frightful tragedy. In the Garden we see him restless and burdened, as though an awful strain were upon him. "He began to be greatly amazed and sore troubled. And he saith unto his disciples, my soul is exceeding sorrowful even unto death." The prayers he utters are cries from a black abyss. "My Father, if it be possible, let this cup pass away from me." At length the horror of great darkness falls upon him, and he feels himself a castaway. "My God, my God, why hast thou forsaken me?"

This is not the way in which brave men, and especially those who stand for a noble cause, face death. Paul under no less terrifying circumstances writes, "If I am poured out as a drink-offering upon the sacrifice and service of your faith, I joy and rejoice with you all." Many a pagan, with not clear hope of a future life, has gone to as excruciating tortures without flinching. Many a coarse hired trooper, for the sake of his honor as a soldier, has marched to the cannon's mouth without a tremor. Many an unremembered Christian martyr—a weak woman, or a convert of only a few weeks' standing—has endured as cruel torments and much more protracted pain, with a boldness and a victorious assurance, quite different from the dejection and dread and utter collapse of the Son of man. Are the disciples above the Master?

How shall we account for Jesus' attitude? By the cause for which he stood, and by this sympathy both with his murderers and with his God.

On the one hand, he felt himself so completely at one with God that every opposition to himself, every stripe given his back, every thorn pressed upon his aching forehead, every nail driven into his quivering flesh was directed against his Father and gave him pain—was sin against God. He might say of his crucifiers, "They know not what they do"; but he knew, and because he knew, he shuddered. His opponents were setting themselves against the universe, of which his Father was Lord, and were dooming themselves to suffer. He was overwhelmed by the awfulness of the tragedy of God's rejection, and the terrible consequences it involved.

And, on the other hand, he felt himself one by ties of brotherhood with the very men who slew him. He had a life in each of their lives, and in every wrong of which they were guilty he was implicated. The want of love that made them blind to him and hostile to the purpose of God was a family disgrace, which he bore as well as they. As the conscientious member of a family feels the shame of a relative's crime, while the culprit himself may not be seriously disturbed, so Jesus was the conscience of his less conscientious brothers, and felt the burden of the shame which they should have felt in thwarting and paining their Father. "The reproaches of them that reproached thee fell on me." He realized, as they did not, the enormity of what they were doing to him. He felt, as they could not, the load of their guilt. In the curse which they brought on themselves he was accursed. He numbered himself among the transgressors; and no one ever appreciated how heavy was the load of transgression, until it was laid on the Son of man and well-nigh crushed him beneath it. In no fictitious sense, but really, in the wounds in his body and the weight of shame on his heart, Jesus bore his brothers' sins in his own body on the tree; he suffered, the just for the unjust.

And yet there is another aspect of his attitude toward the cross. He courted death. He went up of his own accord to Jerusalem. He laid down his life willingly. His life given up in devotion would be the means of freeing many. His blood would seal a new covenant of complete oneness of heart between the Father and his children. Pain and death undergone for love's sake meant not disaster but victory. The Son of man in suffering would save.

How? Jesus himself is not explicit, and as for ourselves—we can never explain all the ins and outs of love. It passeth knowledge. But this we know from the experience of many generations of Christians that the love of Christ—shown in his sympathy, in his devotion to love's cause unto death, in his faith in love's power—takes hold of us and becomes for us the mightiest force we know.

And, when we are drawn to and made one with Christ, we feel that the tragedy of Calvary is not a mere thing of the past. We are ourselves members of the family which slew its elder brother; and, worse yet, we are ourselves moved daily by the same motives that governed Pharisee and Sadducee, a Judas, a Herod, a Pontius Pilate. The crucifixion would be as certain now as it was then. The Son of man must as inevitably suffer. In the social life of today there is the same unbrotherliness, in ourselves the same selfishness. The cross is not an event in ancient history. It comes home to us as something personal and present. It is not merely that Christ, like other martyrs for righteousness' sake, advances the cause of love, and makes me his debtor as an inheritor of all that he gained by his splendid devotion—although that is unspeakably precious. But he is more—he is the embodiment of my conscience; and all that he feels, I ought to feel and, in a sense, I do feel. "I am crucified with Christ." I die to unbrotherliness, to selfishness. They can no longer rule me. They are exposed in the blood of my best friend, and their fascination for me is gone. "I am crucified with Christ; and it is no longer I that live, but Christ liveth in me." I am alive to all he lived for and died for, alive with his interests, his sympathy, his faith, his hopes, his purposes, his love. And that is to be saved.

And that means that I too, like the Son of man, must suffer. At one with Christ in heart, I cannot but feel for, and feel with, every ignorant and abused and wretched and unloved brother the world over. No man is saved—made alive with the life of God, the life that was in his Son—who has not a fellowship with Christ's sufferings, a share in his struggle, a partnership with him in bringing men by love into the new covenant of complete oneness of heart with God. "He laid down his life for us, and we ought to lay down our lives for the brethren:" only insofar as that "ought" takes hold of us, and makes us transform it into our own "I must," are we saved by him, who loved us and gave himself up for us.

To be reconciled to God, to be saved to him, to be in fellowship with him as sons with a Father, to be partakers of the divine nature, alive with his life, animated by his spirit, conformed to his character, is to share his loving purpose for his children, and to give ourselves, as our Father gives himself, to make them wholly his. By suffering with and for us he redeems us, that we by suffering with and for our brethren may redeem them. And every son of man, who would be a son of the Father, must come not to be ministered unto but to minister, and to give his life for the emancipation of many.

**ARTHUR JOHN GOSSIP** (1873–1954) It has been said that the Scottish people love to hear the preaching of a scholarly man; they pride themselves that their preachers are men of intelligence and learning as well as dedicated and spiritual men. Certainly it is because these people loved and expected preaching at its very best that the Scottish church has been blessed with so many outstanding preachers—pearls are not cast before swine. One such preacher of whom they were justly proud was Arthur J. Gossip. He was born in Glasgow and attended Edinburgh University. In 1898, he became a pastor in the Free Church of Scotland (Presbyterian); during the First World War he was a chaplain. For thirty years he was a pastor to several churches in Scotland, and gradually he became recognized as a great preacher. He had an amazing sense of presence and was noted though not appreciated always for occasional use of slang in the pulpit. In 1928, he became professor of practical theology and Christian Ethics at Trinity College, Glasgow, and remained at the university until his retirement in 1945. He had published numerous collections of his sermons in the "Scholar as Preacher Series," and he wrote the exposition for the Gospel of John in *The Interpreter's Bible*. In 1927, his wife died suddenly leaving him with five young children. One sign of the depth and sincerity of his faith can be found in the powerful sermon preached the Sunday after she died. The sermon selected for this collection comes from that same period; it is remarkable for its brilliant ability to evoke images, stimulate the imagination, and move the will to discover again the richness of life that comes only by living in Christ.

# What Shall
# We Choose from Life?*

**D**id you ever notice how much Jesus loved that touch of something extra in a life, that running out over the wall? Yes, you grumble, and how can I give it him—I, planted down in a narrow place, in a set round of petty little drudgeries? Yet even there it can be done, and with enormous consequences. If working men would give, not just a fair day's work, but added to that something extra, the old pride in what they do, a personal interest in the business that thinks of it proudly as their business, and doesn't mind a half-hour more upon occasion, would not that make all the difference, and bring in contracts that are being lost for lack of it, and lift us as a nation out of this dangerous time? And if employers gave, not just a fair day's wage, but added to that something extra, a touch of human interest and friendship, would not that ease many minds that, toil how they may, are never more than a few days or weeks ahead of grim possibilities that set their souls shivering, not for themselves so much as for their dear ones? And so in all our relationships. Let your branches run over the wall; fling in the extra with an eager hand. That is the Christ touch, and our Lord's own way, and what he claims from you and me. "What do ye more than others?" He expects more, not just duty, but that and something added. Always it is the extra that alone suffices.

There is a well-worn gibe against an apocryphal countryman of

* From *The Hero in Thy Soul* (Edinburgh: T. & T. Clark, 1928; New York: Charles Scribner's Sons, 1930). Used by permission of the publishers.

mine, that as he gloomily picked up his money from the counter, he was asked, "Is your change not right, sir?" and replied morosely, "Yes; but just right." Well, that touches the sore. The difficulty is that it is not anything like enough to be just, though that seems all that we can offer; we are asked to love. And less than that means chaos.

The mistake that we keep making is that we will try to run this earth of ours in a mere huckstering way, cautiously paying down the exact amount, measured with meticulous care, for what has with an equally scrupulous accuracy been doled out, drop by drop. And things will never run happily until we learn something of God's enormous generosity, God who never thinks of his own profit, but only of what he can do for others; who does not bother about hours, but, as Christ said, works on and on, all day and every day, week day and resting day alike; who heaps up more on more, and grace on grace, and, sheer bewilderment on sheer bewilderment, is never satisfied to give only the minimum that will suffice. He makes a world, and though seen from his eternities it is only a shadow seen and gone, what infinite skill he lavishes upon it; he grants us life for seventy little years, and what a wonderful life it is, no bleached, lean, unappetizing thing that will pass muster, but gay with color, crowded with endless interests; he thinks out a salvation for our most unworthy souls, and the angels stare at it, stunned and half incredulous, for he has thrown in all God's all, has given his most, his best, God's everything, for us. God, says James in a brilliant metaphor, is like the sun at high noon, always giving all he has. And he expects that we, his children, will live after his own generous way, that our branches will not merely be primly trained in their due place, but that in a riot of liberality they will reach out far over the wall, and right across the road.

Gissing, that needy city sparrow, was staggered, on wandering into the country for the first time, by the lavishness of Nature, who gave him from her bramble bushes not merely a berry or two, as is man's niggardly way, but as much as he could wish, and all for nothing. And Christ tells us that he looks for something similar in us. I want you, he says, to be to others something of what you have found in me. You have never found me fail you. Don't fail them. As in me you have come upon a well of cool and living water, see that in your heart there bubbles up another such at which they can refresh themselves, that in you they have one to whom they feel it matters, who is not outside it all but in it with them, who has a large and leisured sympathy that has time to attend to them and puts that first. They are so weary and dusty and foot-sore, these endless passers-by upon the hot, hard road, let your branches lean invitingly across the wall to them. And strange things will happen. At all events, the Lord Christ will often pass your door; and it was ever his gracious way to stoop to be beholden to the queerest and most impossible people. He took gratefully from the soiled hands of the woman of Samaria, and he will take from yours, often though they have stabbed him. He went upon his way with his heart singing because of the crude faith of an importunate heathen creature; and any little broken bits of faith and trust and courage that you offer him will make his face light up with happiness. And when you come into his presence, ashamed to look him in the eyes, feeling that you have been an utter failure and have nothing to bring home, "Thanks, many thanks," he will say eagerly to you, "for all you did, and all you were, and all the difference that you have made to me and mine."

To be of use to Jesus Christ! What can we conceive to lay alongside that in our boldest day-dreams? And in his infinite condescension he has put that marvellous possibility within the reach of every one, even of you and me!

If our life is to be green and fruitful when others fade, and brown and die, through that terrible mid-time of life when so many souls fall out and perish, it must be near a spring whose waters will come seeping through the hot, dry, dusty earth, and find its roots, and keep it fresh and vigorous. And that is true. As Browning has it, "the real God function," what we need God for most, is not to show us what our lives should be, nearly so much as "to furnish a motive" for doing what we know already, to push us over into the actual living of it out, to keep us at that day by day. We must have something that lays compulsion on us to be what in our hearts we quite agree we ought to be and yet that we are not, something so haunting that it won't be forgotten, so strong that we can't resist it, and so persistent that there is no possible escape. Many things can do that for us in measure. But religion has been far the most efficient. And nothing in any religion has proved to have anything like such masterful power as the Cross of Jesus Christ. Stand upon Calvary, and look at it for yourself. There, where you are now, is the spot where more souls have been won for God than anywhere else. Somehow that grim thing grips the heart; it calls, and one has got to go; it lays on us compelling hands that won't shake off. Do you feel nothing? Jesus thought you would, was sure you must, believed that no one could stand there unmoved. And are you too petty a thing to feel the thrill of it? Can you look at it unconcernedly, and turn away back to your own small hopes, and puny goals, and starveling dreams?

"The value of a really great man," says Harnack, "is that he increases the value of all men." Christ has increased the stature of humanity immeasurably; but has he left you still a crawling earthworm, nothing more? Well, if you really choose so, you must go. But not yet! wait a moment! look once more!

Cynewulf, the old poet, has a wonderful picture of the Day of Judgment. The sun has fallen from the heavens, the moon is darkened, all the stars are out; the only light streams from the Cross; and in that strange and ruddy glow how differently things look from what they used to do in mere deceptive sunshine. Before you make your choice of a life, be certain you have seen things in the light of the Cross. For see how some that seemed so huge have shrunk to nothingness, and some you had thought insignificant have grown how vast! How this light changes everything! And it will be the only light upon the Day of Judgment! God, whom you had resented as an intrusion in your life, whom you had wished away, look at him upon Calvary, and who can keep from loving one who has first so loved us? Our fellowmen, whom we had thought so small, so irritating, so upsetting, with their wretched plans that will clash against ours, how great and wonderful they are beside the Cross, for Jesus Christ has died for them, for each of them, counting them worth his all. Our own life, consider it in that revealing light, and is it not too big a thing to squander upon the poor little dreams to which you meant to give it? And look! why, surely it is not your life at all, but his who bought it at how vast a price. Seeing things as they really are, must you not also lift your hands, and looking up into that dying face, cry out, "I too am thine; and, please God, I will live for thee, and live like thee, so help me Christ, my Christ!"

# Christian

# Piety

# and

# Sacramental

# Living

# JOHN CALVIN (1509–1564)

A French boy of eleven was already on his path toward the priesthood when Martin Luther officially broke with Rome; that same boy received the tonsure when he was twelve, and soon thereafter went to Paris to study theology. When he was about eighteen, John Calvin had doubts about the priestly vocation and went to Orleans to study law. There he became acquainted with some Protestants, and in 1533 he, too, broke with Roman Catholicism. He was for a short time imprisoned; he then fled to Basel where he dedicated himself to private studies. It was there that he wrote his first edition of the *Institutes of the Christian Religion,* which have played so important a role in shaping Protestant thought and life. In 1536, he was called to be a preacher and professor of theology at Geneva, and to assist in organizing the Reformation there. The stern discipline which he demanded led to his expulsion from the city three years later; but in 1541 he was recalled, after his party had secured the upper hand in a political contest. He then established a theocratic regime which proceeded to eliminate all opposition. His intolerance was highly successful; by 1555, all resistance was ended, his chief opponents having been executed or driven out. Until his death he was the unopposed dictator of Geneva. During this time he wrote volumes of commentaries on both the Old and New Testaments; and he preached each alternate weekday and on Sundays.

John Calvin was an irritable man, whose fierce anger did not soon subside, who was always ailing and overburdened with work, who lacked sympathy for the weak and erring, and who was deficient in geniality, humor, and gentleness. These defects show in his preaching. Yet he possessed great courage and candor, unsurpassed love of the truth, fidelity to principle, and sincere consecration to God. These also are evident in his sermons. He had no striking presence and no rich voice, but his commanding will and earnestness, his power of thought and clear style made him one of the most influential preachers of that century. Furthermore his sermons, which are extensions and applications of his commentaries, show the ability for organization which helped to make him a leading Reformer.

# Behavior
# in the Church*

*These things write I unto thee, hoping to come unto thee shortly: but if I tarry long, that thou mayest know how thou oughtest to behave thyself in the house of God, which is the church of the living God, the pillar and ground of the truth.* I TIMOTHY 3:14-15

St. Paul writeth these things to Timothy, that if he tarry long, before he come, he may know how to behave himself in the house of God. Here St. Paul exhorteth Timothy, and in his person all the faithful, to walk warily and carefully in conformity to the spiritual government of the church. For the house of God, if he dwell therein, is the upholder of the truth: yea, that house wherein he has his abode and will make known his majesty: which is, as it were, a closet where his truth is kept.

St. Paul observes that the church is the upholder of the truth; because God will have his truth preached by the mouth of men, therefore he hath appointed the ministration of his Word that we might know his will; for God useth this means, that men may know his truth, and reverence it from age to age. God will not come down from heaven, neither will he send his angels to bring us revelations from above; but he will be made known to us by his Word. Therefore, he will have

* From *The Mystery of Godliness and Other Selected Sermons* (New York: John Forbes, 1830; reprinted in 1950 by Wm. B. Eerdmans Co., Grand Rapids).

ministers of the church preach his truth, and instruct us therein. If we attend not to these things, we are not the church of God, but are guilty, as much as lieth in us, of abolishing his truth; we are traitors and murderers. And why so? Because God could maintain his truth otherwise if he would: he is not bound to these means, neither hath he any need of the help of men. But he will have his truth made known by such preaching as he hath commanded.

And how so? Is it because God hath no other means but by the voice of men? In this sound that vanisheth away in the air? No, no; but yet he hath appointed this means, to the end that when we are restored by his grace, we may attend to the hearing of his Word with all reverence: then shall we feel that his doctrine is not vain and unprofitable but hath its effect, and is of such efficacy as to call us to eternal life. For St. Paul saith, "Faith cometh by hearing," and we know it is faith that quickeneth our souls, which otherwise would be helpless and lost.

Therefore, first of all, those that have charge to preach the doctrine of the gospel, must take heed to themselves. And why so? Because they are set in God's house to govern it. He will have them govern his people in his name, and bear the message of salvation. Seeing they are called to this high station, what carefulness and humility ought there to be in them!

Now we are exhorted to do our duty; God having honored us who were so unworthy, we ought to labor on our part to fill the office whereunto we are called. When the church is called the house of the living God, it ought to awaken us to walk otherwise than we do. Why do we sleep in our sins? Why do we run into wickedness? Do we think that God doth not see us? that we are far out of his sight, and from the presence of our Lord Jesus Christ? Let us remember that the Word of God is preached to us, that God dwelleth among us, and is present with us; as our Lord Jesus Christ saith, "Where two or three are gathered together in my name, there am I in the midst of them." And we know, as it is said, that "in him dwelleth all the fulness of the Godhead bodily."

So then, how oft soever the Devil attempts to rock us to sleep, and tie us to the vanities of this world, or tempt us with wicked lusts, we ought to remember this sentence, and set it before our eyes; that God dwelleth in the midst of us, and that we are his house. Now we must consider that God cannot dwell in a foul place: he must have a holy house and temple. And how? Oh, there is no difficulty in setting out ourselves finely that all the world may gaze at us; but God taketh no pleasure in all these vanities of the world. Our beautifying must be spiritual: we must be clad with the graces of the Holy Ghost: this is the gold and silver, these are the precious stones spoken of by the prophet Isaiah, when he describeth the temple of God (60:6).

Seeing God is so gracious as to have his Word preached among us, let us live in obedience to his divine commands, that he may reside with us, and we be his temple. For this cause, let us see that we cleanse ourselves from all our filthiness, and renounce it, that we may be a fit place for God's holiness to dwell in. If we attend to these things, we shall reap great joy, seeing our Lord joineth himself to us, and maketh his residence in our souls and bodies. What are we? There is nothing but rottenness in us: I speak not of the body only, but more particularly of the soul, which is still more infected; and yet we see the Lord will build us up, that we may be fit temples for his majesty to reside in. We have great occasion to rejoice by reason of this text, and ought to strive to obtain the pureness which is required by the gospel, because God will have us joined to him, and sanctified by his Holy Spirit.

Our text says, "The church of God is the pillar and ground of the truth." God is not under the necessity of borrowing any thing from man, as we before observed; he can cause his truth to reign without our help; but he doth us this honor, and is so gracious as to employ us in this worthy and precious calling. He could instruct us without our hearing the voice of man; he could also send his angels, as he did to his servants in ancient times: but he calleth and gathereth us together in his church; there is his banner which he will set up among his flock; this is the kingly sceptre whereby he will have us ruled.

And indeed, what would it profit us if we knew all other things and were destitute of the knowledge of our God? If we know not God, I say, alas, are we not more than miserable? But as God hath imprinted his image in his Word, it is there he presenteth himself to us, and will have us to behold him, as it were, face to face. Therefore it is not in vain that St. Paul giveth this title to the preaching of the Word of God: namely, "that it is the truth." By this means he maketh himself known to us; it is also the means of our salvation; it is our life, our riches, and the seed whereby we become the children of God: in short, it is the nourishment of our souls, by which we are quickened.

Therefore let us remember that St. Paul saith the truth is maintained among us by the preaching of the gospel, and men are appointed thereunto. First of all, we are miserable (as I before observed) if we know not God. And how shall we know him, unless we suffer ourselves to be taught by his Word? We must learn to seek for this treasure, and apply all our labor to find it: and when God is so gracious, as to offer it to us, let us receive it as poor beggars starved with hunger.

Seeing the truth of God cannot reign among us, unless the gospel be preached, we ought to esteem it highly, knowing that he otherwise holdeth himself afar off. If these things were observed as they ought to be, we should see more reverence for the doctrine of the Word of God.

If we knew how to profit by what is contained in this place, we should have great reason to rejoice; seeing God will have his truth maintained by the means of preaching. There is nothing in men but wickedness; and yet God will use them for witnesses of his truth, having committed it to their keeping. Although there are few that preach the Word of God, yet notwithstanding, this treasure is common to the whole church. Therefore we are keepers of the truth of God; that is to say, of his precious image, of that which concerneth the majesty of the doctrine of our salvation, and the life of the world.

When God calleth us to so honorable a charge, have we not great reason to rejoice and praise his holy name? Let us remember to keep this treasure safe, that it be not profaned among us. St. Paul speaketh not only to instruct those that are called to preach the gospel, but that we may all know what blessings God hath bestowed upon us, when his word is preached in its purity. Our salvation is a matter of great importance; and we must come to it by means of the gospel. For faith is the life of our souls: as the body is quickened by the soul, so is the soul by faith. So then we are dead, until God calleth us to the knowledge of his truth. Therefore we need not fear, for God will adopt us for his children, if we receive the doctrine of the gospel.

We need not soar above the clouds, we need not travel up and down the earth, we need not go beyond the seas, nor to the bottomless pit, to seek God; for we have his word in our hearts, and in our mouths. God openeth to us the door of paradise when we hear the promises that are made to us in his name. It is as much as if he reached out his hand visibly, and received us for his children. God sealeth this doctrine by the signs which are annexed to it: for it is certain that the sacraments have a tendency to this end, that we may know that the church is the house of God, in which he is resident, and that his truth is maintained thereby.

When we are baptized in the name of our Lord Jesus Christ, we are brought into God's household: it is the mark of our adoption. Now, he cannot be our Father, unless we are under his divine protection, and governed by his Holy Spirit: as we have an evident witness in baptism, and a greater in the Lord's Supper: that is, we have a plain declaration that we are joined to God, and made one with him. For our Lord Jesus Christ showeth us that we are his body; that every one is a member; that he is the head whereby we are nourished with his substance and virtue. As the body is not separate from the head, so Jesus Christ showeth us that his life is common with ours, and that we are partakers of all his benefits.

When God exhorteth us to withdraw from all wicked affections, he calleth us to our Savior Jesus Christ, who is our life, who is in heaven; must we not then take pains to come unto him? Now let us meditate upon this subject with solemnity, seeing we are to celebrate the Lord's Supper next Sabbath. Let us see how we are disposed: for God will not have us come to him as liars and deceivers. Therefore, let us see if we are disposed to receive God, not as a guest that travelleth by the way, but as him that hath chosen us for his dwelling place forever: yea, as him that hath dedicated us to himself, as his temples, that we may be as a house built upon a rock. We must receive God by faith, and be made truly one with our Lord Jesus Christ, as I have already shown.

We should so examine and cleanse ourselves that when we receive the supper of our Lord Jesus Christ, we may be more and more confirmed in his grace; that we may be ingrafted into his Body, and be truly made one with him; that all the promises we perceive in the Gospel may be better confirmed in us. We must know that he is our life, and that we live in him, as he dwelleth in us: and thus we know that God owneth and taketh us for his children. Therefore, we should be the more earnest to call upon him, and trust in his goodness that he may so govern us by his Holy Spirit, that poor ignorant creatures may through our example be brought into the right way. For we see many at this day who are in the way to destruction. May we attend to what God hath enjoined upon us, that he would be pleased to show his grace, not only to one city or a little handful of people, but that he would reign over all the world; that every one may serve and worship him in spirit and in truth.

# FREDERICK WILLIAM ROBERTSON (1816–1853) A scholar

wrote that it is an honor to the Anglican church that it was the home of Frederick Robertson. That is great tribute to a man who published but one sermon in his lifetime, occupied no high position in the world or the church, and died at the age of thirty-seven. Though he was becoming an influential preacher shortly before his death, it was the posthumous publication of a collection of his sermons that was responsible for his strong and lasting influence in English-speaking countries and in Germany. These sermons actually were not manuscripts carried into the pulpit; Robertson preached with few notes, if any. They were "recollections" written down by him after each sermon had been preached, to be sent to members of his family who had been unable to hear it.

Frederick Robertson was an unusual and highly gifted man. He was born in London; after a diversified education, he prepared to enter the army. Before graduating from college he decided to enter the ministry of the Church of England; and soon after leaving Oxford he was ordained to its priesthood. He served in several churches, but it was not until he became Vicar of Trinity Chapel, Brighton, that he attracted attention. People came to hear this prophetic voice which spoke with such conviction. He was noted for his keen insight into personal and social problems; as the sermon printed in this chapter indicates, he was excellent in analyzing motives and character. Robertson detested sham and pretense, so that he spoke his mind clearly and forthrightly. Furthermore his sermons were unmistakably biblical; they represent textual preaching at its best. He was considered to be the "preachers' preacher"; yet he was popular with the working classes, upon whom he had marked influence. It was because of his revolutionary ideas for social reform that he encountered stiff opposition while at Brighton. In frustration he resigned his position, and died shortly thereafter. An even greater tribute was paid to him by an inscription on his Brighton tombstone: "He awakened the holiest feelings in poor and rich, in ignorant and learned. Therefore he is lamented as their guide and comforter."

# The Restoration
# of the Erring*

*Brethren, if a man be overtaken in a fault, ye which are spiritual, restore such an one in the spirit of meekness; considering thyself, lest thou also be tempted. Bear ye one another's burdens, and so fulfill the law of Christ.*

GALATIANS 6:1-2

It would be a blessed thing for our Christian society if we could contemplate sin from the same point of view from which Christ and his apostles saw it. But in this matter society is ever oscillating between two extremes, undue laxity and undue severity.

Now the Divine character of the New Testament is shown in nothing more signally than in the stable ground from which it views this matter, in comparison with the shifting and uncertain standing-point from whence the world sees it. It says, never retracting nor bating, "The wages of sin is death." But then it accepts every excuse, admits every palliation: looks upon this world of temptation and these frail human hearts of ours, not from the cell of a monk or the study of a recluse, but in a large, real way: accepts the existence of sin as a fact, without affecting to be shocked or startled: assumes that it must needs be that offences come, and deals with them in a large noble way, as the results of a disease which must be met—which should be, and which can be, cured.

* From *Sermons Preached at Brighton* (New York: Harper & Brothers, 1870).

97

1. *The Christian view of other men's sins.* The first thing noticeable in the apostle's view of sin is that he looks upon it as if it might be sometimes the result of a surprise. "If a man be overtaken in a fault." In the original, it is "anticipated," "taken suddenly in front." As if circumstances had been beforehand with the man: as if sin, supposed to be left far behind, had on a sudden got in front, tripped him up, or led him into ambush.

All sins are not of this character. There are some which are in accordance with the general bent of our disposition: and the opportunity of committing them was only the first occasion for manifesting what was in the heart; so that if they had not been committed, then they probably would or must have been at some other time, and looking back to them we have no right to lay the blame on circumstances —we are to accept the penalty as a severe warning meant to show what was in our hearts.

There are other sins of a different character. It seems as if it were not in us to commit them. They were so to speak unnatural to us: you were going quietly on your way, thinking no evil; suddenly temptation, for which you were not prepared, presented itself, and before you knew where you were, you were in the dust, fallen.

It is shocking, doubtless, to allow ourselves even to admit that this is possible: yet no one knowing human nature from men and not from books, will deny that this might befall even a brave and true man. St. Peter was both: yet this was his history. In a crowd, suddenly, the question was put directly, "This man also was with Jesus of Nazareth." Then came a prevarication—a lie: and yet another. This was a sin of surprise. He was overtaken in a fault.

Again, the apostle considers fault as that which has left a burden on the erring spirit. "Bear ye one another's burdens."

Let us examine this a little more closely. One burden laid on fault is that chain of entanglement which seems to drag down to fresh sins. One step necessitates many others. One fault leads to another, and crime to crime. The soul gravitates downward beneath its burden. It was profound knowledge indeed which prophetically refused to limit

Peter's sin to once. "Verily I say unto thee . . . thou shalt deny me thrice."

We will try to describe that sense of burden. A fault has the power sometimes of distorting life till all seems hideous and unnatural. A man who has left his proper nature, and seems compelled to say and do things unnatural and in false show, who has thus become untrue to himself—to him life and the whole universe becomes untrue. He can grasp nothing—he does not stand on fact—he is living as in a dream—himself a dream. All is ghastly, unreal, spectral. A burden is on him as of a nightmare. He moves about in nothingness and shadows, as if he were not. His own existence, swiftly passing, might seem a phantom life, were it not for the corroding pang of anguish in his soul, for that at least is real!

Add to this the burden of the heart weighing on itself, wearing out itself, against its own thought. One fixed idea—one remembrance, and no other—one stationary, wearing anguish. This is remorse, passing into despair; itself the goad to fresh and wilder crimes. The worst of such a burden is that it keeps down the soul from good.

Then there is the burden of a secret. Some here know the weight of an uncommunicated sin. They know how it lies like ice upon the heart. They know how dreadful a thing the sense of the hypocrisy is; the knowledge of inward depravity, while all without looks pure as snow to men. Such men tread forever on the very verge of a confession: they seem to take a fearful pleasure in talking of their guilt, as if the heart could not bear its own burden, but must give it outness.

Another burden is an intuitive consciousness of the hidden sins of others' hearts. To two states of soul it is given to detect the presence of evil: states the opposite of each other—innocence and guilt.

You would think that one who can deeply read the human heart and track its windings must be himself deeply experienced in evil. But it is not so—at least not always. Purity can detect the presence of the evil which it does not understand: just as the dove which has never seen a hawk trembles at its presence: and just as a horse rears uneasily when the wild beast unknown and new to it is near, so innocence understands, yet understands not the meaning of the unholy look, the guilty tone, the sinful manner. It shudders and shrinks from it by a power given to it, like that which God has conferred on the unreasoning mimosa. Sin gives the same power, but differently. Innocence apprehends the approach of evil by the instinctive tact of contrast. Guilt by the instinctive consciousness of similarity. It is the profound truth contained in the history of the Fall. The eyes are opened: the knowledge of good and evil has come. The soul knows its own nakedness: but it knows also the nakedness of all other souls which have sinned after the similitude of its own sin.

Very marvellous is that test power of guilt: it is vain to think of eluding its fine capacity of penetration. Intimations of evil are perceived and noted, when to other eyes all seems pure. The dropping of an eye—the shunning of a subject—the tremulousness of a tone—the peculiarity of a subterfuge, will tell the tale. "These are tendencies like mine, and here is a spirit conscious as my own is conscious."

This dreadful burden the Scriptures call the knowledge of good and evil: can we not all remember the salient sense of happiness, which we had when all was innocent? when crime was the tale of some far distant hemisphere, and the guilt we heard of was not suspect in the hearts of the beings around us: and can we not recollect, too, how by our own sin, or the cognizance of other's sin, there came a something which hung the heavens with evil? This is the worst burden that comes from transgression: loss of faith in human goodness: the being sentenced to go through life haunted with a presence from which we cannot escape: the presence of Evil in the hearts of all that we approach.

2. *The Christian power of restoration: "Ye which are spiritual, restore such an one."* First, then, restoration is possible. That is a Christian fact. Moralists have taught us what sin is: they have explained how it twines itself into habit: they have shown us its ineffaceable character. It was reserved for Christianity to speak of restoration. Christ, and Christ only, has revealed that he who has erred may be restored, and made pure and clean and whole again.

Next, however, observe that this restoration is accomplished by men. Causatively, of course, and immediately, restoration is the work of

65220

Christ and of God the Spirit. Mediately and instrumentally, it is the work of men. "Brethren . . . restore such an one." God has given to man the power of elevating his brother man. He has conferred on his Church the power of the keys to bind and loose, "Whosoever sins ye remit, they are remitted; and whosoever sins ye retain, they are retained." It is therefore in the power of man, by his conduct, to restore his brother, or to hinder his restoration. He may loose him from his sins, or retain their power upon his soul.

Now the words of the text confine us to two modes in which this is done: by sympathy and by forgiveness. "Bear ye one another's burdens."

By sympathy: we Protestants have one unvarying sneer ready for the system of the Romish confessional. They confess, we say, for the sake of absolution, that absolved they may sin again. A shallow, superficial sneer, as all sneers are. In that craving of the heart which gives the system of the confessional its dangerous power, there is something far more profound than any sneer can fathom. It is not the desire to sin again that makes men long to unburden their consciences; but it is the yearning to be true, which lies at the bottom even of the most depraved hearts, to appear what they are and to lead a false life no longer: and besides this, it is the desire of sympathy. For this comes out of that dreadful sense of loneliness which is the result of sinning— the heart severed from God, feels severed from all other hearts; goes alone as if it had neither part nor lot with other men; itself a shadow among shadows. And its craving is for sympathy: it wants some human heart to know what it feels. Thousands upon thousands of laden hearts around us are crying, "Come and bear my burden with me": and observe here, the apostle says, "Bear ye one another's burden." Nor let the priest bear the burdens of all: that were most unjust. Why should the priest's heart be the common receptacle of all the crimes and wickedness of a congregation? "Bear ye one another's burdens."

Again, by forgiveness. There is a truth in the doctrine of absolution. God has given to man the power to absolve his brother, and so restore him to himself. The forgiveness of man is an echo and an earnest of God's forgiveness. He whom society has restored realizes the possibility of restoration to God's favor. Even the mercifulness of one good man sounds like a voice of pardon from heaven: just as the power and the exclusion of men sound like a knell of hopelessness, and do actually bind the sin upon the soul. The man whom society will not forgive nor restore is driven into recklessness.

Now then let us inquire into the Christianity of our society. Restoration is the essential work of Christianity. The gospel is the declaration of God's sympathy and God's pardon. In these two particulars then, what is our right to be called a Christian community?

Suppose that a man is overtaken in a fault. What does he or what shall he do? Shall he retain it unacknowledged, or go through life a false man? God forbid. Shall he then acknowledge it to his brethren, that by sympathy and merciful caution may restore him? Well, but is it not certain that it is exactly from those to whom the name of "brethren" most peculiarly belongs that he will not receive assistance? Can a man in mental doubt go to the members of the same religious communion? Does he not know that they precisely are the ones who will frown upon his doubts, and proclaim his sins? Will a clergyman unburden his mind to his brethren in the ministry? Are they not in their official rigor the least capable of understanding him? If a woman be overtaken in a fault, will she tell it to a sister-woman? Or does she not feel instinctively, that her sister-woman is ever the most harsh, the most severe, and the most ferocious judge?

The apostle tells us the spirit in which restoration is to be done, and assigns a motive for doing it. The mode is "in the spirit of meekness." For Satan cannot cast out Satan. Sin cannot drive out sin. For instance, my anger cannot drive out another man's covetousness: my petulance or sneer cannot expel another's extravagance. The meekness of Christ alone has power. The charity which desires another's goodness above his well-being; that alone succeeds in the work of restoration.

The motive is, "Considering thyself, lest thou also be tempted." For sin is the result of inclination or weakness, combined with opportunity. It is therefore in a degree the offspring of circumstances. Must you not admit that the majority at least of those who have not fallen are safe because they were not tempted? Well, then, when St. Paul says, "Considering thyself, lest thou also be tempted," it is as if he had written—

Proud Pharisee of a man, complacent in thine integrity, who thankest God that thou art "not as other men are, extortioners, unjust, or as this publican," hast thou gone through the terrible ordeal and come off with unscathed virtue? Or art thou in all these points simply untried? Proud Pharisee of a woman, who passest by an erring sister with an haughty look of conscious superiority, dost thou know what temptation is, with strong feeling and mastering opportunity? Shall the rich cut crystal which stands on the table of the wealthy man, protected from dust and injury, boast that it has escaped the flaws, and the cracks, and the fractures which the earthen jar has sustained, exposed and subjected to rough and general uses? O man or woman! thou who wouldst be a Pharisee, consider, O consider thyself, lest thou also be tempted.

# MARTIN LUTHER (1483–1546)

There is probably no one person more responsible for our appreciation of the importance of preaching than Martin Luther. The reason for this is not only that Luther himself was easily one of the most outstanding and effective preachers of all time, but also because of his recovery of the biblical meaning of justification by grace through faith. In reaction against medieval abuses regarding the doctrine of the necessity and place of works in the Christian life, Luther insisted that one is made righteous only by the divine work of grace; grace creates the faith that receives it. In this sense one is justified by faith alone. Justification by faith occurs by receiving the Word of God. It is by hearing God's Word, which he interpreted as the true preaching of Holy Scriptures, that instills true faith, brings about justification, and inspires good works. For Luther the preaching of the Word was undeniably a sacramental action, and one which was indispensable. It is no wonder that Luther has been so influential upon the preaching of the Christian Church.

In the summer of 1540 the pastor of the church in Wittenberg traveled to Denmark and left Dr. Luther in charge. It was in that town, just twenty-three years before, that the former Augustianian monk had tacked his ninety-five theses to the door of the Castle Church, thus beginning his violent controversy with the papacy which led to his dramatic break with the Church of Rome in 1520. When the elderly Luther entered the pulpit he was nearly a legendary figure to that congregation. Here was a man who had changed the character of life in sixteenth-century Europe. He was then the outstanding leader of the Reformation, the man whose warm and powerful translation of the Bible into the German tongue was heard in the churches regularly and read at home, who had written the catechism by which they and their children had been instructed, whose vigorous and singable hymns enabled them all to take an active part in corporate worship, whose prayers were known, who had taught and inspired their own pastors and preachers and even the secular rulers themselves. He was to them perhaps the most important man in all Europe. However, they felt close to this great man, who talked to them clearly and personally, with a great command of language that was heavily salted with their own colloquialisms and peppered with his own witticisms and obscenities. Occasionally he would reveal to them some deep emotion, a flash of hatred against the papacy, some aspect of his passionate and complex piety, and inevitably the love of Jesus Christ. Luther had been preaching in a verse-by-verse commentary style on the Gospel of St. John, and this particular morning his hearers were to learn something of his own understanding of preaching. They would rarely have received a better sermon from anyone on any occasion.

# Preaching and Perceiving the Word*

*The Samaritan woman said to him, "How is it that you, a Jew, ask a drink of me, a woman of Samaria?" . . . Jesus answered her, "If you knew the gift of God, and who it is that is saying to you, 'Give me a drink,' you would have asked him, and he would have given you living water."* JOHN 4:9–10

Look how gently the Lord deals with this woman! He does not break off talking to her, but continues: "Dear daughter, it is true that I want you to give me a drink; for I am physically fatigued. However, I am not merely interested in a drink for my body; I am looking for something else. I am seeking you Samaritans that you may hear me. I would be happier to reverse the order and give you a drink. In fact, this is the reason for my presence here. I am asking for a drink to quench my physical thirst that I might have occasion to give you a drink. If you only realized what a gift is now to be found on earth, you would ask me for it, and I would give you a drink that would taste better than this water. It is of the utmost importance to recognize this gift and to know him who gives it. But neither the gift nor the giver is known." This is also our lament—and it will eternally remain so—that the great multitude despises this unspeakably precious treasure and

* From Jaroslav Pelikan (ed.), *Luther's Works*, Vol. XXII, "Sermons on the Gospel of Saint John," trans. by Martin H. Bertram (St. Louis: Concordia Publishing House, 1957). Copyright © 1957 by Concordia Publishing House. Used by permission of the publisher.

fails to recognize the Giver of this gift. In fact, we too, who claim to
be saints, pay it no heed and do not fully appreciate the value of this
treasure offered to us through the gospel. My dear friends, how few
there are among us who esteem this as a genuine treasure, as an eternal
gem, as everlasting life! There must be some, however, who will haz-
ard life and limb for it. In Matthew 13 we read of a man who found
a pearl in a field. He sold all his possessions in order to buy pearl and
field. Thus we find many who are willing to endure tortures because
of it; they, too, will receive the drink. But the other crowd says flip-
pantly: "What do I care about it?" You will find a hundred thousand
people who regard silver mined from the earth as a real treasure. They
will not shrink from laboring night and day to acquire such a perishable treasure.

Would to God that we could gradually train our hearts to believe
that the preacher's words are God's Word and that the man addressing us is a scholar and a king. As a matter of fact, it is not an angel
or a hundred thousand angels but the Divine Majesty Himself that
is preaching there. To be sure, I do not hear this with my ears or see
it with my eyes; all I hear is the voice of the preacher, or of my brother
or father, and I behold only a man before me. But I view the picture
correctly if I add that the voice and words of father or pastor are not
his own words and doctrine but those of our Lord and God. It is not
a prince, a king, or an archangel whom I hear; it is he who declares
that he is able to dispense the water of eternal life. If we could believe
this, we would be content indeed. However, a fault which is manifest
throughout the world and also in us is that we fail to recognize the
gift and its giver. I, too, am not at all perfect in this respect; my faith
is not as profound and strong as I should like to have it. Flesh and
blood are an impediment. They merely behold the person of the pastor
and brother and hear only the voice of the father. They cannot be in-
duced to say: "When I hear the Word, I hear a peal of thunder, and
I see the whole world filled with lightning." No, we cannot be brought
to do that, and this is most deplorable. Flesh and blood are at fault.
They refuse to regard the oral word and the ministry as a treasure
costlier and better than heaven and earth. People generally think: "If I

had an opportunity to hear God speak in person, I would run my feet bloody." If someone announced: "I know of a place in the world where God speaks and anyone can hear God there"; if I had gone there and seen and heard a poor pastor baptizing and preaching, and if I had been assured: "This is the place; here God is speaking through the voice of the preacher who brings God's Word"—I would have said: "Well, I have been duped! I see only a pastor." We should like to have God speak to us in his majesty. But I advise you not to run hither and yon for this. I suppose we could learn how people would run if God addressed them in his majesty. This is what happened on Mount Sinai, where only the angels spoke and yet the mountain was wrapped in smoke and quaked. But you now have the Word of God in church, in books, in your home; and this is God's Word as surely as if God himself were speaking to you.

Christ says: "You do not know the gift." We recognize neither the Word nor the Person of Christ, but we take offense at his humble and weak humanity. When God wants to speak and deal with us, he does not avail himself of an angel but of parents, or the pastor, or of my neighbor. This puzzles and blinds me so that I fail to recognize God, who is conversing with me through the person of the pastor or father. This prompts the Lord Christ to say in the text: "If you knew the gift of God, and who it is that is saying to you, 'Give me a drink,' then I would not be obliged to run after you and beg for a drink. You would run after me and ask me for the living water. But since you do not know the gift and do not recognize him who is speaking with you, you despise me." Even if Christ did no more than greet us, it would be a treasure above all treasures; it would be honor and treasure enough. He has another treasure in store for us, however, which he reveals when he brings us forgiveness of sin and redemption from death, Devil, and hell, when he transforms us into heavenly people and illumines our hearts. We can never express the value of this treasure adequately. We shall always fall short of recognizing it fully and of esteeming it as we really and truly should.

It is just beginning to dawn on us that God's speaking to us is an inexpressibly precious gift and that we are honored to be God's pupils and disciples. This is what is meant by knowing the nature of the gift and the person of the Doctor and Teacher. We and our hearers are just beginning to recognize that it is not a man we are listening to, but that it is God who is telling us things that contain an everlasting treasure. Therefore we are told again and again that we cannot speak about this subject enough; we must be like a stammering child. We cannot fathom what an incomprehensibly great treasure we possess in the divine Word. Nor do we really understand who this Person addressing us is or how excellent and exalted this Person is. If we did, it would impel us to boast of being followers, not of a king or of an emperor but of God. People in the world are proud if they have a gracious lord, or if they are privileged to see a prince; it means much to them to stand in his presence and hear him speak. Now it is true that it is a treasure to have a gracious lord or to be a prince's counselor. But look at the glory of the man who can say: "I am God's pupil; I hear him speak—not an angel, not a pastor or a prince, but God himself. I am his counselor." For God says: "My message is an excellent gift, and by comparison the world's riches and glory are nothing but filth."

My dear friends, regard it as a real treasure that God speaks unto your physical ear. The only thing that detracts from this gift is our deficient knowledge of it. To be sure, I do hear the sermon; however, I am wont to ask: "Who is speaking?" The pastor? By no means. You do not hear the pastor. Of course, the voice is his, but the words he employs are really spoken by my God. Therefore I must hold the Word of God in high esteem that I may become an apt pupil of the Word. If we looked upon it as the Word of God, we would be glad to go to church, to listen to the sermon, and to pay attention to the precious Word. There we would hear Christ say: "Give me a drink!" But since we do not honor the Word of God or show any interest in our own salvation, we do not hear the Word. In fact, we do not enjoy listening to any preacher unless he is gifted with a good and clear voice. If you look more at the pastor than at God; if you do not see God's person but merely gape to see whether the pastor is learned and skilled, whether he has good diction and articulates distinctly—then you have already become half a Jacob. For a poor speaker may speak the Word of God just as well as he who is endowed with eloquence. A father speaks the Word of God as well as God does, and your neighbor speaks it as well as the angel Gabriel. There is no difference between the Word when uttered by a schoolboy and when uttered by the angel Gabriel; they vary only in rhetorical ability. It matters not that dishes are made of different material—some of silver, others of tin—or whether they are enameled earthen dishes. The same food may be prepared in silver as in dishes of tin. Venison, properly seasoned and prepared, tastes just as good in a wooden dish as in one of silver. People, however, do not recognize the person of God but only stare at the person of man. This is like a tired and hungry man who would refuse to eat unless the food is served on a silver platter. Such is the attitude that motivates the choice of many preachers today. Many, on the other hand, are forced to quit their office, are driven out and expelled. That is done by those who do not know this gift, who assume that it is a mere man speaking to them, although, as a matter of fact, it is even more than an angel, namely, your dear God, who creates body and soul. This does not imply that we should despise and reject the gifts which God has distributed according to his own measure, more to the one and fewer to the other; for gifts are manifold. However, there is but one God who works through this multiplicity of gifts. One dare not despise the treasure because of the person.

Dear Lord, give us who are truly hungry the real bread and drink. This is what Christ wishes to do to us. But first we must learn to know the gift and the Teacher. Then we should be ready not only to give all to him but also to say: "Oh, dear Lord, give me some of the eternal water too! Without it I must die of eternal thirst and hunger."

# JEREMY TAYLOR (1613–1667)

Born and educated in Cambridge, England, Jeremy Taylor was ordained a priest in the Church of England at the age of twenty. His abilities both as a preacher and as a scholar brought him to the attention of many notable personages of his generation, among them Archbishop Laud and King Charles I; he soon became chaplain to the King. Though imprisoned as a Royalist at the start of the Civil War in 1642, he was soon released and went to Wales to become the chaplain of Richard Vaughan, Earl of Carbery. It was in this capacity that he preached the following sermon as one of a series. It was at that time and place, also, that his best known and still read works were written: *The Rule and Exercise of Holy Living* and *The Rule and Exercise of Holy Dying*. With the Restoration he was appointed to be a Bishop in Ireland in 1660, where he lectured and wrote his famous treatise on moral theology, *Ductor Dubitantium,* which was a significant and helpful work for Anglican priests at that time and is again receiving attention. His genius is best shown in his preaching; therein is revealed his powerful imagination, impressive erudition, his capacity for elucidation and vivid conception, as well as nobility of tone. This sermon reveals his devotion as well as his wit, his deep faith as well as remarkable common sense. The original was much longer; many of the classical allusions and delightfully clever uses of words and ideas in addition to numerous helpful, practical suggestions about the married state have had to be omitted to adhere to limitations of space. Even so the sermon as edited stands as a unit; it is one of the finest expressions of the meaning and nature of Christian marriage that is to be found in English literature.

# The Marriage Ring*

## or The Mysteriousness and Duties of Marriage

*This is a great mystery, but I speak concerning Christ and the Church. Nevertheless let every one of you in particular so love his wife even as himself, and the wife see that she reverence her husband.* EPHESIANS 5:32, 33

Marriage was ordained by God, instituted in paradise, was the relief of a natural necessity, and the first blessing from the Lord; he gave to man not a friend, but a wife, that is, a friend and a wife, too, (for a good woman is in her soul the same that a man is, and she is a woman only in her body; that she may have the excellency of the one and the usefulness of the other, and become amiable in both): it is the seminary of the Church, and daily brings forth sons and daughters unto God; it was ministered to by angels, and Raphael waited upon a young man that he might have a blessed marriage, and that that marriage might repair two sad families, and bless all their relatives. The first miracle that ever Jesus did, was to do honor to a wedding; marriage was in the world before sin, and is in all ages of the world the greatest and most effective antidote against sin, in which all the world had perished if God had not made a remedy; and although sin hath soured marriage, and stuck the man's head with cares and woman's bed with sor-

* From *The Whole Works of the Right Reverend Jeremy Taylor*, Vol. V (London: W. Clowes, 1828).

rows in the production of children, yet these are but throes of life and glory; and "she shall be saved in childbearing, if she be found in faith and righteousness." Marriage is a school and exercise of virtue; and though marriage hath cares, yet the single life hath desires which are more troublesome and more dangerous, and often end in sin, while the cares are but instances of duty and exercises of piety; and therefore if single life hath more privacy of devotion, yet marriage hath more necessities and more variety in it, and is an exercise of more graces.

Here is the proper scene of piety and patience, of the duty of parents and the charity of relatives; here kindness is spread abroad, and love is united and made firm as a center: marriage is the nursery of heaven; the virgin sends prayers to God, but she carries but one soul to him; but the state of marriage fills up the numbers of the elect, and hath in it the labor of love, and the delicacies of friendship, the blessing of society, and the union of hands and hearts; it hath in it less of beauty, but more of safety than the single life; it hath more care, but less danger; it is more merry, and more sad; is fuller of sorrows, and fuller of joys; it lies under more burdens, but it is supported by all the strengths of love and charity, and those burdens are delightful. Marriage is the mother of the world, and preserves kingdoms, and fills cities, and churches, and heaven itself.

Single life makes men in one instance to be like angels, but marriage in very many things makes the chaste pair to be like Christ. "This is a great mystery," but it is the symbolical and sacramental representment of the greatest mysteries of our religion. Christ descended from his Father's bosom, and contracted his divinity with flesh and blood, and married our nature, and we became a Church, the spouse of the bridegroom, which he cleansed with his blood, and gave her his Holy Spirit for a dowry, and heaven for a jointure; begetting children unto God by the gospel.

## The Rights, Duties, and Privileges of Marriage:

Let man and wife be careful to stifle little things, that as fast as they spring, they be cut down and trod upon; for if they be suffered to grow by numbers, they make the spirit peevish, and the society troublesome, and the affections loose and easy by an habitual aversation. Some men are more vexed with a fly than with a wound; and when the gnats disturb his sleep, and the reason is disquieted but not perfectly awakened, it is often seen that he is fuller of trouble than if in the daylight of his reason he were to contest with a potent enemy. In the frequent little accidents of a family, a man's reason cannot always be awake; and when his discourses are imperfect, and a trifling trouble makes him yet more restless, he is soon betrayed to the violence of passion. It is certain that the man or woman are in a state of weakness and folly then, when they can be troubled with a trifling accident; and therefore it is not good to tempt their affections when they are in that state of danger. In this case the caution is, to subtract fuel from the sudden flame; for stubble though it be quickly kindled, yet it is as soon extinguished, if it be not blown by a pertinacious breath, or fed with new materials; add no new provocations to the accident, and do not inflame this, and peace will soon return, and the discontent will pass away soon, as the sparks from the collision of a flint: ever remembering that discontents proceeding from daily little things, do breed a secret discernible disease, which is more dangerous than a fever proceeding from a discerned notorious surfeit.

Let them be sure to abstain from all those things which by experience and observation they find to be contrary to each other. They that govern elephants never appear before them in white, and the masters of bulls keep from them all garments of blood and scarlet, as knowing that they will be impatient of civil usages and discipline when their natures are provoked by their proper antipathies.

Let the husband and wife infinitely avoid a curious distinction of mine and thine; for this hath caused all the laws, and all the suits, and all the wars in the world; let them who have but one person, have also but one interest. The husband and wife are heirs to each other if they die without children, but if there be children, the wife is a partner in the inheritance. But during their life the use and employment is common to both their necessities, and in this there is no other difference of right, but that the man hath the dispensation of all, and may keep it from his wife just as the governor of a town may keep it from the right owner; he hath the power, but no right to do so. And when either of them begins to impropriate, it is like a tumor in the flesh, it draws more than its share, but what it feeds on turns to bile: and therefore the Romans forbade any donations to be made between man and wife, because neither of them could transfer a new right of those things which already they had in common; but this is to be understood only concerning the uses of necessity and personal conveniences; for so all may be the woman's, and all may be the man's in several regards.

These are the duties of them both, which have common regards and equal necessities, and obligations; and indeed, there is scarce any matter of duty, but it concerns them both alike, and is only distinguished by names, and hath its variety by circumstances and little accidents: and what in one is called love, in the other is called reverence; and what in the wife is obedience, the same in the man is duty. He provides, and she dispenses; he gives commandments, and she rules by them; he rules her by authority, and she rules him by love; she ought by all means to please him, and he must by no means displease her. For as the heart is set in the midst of the body, and though it strikes to the one side by the prerogative of nature, yet those throbs and constant motions are felt on the other side also, and the influence is equal to both: so it is in conjugal duties; some motions are to the one side more than to the other, but the interest is on both, and the duty is equal in the several instances. If it be otherwise, the man enjoys a wife as a Periander did his dead Melissa, by an unnatural union, neither pleasing, nor holy, useless to all the purposes of society, and dead to content.

The husband shall prevail, but by sweetness and counsel, by charity and compliance. Yet we cannot discourse of the man's right, without describing the measures of his duty; that therefore follows next. Let him love his wife even as himself: that's his duty, and the measure of it, too. Be not bitter against her; this is the least index and signification of love. A civil man is never bitter against a friend or a stranger, much less to him that enters under his roof, and is secured by the laws of hospitality. But a wife does all that, and more; she quits all her interest for his love, she gives him all that she can give, she is as much the same person as another can be the same, who is conjoined by love and mystery and religion and all that is sacred and profane. They have the same fortune, the same family, the same children, the same religion, the same interest, the same flesh, and therefore this Apostle urges for his injunction (Be not bitter against her), "no man hateth his own flesh, but nourisheth and cherisheth it"; and he certainly is strangely sacrilegious and a violator of the rights of hospitality and sanctuary, who uses her rudely, who is fled for protection, not only to his house, but also to his heart and bosom. A wise man will not wrangle with any one, much less with his dearest relative; and if it be accounted undecent to embrace in public, for the other is in itself lawful, but this never, though it were assisted with the best circumstances of which it is capable. The marital love is infinitely removed from all possibility of such rudenesses; it is a thing pure as light, sacred as a temple, lasting as the world. Such love contains in it all sweetness, and all society, and all felicity, and all prudence, and all wisdom. For there is nothing can please a man without love, and if a man be weary of the wise discourses of the Apostles, and of the innocency of an even and a private fortune, or hates peace or a fruitful year, he hath reaped thorns and thistles from the choicest flowers of paradise; "for nothing can sweeten felicity itself, but love"; but when a man dwells in love, then the breasts of his wife are pleasant as the droppings upon the hill of Hermon, her eyes are fair as the light of heaven, she is a fountain sealed, and he can quench his thirst, and ease his cares, and lay his sorrows down upon her lap, and can retire home as to his sanctuary and refectory, and his gardens of sweetness and chaste refreshments. No man can tell but he that loves his children, how many delicious accents make a man's heart dance in the pretty conversation of those dear pledges; their childishness, their stammering, their little angers, their innocence, their imperfections, their necessities are so many little emanations of joy and comfort to him that delights in their persons and society; but he that loves not his wife and children, feeds a lioness at home, and broods a nest of sorrows, and blessing itself cannot make him happy; so that all the commandments of God enjoining a man to love his wife, are nothing but so many necessities and capacities of joy. She that is loved is safe, and he that loves is joyful. Love is a union of all things excellent; it contains in it proportion and satisfaction, and rest, and confidence; and I wish that this were so much proceeded in, that the heathen themselves could not go beyond us in this virtue, and its proper, and its appendant happiness.

Holy Scripture contains in it that the husband should nourish and cherish his wife, that he should refresh her sorrows and entice her fears into confidence and pretty arts of rest; for even the fig trees that grew in paradise had sharp-pointed leaves, and harshnesses fit to mortify the too forward lusting after the sweetness of the fruit. But it will concern the prudence of the husband's love to make the cares and evils as simple and easy as he can, by doubling the joys and acts of a careful friendship, by tolerating her infirmities (because by so doing, he either cures her, or makes himself better), by fairly expounding all the little traverses of society and communication, by taking everything by the right handle, for there is nothing but may be misinterpreted, and yet if it be capable of a fair construction, it is the office of love to make it.

Above all the instances of love, let him preserve towards her an inviolable faith, and an unspotted chastity, for this is the marriage ring, it ties two hearts by an eternal band; it is like the cherubim's flaming sword set for the guard of paradise; he that passes into that garden, now that it is immured by Christ and the Church, enters into the shades of death. No man must touch the forbidden tree, that is in the midst of the garden, which is the tree of knowledge and life. Chastity is the security of love, and preserves all the mysteriousness like the secrets of a temple. Under this lock is deposited security of families, the union of affections, the repairer of accidental breaches.

I choose this to be the last advice to both. "Remember the days of darkness, for they are many." The joys of the bridal chamber are quickly past, and the remaining portion of the state is dull progress without variety of joys, but not without the change of sorrows; but that portion that shall enter into the grave must be eternal. It is fit that I should infuse a bunch of myrrh into the festival goblet, and after the Egyptian manner serve up a dead man's bones at a feast. I will only show it and take it away again; it will make the wine bitter, but wholesome. All those things that now please us shall pass from us, or we from them, but those things that concern the other life are permanent as the numbers of eternity; and although at the resurrection there shall be no relation of husband and wife, and no marriage shall be celebrated, but the marriage of the Lamb, yet then shall be remembered how men and women passed through this state which is a type of that, and from this sacramental union all holy pairs shall pass to the spiritual and eternal, where love shall be their portion, and joys shall crown their heads, and they shall lie in the bosom of Jesus, and in the heart of God to eternal ages. Amen.

# THEODORE PARKER (1810–1860)

Theodore Parker was born in Lexington, Massachusetts, and was raised on his father's farm. He began to educate himself and then went to Harvard, where he continued self-education by reading for the college courses in which he could not afford to enroll. Harvard later awarded him an honorary degree in 1840 after he had brilliantly passed its examinations. In 1836, he graduated from the Harvard Divinity School as a Unitarian and took a congregation in West Roxbury (Boston). It was in 1841 that he preached an ordination sermon that created a sensation and resulted in his being ostracized by his fellow Unitarian clergymen; the sermon, "The Transient and the Permanent in Christianity" maintained that the essence of Christianity is the influence of Jesus and his religion, which does not need the support of miracles to attest to its veracity. This proved to be even too liberal for the Unitarians, though Parker did receive widespread support of the laity. Soon thereafter he began to write incessantly and traveled widely in the States lecturing and preaching. Though he was awkward in the pulpit and lacked both a good voice and animation, yet he drew large crowds. In 1856, he took charge of what became the Twenty-eighth Congregational Society in Boston. He was a strong agitator for the antislavery movement, and fought for temperance, prison reform, and the education of women. His health broke down, and he died in Florence at the age of fifty. In many ways he is more a contemporary of ours than of the people in his own time; certainly the prophetic element in this unusual sermon that follows speaks as strongly and as relevantly to our situation, if not more so, than it did to the situation of one hundred years ago.

# Of Conventional and Natural Sacraments*

*I will have mercy, and not sacrifice.*   MATTHEW 9:13

The natural and real ordinance of religion is in general a manly life, all the man's faculties of body and spirit developed or developing in their natural and harmonious way, the body ruled by the spirit, its instincts all in their places, the mind active, the conscience, the affections, the soul, all at work in their natural way. Religion is the sacrament of religion; itself its ordinance. Piety and goodness are its substance, and all normal life its form. The love of God and the love of man, with all that belongs thereto, worship with every limb of the body, every faculty of the spirit, every power we possess over matter or men—that is the sacramental substance of religion; a life obedient to the love of God and of man—that is the sacramental form of religion. All else is means, provisional; this the end, a finality. Thus my business, my daily work with the hand, if an honest and manly work, is the ordinance of religion to my body; seeking and expressing truth and beauty is the ordinance of religion to my mind; doing justice to all about me is the moral ordinance of religion; loving men is the natural sacrament of the affections; holiness is the natural ordinance of the soul. Putting all together—my internal consciousness of piety and goodness, my outward life which represents that, is the great nat-

* From *Ten Sermons of Religion* (London: Trubner and Co., 1863).

119

ural sacrament, the one compendious and universal ordinance. Then my religion is not one thing, and my life another; the two are one. Thus religion is the sacrament of religion, morality the test of piety.

If you believe God limited to one spot, then that is counted specifically holy; and your religion draws or drives you thither. If you believe that religion demands only certain particular things, they will be thought sacramental, and the doing thereof the proof of religion. But when you know that God is infinite, is everywhere, then all space is holy ground; all days are holy time; all truth is God's word; all persons are subjects of religious duty, invested with unalienable religious rights, and claiming respect and love as fellow-children of the same dear God. Then, too, all work becomes sacred and venerable; common life, your highest or your humblest toil, is your element of daily communion with men, as your act of prayer is your communion with the Infinite God.

If pains be taken to cultivate piety, and, as it grows up, if it be left to its own natural development, it will have its own form of manifestation. The feeling of love to God, the Infinite Object, will not continue a mere feeling. Directed to the Infinite Object, it will be directed also towards men, and become a deed. As you love God the more, you must also love men the more, and so must serve them better.

At the beginning of your growth in piety, there is, doubtless, need of forms, of special time and place. There need not be another's form, or there may be, just as you like. The girl learning to write imitates carefully each mark on the copy, thinking of the rules for holding the pen. But as you grow, you think less of the form, of the substance more. So the pen becomes not a mere instrument, but almost a limb; the letters are formed even without a thought. Without the form, you have the effect thereof.

If there be piety in the heart, and it be allowed to live and grow and attain its manly form, it will quicken every noble faculty in man. Morality will not be dry, and charity will not be cold; the reason will not grovel with mere ideas, nor the understanding with calculations; the shaft of wit will lose its poison, merriment its levity, common life its tedium. Disappointment, sorrow, suffering, will not break the heart, which will find soothing and comfort in its saddest woe.

The common test of Christianity is not the natural sacrament; it is only this poor conventional thing. Look at this. The land is full of Bibles. I am glad of it. I am no worshipper of the Bible, yet I reverence its wisdom, I honor its beauty of holiness, and love exceedingly the tranquil trust in God which its great authors had. Some of the best things that I have ever learned from man this book has taught me. I am glad the Bible goes everywhere. But men take it for master, not for help. They worship its letter, and the better spirit of Moses, of Esaias, of the Holy Psalms, so old and yet so young, so everlasting in their beauteous faith in God—the sublime spirit of one greater than the temple, and Lord of the Sabbath, who scorned to put the new wine of God into the old and rotten bags of men—that is not in Christendom. O, no! men do not ask for that. The yeasty soul would rend asunder tradition's leathern bags. Worship of Bibles never made men write Bibles; it hinders us from living them. Worship no things for that; not the created, but, O Creator! let us worship Thee. Catholicism is worship of a church, instead of God; Protestantism is worship of a book. Both could not generate a Jesus or a Moses.

For proof of religion men appeal to our churches, built by the self-denial of hard-working men. They prove nothing—nay, nothing at all. The throng of men attending church is small proof of religion. Think of the vain things which lead men to this church or to that; of the vain thoughts which fill them there; of the vain words they hear, or which are only spoken, not even heard! What a small amount of real piety and real morality is needed to make up a popular "Christian!" Alas! we have set up an artificial sacrament; we comply with that, then call ourselves religious—yea Christians. We try ecclesiastic metal by its brassy look and brassy ring, then stamp it with the popular image of our idolatry, and it passes current in the shop, tribute fit for Caesar.

The real test of religion is its natural sacrament—is life. To know whom you worship, let me see you in your shop, let me overhear you in your trade; let me know how you rent your houses, how you get your money, how you keep it, or how it is spent. It is easy to pass the Sunday idle, idly lounging in the twilight of idle words, or basking in the sunshine of some strong man's most earnest speech. It is easy to repeat the words of David, or of Jesus, and to call it prayer. But the sacramental test of your religion is not your Sunday idly spent, not the words of David or of Jesus that you repeat; it is your week-day life, your works, and not your words. Tried by this natural test, the Americans are a heathen people, not religious; far, far from that. Compare us with the Chinese by the artificial standard of the missionary, we are immensely above them; by the natural sacrament of obedience to the law of God, how much is the Christian before the heathen man?

The national test of religion is the nation's justice—justice to other states abroad, the strong, the weak, and justice to all sorts of men at home. The law-book is the nation's creed; the newspapers chant the actual liturgy and service of the day. What avails it that the priest calls us "Christian," while the newspapers and the Congress prove us infidel? The social sacrament of religion is justice to all about you in society—is honesty in trade and work, is friendship and philanthropy; the religious strong must help the weak. The ecclesiastical sacrament of a church must be its effort to promote piety and goodness in its own members first, and then to spread it round the world. Care for the bodies and souls of men, that is the real sacrament and ordinance of religion for society, the Church and State.

For individual man, for you and me, there are two great natural sacraments. One is inward and not directly seen, save by the eye of God and by your own—the continual effort, the great life-long act of prayer to be a man, with a man's body and a man's spirit, doing a man's duties, having a man's rights, and thereby enjoying the welfare of a man. That is one—the internal ordinance of religion. The other is like it—the earnest attempt to embody this in outward life, to make the manly act of prayer a manly act of practice too. These are the only sacraments for the only worship of the only God. Let me undervalue no means of growth, no hope of glory; these are the ends of growth, the glory which men hope.

Is not all this true? You and I—we all know it. There is but one religion, natural and revealed by nature—by outward nature poorly and in hints, but by man's inward spirit copiously and at large. It is piety in your prayer; in your practice it is morality. But try the nations, society, the Church, persons, by this sacramental test, and what a spectacle we are! For the religion of the State, study the ends and actions of the State; study the religion of the Church by the doctrines and the practice of the Church; the religion of society—read it in the great cities of the land. "Thy kingdom come, Thy will be done," prays the minister. Listen to the "Amen" of the courts and the market, responding all the week! The actual religion of mankind is always summed up in the most conspicuous men. Is that religion Christian? Spirit of the Crucified! how we take thy honored name in vain! Yet we did not mean to be led astray: the nations did not mean it; the cities meant it not; the churches prayed for better things; the chief men stumbled and fell. We have altogether mistaken the ordinance of religion, and must mend that.

The New England Indian insisted upon his poor, hungry sacrament; so did the barbarian German; so the Jew, the Catholic, the Protestant; and each sectarian has his Shibboleth of ritual and creed. How poor and puerile are all these things! How puerile and poor the idea of God asking such trifles of mortal man! We shall never mend matters till we take the real religious sacrament, scorning to be deluded longer by such idle shows.

Now it has come to such a pass, that men wish to limit all religion to their artificial sacraments. The natural ordinance of human piety must not be even commended in the church. You must not apply religion to politics; it makes men mad. There is no law of God above the written laws of men. You must not apply it to trade: business is business; religion is religion. Business has the week for his time, the world for his market-place; religion has her Sunday and her meeting-house; let each pursue his own affairs. So the minister must not expose the sins of trade nor the sins of politics. Then, too, public opinion must be equally free from the incursions of piety. "O Religion!" say men, "be busy with thy sacramental creeds, thy sacramental rites, thy crumb of bread, thy sip of wine, thy thimbleful of water sprinkled on a baby's face, but leave the state, the market and all men, to serve the Devil, and be lost." "Very well," says the priest, "I accept the condition. Come and take our blessed religion!"

I love to study real piety in the forms of the past, in the mystic forms of Thomas à Kempis and Williaw Law, in Fénelon and Swedenborg, in John Tauler, in St. Bernard and St. Victor, in Taylor and Herbert. But there it appears not in its fairest form. I love to see piety at its work better than in its play or its repose; in philanthropists better than in monks and nuns, who gave their lives to contemplation and to wordy prayer, and their bodies to be burned. I love piety embodied in a Gothic or Roman cathedral, an artistic prayer in stone, but better in a nation well fed, well housed, well clad, instructed well, a natural prayer in man or woman. What is so fair as sentiment, is lovelier as life.

All the triumphs of ancient piety are for you and me; the lofty sentiment, the high resolve, the vision filled with justice, beauty, truth, and love. The great, ascending prayer, the manly consciousness of God, his income to your soul as justice, beauty, truth, and faith, and love—all these wait there for you—happiness now and here; hereafter the certain blessedness which cannot pass away.

# FRANCOIS de SALIGNAC de La MOTHE FENELON

(1651–1715) One of the great masters of the spiritual life was Francois Fénelon. He came from an aristocratic family in the southwest of France to study for the priesthood at Cahors and later at Paris. When he was twenty-four he was ordained a priest and subsequently made superior of a center for women converts from Protestantism. Later he became a tutor to the grandson of Louis XIV. It was during this time that he became acquainted with Madam Guyon; his sympathy with her Quietism brought him eventually into bitter controversy with the able and eloquent Bossuet. Bossuet was successful in his case against Fénelon, so that the pope condemned his book which had defended some of the Quietistic principles. Fénelon's gracious submission to the papal judgment is generally regarded as a mark of his greatness of character, an indication of unusual and sincere humility. Even though some were against him, he was admired as a holy person, and many turned to him for spiritual guidance. He was widely known for his writings and letters, which advised those mindful of spiritual growth. He was a man of practical charity as well; he was known for his kindness toward the poor and unfortunate, particularly while he was Bishop of Cambrai during the last eighteen years of his life. He was also noted for his preaching; although he did not match the eloquence of Bossuet, he was admired for his clear, thoughtful, and elevating sermons. In his *Dialogues on Eloquence* he argued against the prevailing mannerisms of his day, pleading that eloquence is not to entertain but to instruct the intelligence and to improve morals by the use of clear description, vivid pictures, and natural utterance. It is perhaps because he was basically honest and natural that his simple, unadorned sermon on prayer still speaks meaningfully to us today.

# The Saint's Converse with God*

*Pray without ceasing.* I THESSALONIANS 5:17

O f all the duties enjoined by Christianity, none is more essential and yet more neglected, than prayer. Most people consider this exercise a wearisome ceremony, which they are justified in abridging as much as possible. Even those whose profession or fears lead them to pray, do it with such languor and wanderings of mind, that their prayers, far from drawing down blessings, only increase their condemnation. I wish to demonstrate in this discourse, first, the general necessity of prayer; secondly, its peculiar duty; thirdly, the manner in which we ought to pray.

First. God alone can instruct us in our duty. The teachings of men, however wise and well disposed they may be, are still ineffectual, if God does not shed on the soul that light which opens the mind to truth. The imperfections of our fellow creatures cast a shade over the truths that we learn from them. Such is our weakness that we do not receive, with sufficient docility, the instructions of those who are as

*From Sidney Dark (ed.), *The World's Great Sermons* (London: Arthur Barker, Ltd., 1933). Used by permission of the publisher.

127

imperfect as ourselves. A thousand suspicions, jealousies, fears, and prejudices prevent us from profiting, as we might, by what we hear from men; and though they announce the most serious truths, yet what they do, weakens the effect of what they say. In a word, it is God alone who can perfectly teach us.

St. Bernard said, in writing to a pious friend: If you are seeking less to satisfy a vain curiosity than to get true wisdom, you will sooner find it in deserts than in books. The silence of the rocks and the pathless forests will teach you better than the eloquence of the most gifted men. "All," says St. Augustine, "that we possess of truth and wisdom, is a borrowed good, flowing from that fountain, for which we ought to thirst in the fearful desert of this world, that, being refreshed and invigorated by these dews from heaven, we may not faint upon the road that conducts us to a better country. Every attempt to satisfy the cravings of our hearts at other sources, only increases the void. You will be always poor if you do not possess the only true riches." All light that does not proceed from God is false; it only dazzles us; it sheds no illumination upon the difficult paths in which we must walk, along the precipices that are about us.

Be assured that the greatest obstacle to true wisdom is the self-confidence inspired by that which is false. The first step toward this precious knowledge is earnestly to desire it, to feel the want of it, and to be convinced that they who seek it must address themselves to the Father of lights who freely gives to him who asks in faith.

Do not think that it is necessary to pronounce many words. To pray is to say, Let Thy will be done. It is to form a good purpose; to raise your heart to God; to lament your weakness; to sigh at the recollection of your frequent disobedience. This prayer demands neither method, nor science, nor reasoning; it is not essential to quit one's employment; it is a simple movement of the heart toward its Creator, and a desire that whatever you are doing you may do it to his glory. The best of all prayers is to act with a pure intention, and with a continual reference to the will of God. It depends much upon ourselves whether our prayers be efficacious. It is not by a miracle, but by a movement of the heart, that we are benefited; by a submissive spirit. Let us believe, let us trust, let us hope, and God never will reject our prayer. Yet how many Christians do we see strangers to the privilege, aliens from God, who seldom think of him, who never open their hearts to him; who seek elsewhere the counsels of a false wisdom, and vain and dangerous consolations; who cannot resolve to seek, in humble, fervent prayer to God, a remedy for their griefs and a true knowledge of their defects, the necessary power to conquer their vicious and perverse inclinations, and the consolations and assistance they require, that they may not be discouraged in a virtuous life.

But some will say, "I have no interest in prayer; it wearies me; my imagination is excited by sensible and more agreeable objects, and wanders in spite of me."

If neither your reverence for the great truths of religion, nor the majesty of the ever-present Deity, nor the interest of your eternal salvation, have power to arrest your mind, and engage it in prayer, at least mourn with me for your infidelity; be ashamed of your weakness, and wish that your thoughts were more under your control; and desire to become less frivolous and inconstant. Make an effort to subject your mind to this discipline. You will gradually acquire habit and facility. What is now tedious will become delightful; and you will then feel, with a peace that the world cannot give nor take away, that God is good.

Secondly. The peculiar obligation of prayer. Were I to give all the proofs that the subject affords, I should describe every condition of life, that I might point out its dangers, and the necessity of recourse to God in prayer. But I will simply state that under all circumstances we have need of prayer. There is no situation in which it is possible to be placed where we have not many virtues to acquire, and many faults to correct. We find in our temperament, or in our habits, or in the peculiar character of our minds, qualities that do not suit our occupations, and that oppose our duties. One person is connected by marriage with another whose temper is so unequal that life becomes a perpetual warfare. Some, who are exposed to the contagious atmosphere of the world, find themselves so susceptible to the vanity which they inhale, that all their pure desires vanish. Others have solemnly promised to renounce their resentments, to conquer aversions, to suffer with patience certain crosses, and to repress their eagerness for wealth; but nature prevails, and they are vindictive, violent, impatient, and avaricious.

Whence comes it that these resolutions are so frail? that all these people wish to improve, desire to perform their duty toward God and man better, and yet fail? It is because our own strength and wisdom, alone, are not enough. We undertake to do everything without God; therefore we do not succeed. It is at the foot of the altar that we must seek for counsel which will aid us. It is with God that we must lay our plans of virtue and usefulness; it is he alone that can render them successful. Without him, all our designs, however good they may appear, are only temerity and delusion. Let us then pray, that we may learn what we are and what we ought to be. By this means, we shall not only learn the number and the evil effects of our peculiar faults, but we shall also learn to what virtues we are called, and the way to practice them.

In the most holy occupation, a certain degree of precaution is necessary. Do not devote all your time to action, but reserve a certain portion of it for meditation upon eternity. We see Jesus Christ inviting his disciples to go apart, in a desert place, and rest awhile, after their return from the cities, where they had been to announce his religion. How much more necessary it is for us to approach the source of all virtue, that we may revive our declining faith and charity, when we return from the busy scenes of life, where men speak and act as if they had never known that there is a God! We should look upon prayer as the remedy for our weaknesses, the rectifier of our faults. He who was without sin, prayed constantly; how much more ought we, who are sinners, to be faithful in prayer!

Even the exercise of charity is often a snare to us. It calls us to certain occupations that dissipate the mind, and that may degenerate into mere amusement. It is for this reason that St. Chrysostom says that nothing

is so important as to keep exact proportion between the interior source
of virtue, and the external practice of it; else, like the foolish virgins,
we shall find that the oil in our lamp is exhausted when the bridegroom comes.

Thirdly. Of the manner in which we ought to pray. 1. We must
pray with attention. God listens to the voice of the heart, not to that
of the lips. Our whole heart must be engaged in prayer. It must fasten
upon what it prays for; and every human object must disappear from
our minds. To whom should we speak with attention, if not to God?
Can he demand less of us than that we should think of what we say
to him? Dare we hope that he will listen to us, and think of us, when
we forget ourselves in the midst of our prayers? This attention to
prayer, which it is so just to exact from Christians, may be practiced
with less difficulty than we imagine. It is true, that the most faithful
souls suffer from occasional involuntary distractions. They cannot always control their imaginations, and, in the silence of their spirits, enter
into the presence of God. But these unbidden wanderings of the mind
ought not to trouble us; and they may conduce to our perfection even
more than the most sublime and affecting prayers, if we earnestly strive
to overcome them, and submit with humility to this experience of our
infirmity. But to dwell willingly on frivolous and worldly things, during prayer, to make no effort to check the vain thoughts that intrude
upon this sacred employment, and come between us and the Father
of our spirits—is not this choosing to live the sport of our senses, and
separated from God?

2. We must also ask with faith; a faith so firm that it never falters.
He who prays without confidence cannot hope that his prayer will be
granted. Will not God love the heart that trusts in him? Will he reject
those who bring all their treasures to him, and repose everything upon
his goodness? When we pray to God, says St. Cyprian, with entire
assurance, it is himself who has given us the spirit of our prayer. Then
it is the Father listening to the words of his child; it is he who dwells
in our hearts, teaching us to pray.

3. We must join humility with trust. Great God, said Daniel, when

we prostrate ourselves at thy feet, we do not place our hopes for the success of our prayers upon our righteousness, but upon thy mercy. Without this disposition in our hearts, all others, however pious they may be, cannot please God. Saint Augustine observes that the failure of Peter should not be attributed to insincerity in his zeal for Jesus Christ. He loved his Master in good faith; in good faith he would rather have died than have forsaken him; but his fault lay in trusting to his own strength to do what his own heart dictated.

It is the humble and contrite heart that God will not despise. Remark the difference which the Evangelist has pointed out between the prayer of the proud and presumptuous Pharisee, and the humble and penitent Publican. The one relates his virtues, the other deplores his sins. The good works of the one shall be set aside, while the penitence of the other shall be accepted. It will be thus with many Christians. Sinners, vile in their own eyes, will be objects of the mercy of God; while some who have made their professions of piety will be condemned, on account of the pride and arrogance that have contaminated their good works. It will be so, because these have said in their hearts, "Lord, I thank thee that I am not as other men are." They imagine themselves privileged souls; they pretend that they alone have penetrated the mysteries of the kingdom of God; they have a language and science of their own; they believe that their zeal can accomplish everything. Their regular lives favor their vanity; but in truth they are incapable of self-sacrifice, and they go to their devotions with their hearts full of pride and presumption. Unhappy are those who pray in this manner! Unhappy are they whose prayers do not render them more humble, more submissive, more watchful over their faults, and more willing to live in obscurity!

4. We must pray with love. It is love, says St. Augustine, that asks, that seeks, that knocks, that finds, and that is faithful to what it finds. We cease to pray to God as soon as we cease to love him, as soon as we cease to thirst for his perfections. The coldness of our love is the silence of our hearts toward God. Without this we may pronounce prayers, but we do not pray; for what shall lead us to meditate upon

the laws of God, if it be not the love of him who has made these laws? Let our hearts be full of love, then, and they will pray. Happy are they who think seriously of the truths of religion; but far more happy are they who feel and love them!

# HORACE BUSHNELL (1802–1876)

Born near Litchfield, Connecticut, Horace Bushnell later went to college at Yale. It was there, when studying law, that he overcame his religious doubts during a religious revival and entered upon theological studies. In 1833, he became pastor of the North Congregational Church in Hartford, Connecticut, and remained there until his retirement. He was not a forceful or dramatic preacher, yet he acquired widespread reputation for his sermons and later for his theological writings. He was of medium stature, and though he had been handsome during his youth, he had become thin and bony; so it was not his appearance which drew crowds. His voice was good, but not outstanding, and even that was lost later in life. And in preaching he was chained to his manuscript. Yet there was a natural manner about him which personified his understanding of the Christian life. He avoided clerical garb, dressing as an ordinary man, and there was an unmistakable homespun character about his appearance; furthermore there was a conversational quality in his sermons. As was made clear in his famous book, *Christian Nurture* (1847), he was convinced that the mark of the true Christian life is naturalness.

In the sermon presented here, Bushnell rejects much self-examination as it has been encouraged and practiced because it breeds scrupulosity and Pharisaism; Christian self-examination occurs naturally as God reveals what he will to the person who is responsive to him. It was his deep faith in the immanence of God who works naturally through the natural order which led Bushnell to re-examine many traditional doctrinal formulations and to restate them. A man of intellectual independence and conviction, he became the pioneer of liberal theology in New England, although he held no official positions in his church. In 1859, he resigned from his pastorate because of ill health.

# Self-examination Examined*

*Examine me, O Lord, and prove me, try my reins and my heart.* PSALM 26:2

Self-examination is to many disciples a kind of first point in practical religion. We have also labored treatises from the press, in which set rules are drawn out, whereby the self-examining process may be skillfully and scientifically conducted. In one way or another, this particular type of Christian exercise has come so near being the staple matter of a good life, that any common disciple called to address some brotherhood of strangers will probably not get on many sentences without falling into the exhortational mood and beginning to say—"Brethren, let us examine ourselves." All which is the more wearisome that it signifies so little, and requires only the driest kind of sanctimony to carry it on. We might very naturally presume that there must be a great deal of Scripture for this kind of practice; and yet I do not know more than two passages that can be cited for it at all; one of which certainly has no such meaning, and the other of which has, at most, only a doubtful, or variantly shaded meaning, such as carries no sufficient authority for the practice.

The Scripture sends us to God for the examinations wanted, and not, in any case, to ourselves; knowing that when God proves us, we

---

* From *Sermons on Living Subjects* (New York: Charles Scribner's Sons, 1877).

shall be thoroughly and truly proved, and that what assurance he may give us will be more than a guess, or opinion, or conclusion of our own, a veritable witness of God in our hearts. In this way the Psalmist prays—"Examine me, O Lord, and prove me, try my reins and my heart." And again—"Search me, O God, and know my heart, try me and know my thoughts, and see if there be any wicked way in me, and lead me in the way everlasting." It was also an accepted Proverb even in the same view—"The fining pot is for silver, and the furnace for gold, but the Lord trieth the hearts." Here is the true and proper method of examination; it must be accomplished under and through the scrutiny, or inspecting power of God; we truly prove ourselves, when he proves us, and may rightly approve ourselves, only when he approves us.

If we are in a truly right state towards him, he will know it, and he has planned to give us witness, infallible and immediate witness of the fact. For as unbelief and wrong separate the soul forthwith from God, so where there is no such separation, or where the separating force is abated, God is immediately revealed in the soul's consciousness. It abideth in the light, it recognizes God as a divine other, present within, even as the Savior himself declared—"But ye see me," and again —"I will manifest myself unto him." God then is manifested always in the consciousness of them that love him, and are right towards him. They need not go into any curious self-examination that will only confuse and obscure the witness. They will know God by an immediate knowledge or revelation. They will have his spirit witnessing with theirs. They will have the testimony that they please God. In their simple love they will know God's love to them; for he that loveth knoweth God. For a man then to be obliged to examine himself, and study and cipher over himself to find out whether he is a child of God or not, is no good sign; for if he is, he should have a witness more immediate, and should want no such information at all. God knows him perfectly, and if God has revealed himself in the consciousness, if he has the witness of God and the testimony that he pleases God, what more can he have? And if he has not this at all, what can he have, or what, by self-scrutiny, find to make good the want of it?

But we have a great many defects and errors and bad qualities lurking in us, and here again we shall discover that God has planned to bring us into a perception of these, and set us in the same judgment of them that he has himself. As the fining pot is for silver, and the furnace for gold, so the Lord trieth the hearts. It is wonderful to see with what skill God has adjusted all our experiences, in this mortal life, so as to make us sensible of our errors and defects. As the invisible ink is brought out in a distinct color, by holding what is written to the fire, so God brings out all our faults and our sins by the scorches of experience through which we are ever passing in the fiery trials of life. If we are proud, he has a way to make us see it, and to break down our pride. If we cherish any subtle grudge, or animosity, he will somehow call it out and make us see it. If we are selfish, or covetous, or jealous, or frivolous, or captious, or self-indulgent, or sensual, or self-confident, or fanatical, or self-righteous, or partial, or obstinate, or prejudiced, or uncharitable, or censorious—whatever fault we have in us, whether it be in the mind, or the head, or the body, or I might almost say the bones, no matter how subtle, or how ingeniously covered it may be, he has us in the furnace of trial and correction, where he is turning us round and round, lifting us in prosperity, crushing us in adversity, subduing us with afflictions, tempting out our faults and then chastising them, humbling us, correcting us, softening, tempering, soothing, fortifying, refining, healing, and so managing us as to detect all our drossy and bad qualities, and separate them from us. He sits as a refiner and purifier of silver, and allows nothing to escape either his discovery or our correction. No self-examination we could make would discover, at all, what he is continually bringing to the light, and exposing to our detection. The very plan of our life is so to handle us that we shall come into the full advantage of his perfect knowledge of our state and character. He is proving us at every turn, making us apprised of ourselves, trying even the reins and the heart, that our most secret things may be revealed.

It can not then be said that there is no way of making God's examination of us available; for he is, all the while, and in every possible manner, giving us advantage of it. If the trial of our faith is precious, he for just that reason leaves it not to us alone to make the trial, but his plan is, knowing what we are and what we want, to conduct every point of the trial himself.

I will only add, and this perhaps I ought to add, that if there be any legitimate place for self-examination, it is in the field last mentioned, where we go into self-inspection just to discover our faults, and the sins that require to be forsaken or put away. This would be a very honest kind of endeavor, and I see no objection to it, save that it is very likely, when pursued too closely, to produce a morbid state, and sink the soul in the disabilities of fatal discouragement. No prudent Christian, therefore, will even dare to set himself down upon the discovery of his sins, and make it his chief engagement. He can not be always looking down this gulf, and not wither in a prospect so ungenial. He must have a little gospel somehow, and if he does not have a great deal, so much sin will starve him to death. It will generally be much better to just let God put him on such ways of discovery here as will be best for him. But this is not what most disciples go to self-examination, or by their teachers are put on self-examination, for; they are set to it, not to find out their faults, and correct them, but to settle and try out their Christian evidences. Our great and godly Edwards writes his book on the Affections, for exactly this, and taking his book for what he verily thought was to be the use of it, I as verily think it one of the most mistaken books that a good and saintly man was ever allowed to write—it is a kind of morbid anatomy for the mind. And we have hundreds of others in the same strain. Evidences of piety are a great deal more likely to be hidden, or ruled out in that way, than they are to be found, and the most sensitively delicate disciple is the one that will suffer. It is well if he does not push himself into spiritual distraction by it. On the other hand, when evidences are sought in this manner, that class of persons who are commonly finding what they look for, will be almost certain to fish up the evidences they want. This whole method of self-examination, to settle the question of Christian evidence, is deceptive, unscriptural, and bitterly injurious.

And it is injurious, I must add, not only in misleading, but also in hindering the disciple. How can he get on with any sort of growth when totally occupied in the matter of self-inspection? The very engagement becomes a dry and weary fumbling of his own state. Even as the lad I knew, who had undertaken to grow a patch of watermelons, looked to see them ripen long before they were grown; went to them every day and examined and tested them, pressing his thumb down hard upon them, to see if the rind would snap; for that was to be the sign when they were ripe. But the poor things, under so many indentations, fell to rotting, and did not ripen at all. They were examined to death. God's winds, and rains, and suns, and dews, were doing a much better examination upon them—with the advantage that it gave them time to grow, and a chance to naturally live.

The real wisdom of the Christian, then, for this is the conclusion to which we are brought, is that he shall be more natural; not facing round as he walks, to examine the tracks he makes, but asking the way to Zion with his face thitherward. This dismal retroversion is the bane of character, giving it a twisted and hard look, a sorely and even selfishly circumspective look. You see at a glance, how often, that the man or woman writes a diary, and puts down all the frames passed through, keeping them in tally, and considering the figure they make. Not that every man who writes a diary does it of course in this self-regarding way. George Fox writes two heavy volumes of diary, and after he has fairly opened his Christian story, from its birthday beginning, he scarcely so much as alludes to any frame of feeling, or score of evidence in his life, but simply puts his face right onward, telling where he went, and whom he saw, and what in God's name he did. He never once intimates a misgiving, and when he comes to die, he is so little concerned for it, that in what is called his death, he simply forgot to live! Such a disciple grows less conscious and not more conscious in his habit, and there is such plain, forward-going simplicity in him, that he visibly bears the stamp of God's approving, not of his own self-approving.

God forbid, my hearers, that in ruling out so much that has been held in sacred esteem and reverence, and carefully observed and practiced by the faithful and godly in Christ Jesus, I should seem willing to encourage lightness and looseness of life. Is it a light thing to be said,

or only a true, that a man does not want to examine himself to find
whether he is cold or hungry, whether he loves his child, whether he
is an honest man? No, the sturdy fact is that all such answers sought
come and ought to come without seeking, and can only come to themselves in simply being true. And if they do not, if a man has to make
a case on the question of his honesty, he is very certainly a good deal
less honest than he should be. No, my friends, the thing wanted here,
and that which only yields the true evidence, is the genuine down-
rightness of our life—that it covers no shams, gets up no mock virtues
and no pretexts of proceeding scientifically, but goes right on, putting
its face the way it goes, and not backwards. It is consciously right, and
God is consciously yielding it his immediate testimony. And let there
be no doubt of this, as if it were a way not safe. God will make it safe
as he only can. And if you are afraid that some looseness may creep in,
or some false hope steal you away, be upon your watch, for watching
is one thing, and self-examination a very different thing. Watch and
pray that you may not enter into temptation, and let the prayer be this,
which God will never disregard—"Search me, O God, and know my
thoughts, and see if there be any wicked way in me, and lead me in the
way everlasting." Then forward, forward in that way.

# GEORGE HERBERT MORRISON (1866–1928) George Morrison was born in Glasgow, graduated from the university there, and was ordained to the ministry in the Free Church of Scotland. After a four-year ministry in a small town in northern Scotland, he took charge of St. John's Church in the industrial town of Dundee; it was there that his wife died, leaving him with four small children. Though he had already become a respected preacher, it was not until he came to the United Presbyterian Church of Wellington, adjacent to the University of Glasgow, that his truly great ministry of preaching began. His sermons drew large crowds from both the university and the city. His most "popular" sermons were those delivered Sunday evenings, of which the following is one. Though a great preacher, Morrison considered himself primarily a pastor. He called on his flock extensively, once traveling to London to visit a young parishioner who had written that she was lonely and depressed; and still there are people in Glasgow who will point proudly to the chair in which Dr. Morrison used to sit.

His sermons reveal his deep pastoral concern. They are marked by the combination of simplicity and profundity; and in the tradition of fine Scottish preaching, they display remarkable erudition. Morrison did not preach evangelical sermons to nonbelievers; his hearers were mostly Christian, and he spoke to them as such, seeking to enliven and deepen their faith. His emphasis was upon personal religion. His sermons are definitely biblical, never prepared without a thorough study of his text. One will also notice an unmistakable touch of the poet in his remarkable prose. Morrison preached in an undramatic fashion, standing still, with his hands behind his back, without notes, and speaking quietly, because an early illness had seriously impaired his vocal cords. Two years before his death he was honored to be elected Moderator of the General Assembly of his church.

# The Ministry
# of Silence*

*Be still, and know that I am God.* PSALM 46:10

There are certain voices which we never hear save when everything is silent. They reach us as a revelation of the stillness. Sometimes on a summer afternoon one gets away from city or from town, and climbs up the grassy hillside till all the noise of human life is lost, and it is often then that there breaks upon the ear a certain indistinguishable murmur as of the moving of innumerable wings. Travellers tell us that there are rivers flowing beneath the streets of the ancient city of Shechem. During the hours of the day you cannot hear them, for the noise of the narrow streets and the bazaars. But evening comes, and the clamor dies away, and the dews of kindly sleep rest on the city; and then quite audibly, in the hush of night, you may hear the music of the buried streams. There are many voices like those hidden waters. You never can hear them save when things are still. There are whisperings of conscience in the bosom which a very little stir can easily drown. There are tidings from the eternal Spirit who is not far away from any one of us; tidings that will come and go unnoticed, unless we have won the grace of being still.

* From George M. Docherty (ed.), *The Greatest Sermons of George H. Morrison* (New York: Harper & Brothers, 1959). Copyright © 1959 by Harper & Brothers. Used by permission of the publisher.

And yet that very element of stillness is one which is conspicuously lacking now. We have been taught the art of being strenuous, and we have lost the art of being still. A recent writer, in an essay on the orchestral music of today, tells us that we are living nowadays under "the dominion of din." And whether or not that be true of orchestral music, it is certainly true of ordinary life. Our forefathers in the religious life may have had very imperfect ideals of Christian service. They may have tolerated social abuses which we should never tolerate today. But they had one element in their religious life in an ampler measure than we have it, and that was the blessed element of silence. What peace there was in the old-fashioned Sabbath—what a reverent stillness in the house of God—what a quiet and leisurely solemnity in the morning worship at the family altar! And if today we cannot but be conscious that something of that old spirit has departed, we know that something precious has been lost. It is a gain to be immersed in service. It is a high ambition to be strenuous. "Whatsoever thy hand findeth to do, do it with thy might" (Eccl. 1:10). And yet the Bible never says to us, "Be strenuous, and know that I am God." It says, "Be still, and know that I am God."

Indeed, so in love are we with noise today that stillness is commonly looked upon as weakness. And it is well to remind ourselves occasionally that often the very opposite is true. When the rain beats against the windowpane we are awakened by the driving of it. But the snow falls so silently, that never an infant stirs within its cradle. And yet the snow may block up every road quite as effectually as soldiery, and dislocate the traffic of a kingdom. Set a thousand scratching spades to work, and you produce a certain effect upon the soil. But now the frost comes, with her silent fingers, and lightly touches field and meadow with them; and in a single night that silent frost will work more effectually than a thousand spades. God does not work in this strange world by hustling. God works in the world far oftener by hush. In all the mightiest powers which enkindle us there is a certain element of stillness. And if I did not find in Jesus Christ something of that divine inaudibility, I confess I should be tempted to distrust him. When Epictetus had had his arm broken by the savage cruelty of his master, he turned round without one trace of anger, and said to him quietly, "I told you so." When a heathen satirist then taunted the Christians, asking what nobler thing their Master did, one of them answered, "He kept silence." There is a silence that may speak of weakness. There is another silence that is full of power. And it is well to remember that we are tempted to associate quietness with weakness.

There is, of course, a certain kind of silence which is but the outward sign of self-absorption. It does not indicate that a man is hearing anything; it just means that he is withdrawn into himself. I have heard runners say that in great races they have been oblivious of every sound. There may have been a thousand voices cheering them, and yet they seemed to run in a great silence. Perhaps all of us have had hours such as that—hours of suffering or of intense activity—when we felt ourselves alone in a great solitude. That is the stillness of absorption. It is not the stillness to which our text refers. It is of another quietness that it speaks; the quietness which is the basis of communion. For there are times when we never speak so tellingly, and times when we never hear so finely, as when the tongue is silent, and the lips are closed, and the spirit is the one interpreter. A love that has no silence has no depth. "Methinks the lady doth protest too much." There are people whose love we instinctively distrust because they are always telling us about it. And perhaps it is simply because God is love, in all the glorious fulness of that word, that we have to be still if we would know him.

Indeed, there is often no surer sign than silence that the heart has been reached and the depths been broken up. In their greatest hours men are seldom noisy. I have watched sometimes an audience at a concert—for to me the audience is more interesting than the music— I have watched the listless attention which they gave to music that reached no farther than the ear. And then perhaps there was some perfect melody—some chord which had the insistence of a message— and it was as if a voice had cried aloud, *Be still, and know that I am God*. We do not clamber to God by the steps of logic; we reach him by the feelings of the heart. And it is just because, when the heart is moved profoundly, there falls upon it a silence and a stillness, that we are bidden in our text to be still, and know that he is God.

Probably that is the reason, too, why great silences have a divine suggestion. Great silent spaces speak to us of God. I remember visiting the cathedral at Cologne. Passing in from the crowded city streets, the thought of the presence of God was overwhelming. I knew he was present in the teeming city. I knew he was present in the crowded thoroughfare. I knew that where the stir and traffic were the infinite Spirit was not far away. And yet it is one thing to know, and it is quite another thing to feel; and in the calm and solemn quiet of the cathedral I felt that God was there. That is what spiritual men have always felt under the silence of the starry sky. That is why they have always thought of God when they lifted up their eyes unto the hills. Our noisy talkative life is like the surge breaking on the margin of the shore, and away beyond it is the silent ocean carrying the message of infinity. We lose our sense of God in a great city far more readily than lonely dwellers do. And we lay the blame of that upon a score of things —on the strain of business, on our abundant pleasures. Perhaps there is a deeper reason than all these; it is the loss of the ministry of silence: of the moor, of the glen, and of the hill: of the solitudes which are quivering with God.

I close by suggesting that this is the reason why God makes silences in every life; the silence of sleep—the silences of sorrow—and then the last great silence at the end. One of the hardest things in the world, as you all know, is to get little children to keep still. They are in a state of perpetual activity, restless, eager, questioning, alert. And just as a mother says to her child, "Be still," and hushes it to sleep that it may rest, so God does sooner or later with us all. What a quiet, still place the sickroom is! What a silence there is over a house of mourning! How the voices are hushed, and every footstep soft. Had we the choosing of our own affairs we should never have chosen such an hour as that; and yet how often it is rich in blessing. All the activities of eager years may not have taught us quite so much as that. There are things which we never learn when we are active. There are things which we only learn when we are passive. And so God comes, in his resistless way, which never ceases to be a way of love, and says, *Be still, and know that I am God*. If that be so with the passive hours of life, may it not be so with the passive hour of death? What is death but the Almighty Father saying to our talking lips, *Be still?* And I for one believe that in that stillness we shall awaken to know that he is God, in such a love and power as will be heaven.

# part three

# Christian

# Seasons

# and

# Festivals

# GERARD MANLEY HOPKINS (1844-1889)

Born in Stratford, Essex, the eldest of eight children, Gerard Manley Hopkins was reared in an artistic family. As a young boy he thought of becoming a painter; when a student at Oxford he began to write poetry seriously and was later to become a significant English poet. Though he had been an Anglo-Catholic at Oxford, he was converted to Roman Catholicism and was received by another famous Oxfordian represented in this collection of sermons who had some twenty years before followed a similar road—John Henry Newman. Hopkins soon entered the Society of Jesus and began his training for the priesthood, to which he was ordained in 1877. He spent four years as a parish priest in various places including London, Oxford, and Liverpool. The sermon "A Hero All the World Wants" was preached in 1879 and shows his gifts for striking phraseology and an almost musical sense of language as well as a rare, sensitive imagination. His poetry shows on occasion his deep inner struggle with doubt and occasional rebellious feelings, but this sermon, like many of his poems, reveals his underlying deep personal faith. Though he was devout and conscientious in his work as a priest, his slight frame and delicate physical condition did not suit him for a parochial ministry nor for preaching. He became a teacher of Latin and then a professor of classics at Dublin University in Ireland; at the age of forty-five he died there of typhoid fever.

# A Hero
# All the World Wants*

*And his father and mother marvelled at what was said about him.* LUKE 2:33

St. Joseph, though he often carried our Lord Jesus Christ in his arms, and the Blessed Virgin, though she gave him birth and suckled him at her breast, though they seldom either of them had the Holy Child out of their sight and knew more of him far than all others, yet when they heard what Holy Simeon a stranger had to say of him, the Scripture says they wondered. Not indeed that they were surprised and had thought to hear something different, but that they gave their minds up to admiration and dwelt with reverent wonder on all God's doings about the child, their sacred charge. Brethren, see what a thing it is to hear about our Lord Jesus Christ, to think of him and dwell upon him; it did good to these two holiest people, the Blessed Virgin and St. Joseph. Even with him in the house, God thought fit to give them lights by the mouth of strangers. It cannot but do good to us, who have more need of holiness, who easily forget Christ, who have not got him before our eyes to look at.

Our Lord Jesus Christ, my brethren, is our hero, a hero all the world wants. You know how books of tales are written, that put one man

* Christopher Devlin, S.J. (ed.), *The Sermons and Devotional Writings of Gerard Manley Hopkins* (London: Oxford University Press, 1959). Used by permission of the publisher.

before the reader and shew him off handsome for the most part and brag and call him, My hero or Our hero. Often mothers make a hero of a son; girls of a sweetheart and good wives of a husband. Soldiers make a hero of a great general, a party of its leader, a nation of any great man that brings it glory, whether king, warrior, statesman, thinker, poet, or whatever it shall be. But Christ, he is the hero. He too is the hero of a book or books, of the divine Gospels. He is a warrior and a conqueror; of whom it is written he went forth conquering and to conquer. He is a king, Jesus of Nazareth king of the Jews, though when he came to his own kingdom his own did not receive him, and now, his people having cast him off, we Gentiles are his inheritance. He is a statesman, that drew up the New Testament in his blood. He is a thinker, that taught us divine mysteries. He is an orator and poet, as in his eloquent words and parables appears. He is all the world's hero, the desire of nations. But besides he is the hero of single souls; his mother's hero, not out of motherly foolish fondness but because he was, as the angel told her, great and the son of the Most High and all that he did and said and was done and said about him she laid up in her heart. He is the true love and the bridegroom of men's souls: the virgins and martyrs follow him; all his servants take up their cross and follow him. And those even that do not follow him, yet they look wistfully after him, own him a hero, and wish they dared answer to his call. Children as soon as they can understand ought to be told about him, that they may make him the hero of their young hearts.

There met in Jesus Christ all things that can make man lovely and lovable. In his body he was most beautiful. Accounts of him written in early times tell us that he was moderately tall, well built and tender in frame, his features straight and beautiful, his hair inclining to auburn, parted in the midst, curling and clustering about the ears and neck as the leaves of a filbert, so they speak, upon the nut. He wore also a forked beard and this as well as the locks upon his head were never touched by razor or shears. The account I have been quoting, we do not indeed for certain know to be correct, but it has been current in the Church and many generations have drawn our Lord accordingly either in their own minds or in his images. His constitution too was tempered perfectly, he had neither disease nor the seeds of any; weariness he felt when he was wearied, hunger when he fasted, thirst when he had long gone without drink, but to the touch of sickness he was a stranger. I leave it to you, brethren, then to picture him, in whom the fulness of the Godhead dwelt bodily, in his bearing how majestic, how strong and yet how lovely and lissome in his limbs, in his look how earnest, grave but kind. In his Passion all this strength was spent, this lissomeness crippled, this beauty wrecked, this majesty beaten down. But now it is more than all restored, and for myself I make no secret I look forward with eager desire to seeing the matchless beauty of Christ's body in the heavenly light.

I come to his mind. He was the greatest genius that ever lived. You know what genius is, brethren—beauty and perfection in the mind. For perfection in the bodily frame distinguishes a man among other men his fellows: so may the mind be distinguished for its beauty above other minds and that is genius. Then when this genius is duly taught and trained, that is wisdom; for without training genius is imperfect and again wisdom is imperfect without genius. But Christ, we read, advanced in wisdom and in favor with God and men; now this wisdom, in which he excelled all men, had to be founded on an unrivalled genius. Christ then was the greatest genius that ever lived. You must not say, Christ needed no such thing as genius; his wisdom came from heaven, for he was God. To say so is to speak like the heretic Apollinaris. Christ was perfect man and must have mind as well as body and that mind was, no question, of the rarest excellence and beauty; it was genius. As Christ lived and breathed and moved in a true and not a phantom human body and in that labored, suffered, was crucified, died, and was buried; as he merited by acts of his human will; so he reasoned and planned and invented by acts of his own human genius, genius made perfect by wisdom of its own, not the divine wisdom only.

A witness to his genius we have in those men who being sent to arrest him came back empty handed, spellbound by his eloquence, saying, "Never man spoke like this man."

A better proof we have in his own words, his Sermon on the Mount, his parables and all his sayings recorded in the Gospel. My brethren, we are so accustomed to them that they do not strike us as they do a stranger that hears them first, else we too should say, "Never man spoke like this man." No stories or parables are like Christ's, so bright, so pithy, so touching; no proverbs or sayings are such jewellery; they stand off from other men's thoughts like stars, like lilies in the sun; nowhere in literature is there anything to match the Sermon on the Mount: if there is let men bring it forward. Time does not allow me to call your minds to proofs or instances. Besides Christ's sayings in the Gospels a dozen or so more have been kept by tradition. Though one cannot feel sure of every one, yet reading all in one view they make me say, "These must be Christ's, never man spoke like this." One is: "Never rejoice but when you look upon your brother in love." Another is: "My mystery is for me and for the children of my house."

Now in the third place, far higher than beauty of the body, higher than genius and wisdom—the beauty of the mind, comes the beauty of his character, his character as man. For the most part his very enemies, those that do not believe in him, allow that a character so noble was never seen in human mold. Plato the heathen, the greatest of the Greek philosophers, foretold of him: he drew by his wisdom a picture of the just man in his justice crucified and it was fulfilled in Christ. Poor was his station, laborious his life, bitter his ending: through poverty, through labor, through crucifixion his majesty of nature more shines. No heart as his was ever so tender, but tenderness was not all: this heart so tender was as brave, it could be stern. He found the thought of his Passion past bearing, yet he went through with it. He was feared when he chose: he took a whip and singlehanded cleared the temple. The thought of his gentleness towards children, towards the afflicted, towards sinners, is often dwelt on; that of his courage less. But for my part I like to feel that I should have feared him. We hear also of his love, as for John and Lazarus; and even love at first sight, as of the young man that had kept all the commandments from his childhood. But he warned or rebuked his best friends when need was, as Peter, Martha, and even his mother. For, as St. John says, he was full both of grace and truth.

But, brethren, from all that might be said of his character I single out one point and beg you to notice that. He loved to praise, he loved to reward. He knew what was in man, he best knew men's faults and yet he was the warmest in their praise. When he worked a miracle he would grace it with: "Thy faith hath saved thee," that it might almost seem the receiver's work, not his. He said of Nathanael that he was an Israelite without guile; he that searches hearts said this, and yet what praise that was to give! He called the two sons of Zebedee Sons of Thunder, kind and stately and honorable name! We read of nothing thunderlike that they did except, what was sinful, to wish fire down from heaven on some sinners, but they deserved the name or he would not have given it, and he has given it them for all time. Of John the Baptist he said that his greater was not born of women. He said to Peter, "Thou art the Rock," and rewarded a moment's acknowledgment of him with headship of his Church. He defended Magdalen and took means that the story of generosity should be told for ever. And though he bids us say we are unprofitable servants, yet he himself will say to each of us, "Good and faithful servant, well done."

And this man whose picture I have tried to draw for you, brethren, is your God. He was your maker in time past; hereafter he will be your judge. Make him your hero now. Take some time to think of him; praise him in your hearts. You can over your work or on your road praise him, saying over and over again: Glory be to Christ's body; Glory to the body of the Word made flesh; Glory to Christ's body in its beauty; Glory to Christ's body in its weariness; Glory to its courage and manliness; Glory to its meekness and mercy; Glory to its every heartbeat, to its joys and sorrows, wishes, fears; glory to Christ's body risen and in the Blessed Sacrament. Glory in all things to Jesus Christ God and man. If you try this when you can you will find your heart kindle and while you praise him he will praise you.

**AURELIUS AUGUSTINE** (354-430) There is no one theologian who has been more influential in the shaping of Western Christian theology than St. Augustine; and there is probably no theologian whose life is more familiar than his, at least the first forty years of it which are covered by his *Confessions*. Born in Tagaste, North Africa, he was sent to the University of Carthage where he studied rhetoric with the intention of practicing law. There he acquired a mistress, to whom he was faithful for fifteen years, and abandoned whatever Christianity he had acquired from his mother, Monica. He became a Manichean until dissatisfied with it some ten years later; eventually he became a Christian critic of Manicheism. After turning from rhetoric to philosophy and eventually to neo-Platonism, and having taught in Carthage and Rome, he moved to Milan to teach, where he came under the influence of the Bishop, St. Ambrose. In 387, he and his son were baptized by the bishop, and Augustine returned to Tagaste to live in monastic retirement. While visiting the city of Hippo, he was taken by the people and presented to the bishop for ordination. In 391 he was ordained a priest, and in 396 he became the Bishop of Hippo, and remained so until his death.

In addition to disputing with the Manicheans, the Donatists, and Pelagius, three challenges to Christian orthodoxy, running his diocese, and writing voluminous material on biblical, political, and theological matters, he was also a frequent preacher, sometimes preaching as often as five times a week. His brilliant and orderly mind, his passionate faith, his rhetorical abilities, and his vast learning and sensitive awareness to his total environment combined to make him an outstanding preacher; he is generally regarded as the greatest Latin preacher. It is recorded that he was able to gain the attention of the roughest crowd and to move the most contentious people to tears and repentance. He had high esteem for the office of preacher, and he emphasized the importance of preaching, though he himself was not always well prepared. Many of his sermons contain polemical material, and some exhibit traces of his own mystical piety; this sermon presents him as a bishop teaching his flock. It was probably preached shortly before A.D. 410. It also provides an exmaple of the allegorical method of interpreting the Scriptures which was popular in the Church at that time.

# Epiphany*

Today's feast is known throughout the whole world. What joy it brings us, or what lesson the feast has for us on its annual return—the season suggests that we also make this the topic of the sermon which we give at this time each year.

The Greek *Epiphania*, it is clear, can be rendered in Latin by the word *Manifestatio* [and in English by "manifestation"]. It is on this day that the Magi are said to have adored the Lord. They were prevailed upon to do this by a star which appeared to them and were led on by the star going before them. On the day he was born they saw the star in the East; and they knew whose birth was signified by the star. From that day, then, to this did they hasten to find him. They frightened King Herod with the news. When in answer to their inquiry the Jews had quoted to them the prophecies contained in the Scriptures, they found the city of Bethlehem where the Lord had been born. Then, with the same star as their guide, they came to the place where the Lord was. When they recognized him, they adored him. They offered him gold, incense, and myrrh. They returned by another way.

The Lord was also made manifest, and that on the day of his birth, to the shepherds who were informed by an angel. And on that day news of him was given by a star also to those men still far off in the East; and this is the day on which they adored him. Therefore, the

* From *Sermons for Christmas and Epiphany*, "Ancient Christian Writers," No. XV, trans. by T. C. Lawlor (Westminster, Md.: The Newman Press, 1952). Copyright 1952 by Rev. Johannes Quasten and Rev. Joseph C. Plumpe. Used by permission of the publisher.

universal Church of the Gentiles adopted this day as a day to be celebrated in a most devout manner; for even these Magi, what were they
but the first fruits of the Gentiles?

The shepherds were Israelites, the Magi, Gentiles. The first lived
nearby, the latter, far away; yet both met at the Cornerstone. "Coming,"
to be sure, as the Apostle says, "he preached peace to us that were afar
off, and peace to these that were high. For he is our peace who has
made both one, and has made the two in himself into one new man,
making peace, and has changed both to God in one body, killing the
enmities in himself."

Let us celebrate the manifestation of our Lord and Savior Jesus Christ
on which he harvested the first fruits of the Gentiles, in the unity of
the Gentiles.

For at that time when he was a child, before he knew how to call
his father or mother, as had been prophesied of him, he accepted "the
strength of Damascus and the spoils of Samaria"; that is, before he
uttered human words through his human flesh, he accepted the strength
of Damascus, namely, that on which Damascus prided itself. Indeed,
by the standards of the world it was a flourishing city and because of
its riches had once given itself airs. But among riches the first place is
given to gold, and this the Magi humbly offered to Christ. As for the
spoils of Samaria, these were quite the same as the people who were
living there: "Samaria" was taken as synonymous with "idolatry;" for
there the people of Israel turned away from the Lord and gave themselves to worship idols. Christ, who was of course going to vanquish
the kingdom of the Devil throughout the world with a spiritual sword,
as a child took these first spoils away from the domination of idolatry.
Thus he was to convert the Magi from the curse of their superstition
to the adoration of himself; and because he was not yet speaking on
this earth through his tongue, he was to speak from heaven through a
star. He was to show, not by a voice of flesh, but by the power of the
Word made flesh, who he was, whither he had come, and for whose
sake he had come.

This Word, which in the beginning was God with God, now also
made flesh that he might dwell among us, had come to us—but he was

also remaining with the Father. Without deserting the angels on high,
he was employing the angels to gather men to himself below. Because
he was the Word, he shone with the light of unchangeable truth upon
the dwellers in heaven; and at the same time, because his lodging was
so small, he was lying in a manger.

It was he who showed the star in the sky, and it was he who showed
himself to be adored on earth. And yet this infant, so powerful, so
great, fled into Egypt, a child borne there by his parents—because of
the hostility of Herod. Thus he says to his members, though not yet
in words but as implied by his actions: "If you are persecuted in one
city, flee into another."

He was, to be sure, wearing the garment of mortal flesh, that therein
he might serve us as a model; and in it he was also to die for us at
the opportune time. This is why he had received from the Magi not
only the gold of honor and the incense of adoration, but also the myrrh
of burial. In the little ones whom Herod had slain, he also showed
what kind of people were going to die for his name, how innocent, how
humble they would be.

But whose thoughts are not already directed to the significance of
the fact that the Jews quoted Scripture when replying to the question
of the Magi concerning the place where Christ was born, but themselves refrained from adoring him? Do we not see this even now, when
the very practices of religion to which their obduracy is exposed, point
to nothing else but the Christ in whom they do not want to believe?
Even when they kill their sheep and eat the Passover, do they not point
out to the Gentiles the Christ whom they themselves do not adore with
them? Indeed, what of the fact that in the case of prophetic testimonies
by which Christ was announced beforehand and regarding which
doubting individuals think that Christians may have composed them—
not when they were still in the future, but when they were accomplished facts—we often cite the writings of the Jews to settle the doubts
they have in their minds? Do not the Jews even then show the Gentiles
the Christ whom they do not wish to adore with the Gentiles?

We, therefore, beloved, of whom the Magi were the first fruits, we
are the inheritance of Christ even to the ends of the earth. For our

sake a part of Israel was overtaken by blindness that the fullness of the Gentiles might come in. We have learned to know our Lord and Savior Jesus Christ, who that he might console us, did then lie in a tiny lodging, who that he may raise us up, now sits in heaven. Let us so proclaim him on this earth, in this our mortal life, that we may not return the way we have come, nor retrace the footsteps of our former way of life. This is why, too, the Magi did not return the way by which they had come. A change of way meant a change of life.

To us also did "the heavens show forth the glory of God"; we, too, have been led to the adoration of Christ by the truth shining forth from the Gospel, like a star from the sky; we, too, have listened faithfully and have understood the prophecy honored in the Jewish race— a testimony, as it were, of the Jews refusing to go on with us; we, too, by acknowledging and praising the King, the Priest, the Christ who died for us, have honored him, so to speak, in gold and incense and myrrh. It only remains for us to be heralds of his Gospel and go a new way, and not return the way we have come.

# JOHN CHRYSOSTOM (347-407)

**JOHN CHRYSOSTOM** (347-407) Born in Antioch, John, like his contemporary St. Augustine, was raised by his pious, widowed mother. While a student of law and literature, he was baptized, in his early twenties, and not many years later left his studies to become a monk. The rigorousness of that extremely ascetic life broke his health, and he returned to Antioch to become a priest in 386. Though small in stature and having an emaciated frame, this man became a powerful preacher with a winning manner and eloquent delivery. So memorable and striking were his phrases that he was nicknamed "golden mouthed," which is the meaning of "chrysostom."

This sermon "On Fasting," which is part of a much longer one, was preached in a turbulent historical period. It was the spring of 387, and the Emperor Theodosius had announced his intention to destroy Antioch because of the people's recalcitrance with regard to imperial taxes; while Bishop Flavian was interceding with the emperor for the city, John preached a series of sermons to comfort, instruct, and guide the people. His timely remarks about the appropriate manner of observing the fast of Lent have relevance even today, and fortunately they could be applied by his listeners long after the sermon was delivered; the city was spared. In 398, he became Patriarch of Constantinople; here again he was noted for his eloquent sermons and his reforming zeal, particularly as this was directed against the sins and failures of the clergy. During politically stormy years he was maligned and subsequently exiled, in 404. Three years later he died a martyr, his death resulting from enforced travel in a feeble condition on route to a newly selected place of exile. The Eastern Orthodox Church honors him not only as a saint, but has given his name to the liturgy which is generally used in its services.

# On Fasting*

Let us not then despair of our safety, but let us pray; let us make invocation; let us supplicate; let us go on embassy to the King that is above with many tears! We have this fast, too, as an ally, and as an assistant in this good intercession. Therefore, as when the winter is over and the summer is appearing, the sailor draws his vessel to the deep; and the soldier burnishes his arms, and makes ready his steed for the battle; and the husbandman sharpens his sickle; and the traveller boldly undertakes a long journey, and the wrestler strips and bares himself for the contest. So too, when Lent makes its appearance, like a kind of spiritual summer, let us as soldiers burnish our weapons; and as husbandmen let us sharpen our sickles; and as sailors let us order our thoughts against the waves of extravagant desires; and as travellers let us set out on the journey towards heaven; and as wrestlers let us strip for the contest. For the believer is at once a husbandman, and a sailor, and a soldier, a wrestler, and a traveller. Hence St. Paul saith, "We wrestle not against flesh and blood, but against principalities, against powers. Put on therefore the whole armor of God." Hast thou observed the wrestler? Hast thou observed the soldier? If thou art a

* From Philip Schaff (ed.), *A Select Library of the Nicene and Post-Nicene Fathers of the Christian Church,* Vol. IX, trans. by W. R. W. Stephens (New York: The Christian Literature Co., 1889; reissued in 1956 by Wm. B. Eerdmans Publishing Co., Grand Rapids).

wrestler, it is necessary for thee to engage in the conflict naked. If a soldier, it behooves thee to stand in the battle line armed at all points. How then are both these things possible, to be naked, and yet not naked; to be clothed, and yet not clothed? How? I will tell thee. Divest thyself of worldly business, and thou hast become a wrestler. Put on the spiritual armor, and thou hast become a soldier. Strip thyself of worldly cares, for the season is one of wrestling. Clothe thyself with the spiritual armor, for we have a heavy warfare to wage with demons. Therefore also it is needful we should be naked, so as to offer nothing that the Devil may take hold of, while he is wrestling with us; and to be fully armed at all points, so as on no side to receive a deadly blow. Cultivate thy soul. Cut away the thorns. Sow the word of godliness. Propagate and nurse with much care the fair plants of divine wisdom, and thou hast become a husbandman. And Paul will say to thee, "The husbandman that laboreth must be first partaker of the fruits." He, too, himself practiced this art. Therefore, writing to the Corinthians, he said, "I have planted, Apollos watered, but God gave the increase." Sharpen thy sickle, which thou hast blunted through gluttony—sharpen it by fasting. Lay hold of the pathway which leads towards heaven; rugged and narrow as it is, lay hold of it, and journey on. And how mayest thou be able to do these things? By subduing the body, and bringing it into subjection. For when the way grows narrow, the corpulence that comes of gluttony is a great hindrance. Keep down the waves of inordinate desires. Repel the tempest of evil thoughts. Preserve the bark; display much skill, and thou hast become a pilot. But we shall have the fast for a groundwork and instructor in all these things.

I speak not, indeed, of such a fast as most persons keep, but of real fasting; not merely an abstinence from meats; but from sins, too. For the nature of a fast is such, that it does not suffice to deliver those who practice it, unless it be done according to a suitable law. "For the wrestler," it is said, "is not crowned unless he strive lawfully." To the end then, that when we have gone through the labor of fasting, we forfeit not the crown of fasting, we should understand how, and after what manner, it is necessary to conduct this business; since that Pharisee also fasted, but afterwards went down empty, and destitute of the fruit of fasting. The Publican fasted not; and yet he was accepted in preference to him who had fasted, in order that thou mayest learn that fasting is unprofitable, except all other duties follow with it. The Ninevites fasted, and won favor of God. The Jews fasted, too, and profited nothing, nay, they departed with blame. Since then the danger in fasting is so great to those who do not know how they ought to fast, we should learn the laws of this exercise, in order that we may not "run uncertainly," nor "beat the air," nor while we are fighting contend with a shadow. Fasting is a medicine; but a medicine, though it be never so profitable, becomes frequently useless owing to the unskillfulness of him who employs it. For it is necessary to know, moreover, the time when it should be applied, and the requisite quantity of it; and the corresponding diet; as well as various other particulars; any of which, if one overlooks, he will mar all the rest that have been named.

I have said these things, not that we may disparage fasting, but that we may honor fasting; for the honor of it consists not in abstinence from food, but in withdrawing from sinful practices, since he who limits his fasting only to an abstinence from meats is one who especially disparages it. Dost thou fast? Give me proof of it by thy works! Is it said by what kind of works? If thou seest a poor man, take pity on him! If thou seest an enemy, be reconciled to him! If thou seest a friend gaining honor, envy him not! If thou seest a handsome woman, pass her by! For let not the mouth only fast, but also the eye, and the ear, and the feet, and the hands, and all members of our bodies. Let the hands fast, by being pure from plunder and avarice. Let the feet fast, by ceasing from running to the unlawful spectacles. Let the eyes fast, being taught never to fix themselves rudely upon handsome countenances, or to busy themselves with strange beauties. For looking is the food of the eyes, but if this be such as is unlawful or forbidden, it mars the fast; and upsets the whole safety of the soul; but if it be lawful and safe, it adorns fasting. For it would be among things the most absurd to abstain from lawful food because of the fast, but with the eyes to touch even what is forbidden. Dost thou not eat flesh? Feed not upon lasciviousness by means of the eyes. Let the ear fast also. The fasting of the ear consists in refusing to receive evil speakings and calumnies. "Thou shalt not receive a false report," it says.

Let the mouth too fast from disgraceful speeches and railing. For what doth it profit if we abstain from birds and fishes; and yet bite and devour our brethren? The evil speaker eateth the flesh of his brother, and biteth the body of his neighbor. Because of this Paul utters the fearful saying, "If ye bite and devour another, take heed that ye be not consumed one of another." Thou hast not fixed thy teeth in the flesh, but thou hast fixed the slander in the soul, and inflicted the wound of evil suspicion; thou hast harmed, in a thousand ways, thyself and him, and many others, for in slandering a neighbor thou hast made him who listens to the slander worse; for should he be a wicked man, he becomes more careless when he finds a partner in his wickedness; and should he be a just man, he is lifted up to arrogance, and puffed up, being led on by the sin of others to imagine great things concerning himself. Besides, thou hast struck at the common welfare of the Church; for all those who hear not only accuse the supposed sinner, but the reproach is fastened on the Christian community; neither dost thou hear the unbelievers saying, "Such a person is a fornicator, or a libertine"; but instead of the individual who hath sinned, they accuse all Christians. In addition to this, thou hast caused the glory of God to be blasphemed; for as his name is glorified when we have good report, so when we sin, it is blasphemed and insulted.

In the meanwhile I desire to fix these precepts in your mind, to the end that you may accomplish me these during your fast: to speak ill of no one, and to hold no one for an enemy. As in a given field, the husbandman, digging it all up piecemeal, gradually comes to the end of his task; so we, too, if we make this rule for ourselves, in any wise to reduce to a correct practice these precepts during our present fast, and to commit them to the safe custody of good habit, we shall proceed with greater ease to the rest; and by this means arriving at the summit of spiritual wisdom, we shall both reap the fruit of a favorable hope in the present life; and in the life to come we shall stand before Christ with great confidence, and enjoy those unspeakable blessings; which, God grant, we may all be found worthy of, through the grace and loving kindness of Jesus Christ our Lord, with whom be glory to the Father and the Holy Spirit forever and ever. Amen.

# THOMAS AQUINAS

(1225–1274) Count Landulf of Aquino intended that his youngest son, Thomas, become a Benedictine abbot, but even a fifteen-month imprisonment by his parents could not prevent Thomas from joining his beloved Dominican Order when he was nineteen. As a Dominican, Thomas studied at the University of Paris, where he was at first called the "Dumb Ox," because of his large frame, awkward movements, and apparently slow-working mind. A legend tells of a bright student who came to help Thomas with his studies; at the end of the evening, this student was sitting at Thomas' feet, learning from the usually silent Italian. The famous Albertus Magnus soon recognized his extraordinary talent and became both his teacher and his friend. Thomas' massive intellect, enormous power of concentration, and naturally steady, quiet temperament ideally suited him for a life of teaching at universities in Germany, France, and Italy. His was by no means a quiet life; he was engaged in the many controversies that raged in the universities as well as in the Church, and during the last twenty years of his life he did not remain in any one place or position more than a few years. In addition to teaching, preaching, and debating he produced an unusually large body of writing, particularly impressive when it is remembered that he did not have a long life. In December of 1273, Thomas returned from saying Mass and told one of his stenographers that he could not go on with the *Summa Theologica,* which remains unfinished; he had had a vision, and in comparison to what he had seen then all his writing appeared to him as straw. His silence lasted a winter; on his way to the Council of Lyons he died, before reaching the age of fifty.

Students have at times wondered if the *Summa Contra Gentiles* and the *Summa Theologica,* two of the last and best known works issuing from the Angelic Doctor, were composed by a human being or a machine. His theological writings lack the strong personal element found in the works of St. Augustine and Luther, for example; yet they are gems of precision, profundity, erudition, and comprehensiveness, even though somewhat inappropriate to current theological discussion. Certainly they do not immediately reflect the passionately devout and happy nature of this man as do his Eucharistic hymns and this "Sermon on the Body of the Lord." Here the unity of his heart, faith, and reason is uninhibitedly revealed, as he expresses, in the form of a sermon, his devotion to the God whom he loved. It is almost a hymn of praise, displaying deep Christian reverence for the creation, which is basic to his theology. This sermon is also noteworthy in that it succinctly captures and represents a most important aspect of the thinking and piety of the high Middle Ages.

Thomas preached this sermon before Pope Urban IV and his cardinals at Orvieto on Maundy Thursday in the year 1264, and it was instrumental in establishing the Feast of Corpus Christi in the fall of that same year. Included in this sermon is Thomas' doctrine of transubstantiation, which, in view of the other preachers and traditions represented in this book, is unquestionably a sectarian teaching; non-Roman Catholic interpretations of the Holy Communion tend to emphasize the divine creative action upon and within the community rather than to focus upon and to attempt to define a change in the elements. Apart from the obvious controversial aspect, this sermon is a fine affirmation of the divine sacramental principle which focuses and culminates in the person of Jesus Christ who is yet present in and to his Church, particularly when it celebrates the Holy Communion.

# Sermon on
# the Body of the Lord*

The joyful memory of the feast we keep today reminds us that it is our duty and our privilege ever to find our gladness in praising the most sacred Body of Christ. Is there any employment, indeed, more congenial to Christian men than eulogizing the abyss of divine charity? Could there be for the panegyrist a more attractive theme than this love? It overflows, and it is like a furnace, this love of God, Who, in the banquet of regenerating grace gives unceasingly, through the ministry of His priests, His own flesh to be eaten and His own precious blood to be drunk by them who are His own sons and the heirs of the kingdom He has promised to them that love Him.

Thine is this august work, O Christ, Thine Whose power is without limits and Who art faithful and kind. It is Thou Who, recalling the memory of former marvels, hast, in this sacred food and supersubstantial bread, wonderfully found means and the way whereby, in the eating of the Lamb without spot or stain, they may be healed who, through the eating of the forbidden tree, had been made sick, and had lost the unfading and imperishable crown of everlasting glory.

Wonderful, indeed, in our regard, and most worthy of all praise, is the goodness of God, bounteous and unweariedly loving, who, to meet and greet His children, in the sacrament which is the term and final realization of all sacrifices everywhere, dwells without end till the

*From the book *Thomas Aquinas: Selected Writings*. Selected and edited by the Rev. Father M. C. D'Arcy. Everyman's Library Edition. Reprinted by permission of E. P. Dutton & Co., Inc.

world's end. He gives us men for our refreshment the bread of angels, and for our drink (ours, who are but children of adoption) strong wine, the Blood of His Son, though we are not of His blood. Lowliness, we know, is pleasing to God and it was extolled by Christ; and surely in this sacrament He preaches by the example of an unrivalled lowliness, which disdains no dwelling, but consents to come as a guest to any, even a defiled, heart.

O purity, clean as the sun's ray, near which no tainted thing should come, which no sullied thing has power to stain, which casts out all earthly lusts from the heart it enters! O food, truly, of the blessed spirits, Thou who every day unfailingly dost nourish us, and who in Thyself dost never fail! In the breaking of the bread Thou art not broken, nor art Thou divided. Thou art eaten, but, like the burning bush, Thou art not consumed. Nay, Thou continuest whole and entire, even as that meal and oil of old which lasted miraculously without diminution or waste.

O marvellous sacrament in which God lies concealed, and our Jesus, like another Moses, cloaks His face under the creatures He has made! May all generations praise Him! Wonderful is this sacrament in which, in virtue of the words of institution, charged with the Divine power, the symbolic species are changed into flesh and blood; in which accidents subsist without a subject; and in which, without violation of nature's law, by consecration the single and whole Christ self-identically exists in different places—as a voice is heard and exists in many places —continuing unchanged, remaining inviolable when partaken, nor suffering any diminution; nay, He is whole and entire and perfect in each and every fragment of the host, as visual appearances are multiplied in a hundred mirrors.

Christ is fittingly offered by the faithful under the twofold species (though He truly exists whole under either) to signify that the salvation He brings to men affects both their constituent parts, soul and body, and to remind them that His bitter passion was likewise twofold. O unspeakable efficacy of this sacrament, which sets the affections ablaze with the fire of charity, and sprinkles our home's lintel, on either doorpost, with the blood of the immaculate Lamb! What wholesome

journey-provision have we in this food for our precarious sojourning!
What strengthening manna here regales the traveller! It restores vigour
to the weak, health to the sick; it gives increase of virtue, makes grace
to abound, purges away vices, refreshes the soul, renews the life of the
ailing, knits together all the faithful in the union of charity! This Sacrament of Faith also inspires hope and increases charity. It is the central
pillar of the Church, the consolation of the dead, and the completion
of Christ's Mystical Body.

By these sacred species we recognize the tree of life. Here, Lord
Jesus, art Thou both shepherd and green pasture, priest and victim,
meat and drink of the elect, living bread, a food for spirits, a remedy
for daily falls, the fare of the twice-born. O sacrifice of praise and
righteousness, holocaust of the New Covenant, heavenly repast, not of
beeves and fatlings, but of strong meats full of marrow and of wine
purified from the lees, at which Thy friends on earth renew their
strength and in heaven the blessed are made drunk with Thy love!

O table of the infinite God! The many marvels of this Feast amaze
the mind: it is luscious beyond all dainties, delicious beyond the rarest
delicacies, more fragrant than any odour, more pleasing than any form
of grace, more desirable than every other food. This is the banquet to
which Christ entertained those who on earth were His companions,
sitting with Him at table. It is the supper to which the householder
invited his son on his return from the feast of the prefiguring lamb. O
cleansing waters foreshown in earlier springs! This pasch in which
Christ is immolated requires that virtue supersede vice; it makes free
those who are Hebrews after the spirit. This is the food that appeases
the hunger of the devoted heart. Faith is its seasoning, and devotion
and fraternal charity its relish. The teeth of the body may break this
food, but only an unfaltering faith can savour it. What a ration for
the march is this, which brings the traveller even to the mountain of
virtues! O living Bread, begotten in heaven, barmed in the womb of
the Virgin, baked in the furnace of the Cross, brought forth to the altar
under the disguise of the wafer: strengthen my heart unto good, make
it steadfast on the path through life, make glad my mind, make my
thoughts pure!

This is the true Bread which is eaten and not consumed, eaten and not dissolved, which conveys, without losing, energy. It has power to save, and it completes the work. It is the source of life and the fount of grace. It forgives sin and weakens concupiscence. The faithful find here their repast, and souls a food which enlightens the intelligence, inflames the affections, purges away defects, elevates the desires. O chalice of sweetness which devout souls drain! O fiery cup, which sealed in Christ's blood His covenant: purge out the old leaven, make full the spirit of our minds, that we may be a new paste, feasting with the unleavened bread of sincerity and truth! O dish of Solomon, cenacle of consolation, sovereign remedy of life's disease, sweet nourishment, nurse of virtues, seal of sanctity, bread that fosters harmony and is a pledge of eternal felicity!

We are reminded by the smallness of the host to be humble, by its roundness to be obedient, to be thrifty by its little substance, by its whiteness to be pure, by its lacking leaven to be patient and kind, by its being baked to be charitable, by its inscription to be discreet, by its sensible appearances to be solid and enduring, by its circularity to round off a life of holiness. O rich unleavened bread! O hiding-place of most high power! What the eye sees is small; yet what is therein contained is wonderful and excellent. O body and soul of the Divinity, and divine substance inseparable from both!

This sublime sacrament, good Jesus, declares to the believing soul Thy wonderful works. For after the consecration the accidents subsist alone; that which is eaten is not changed nor lessened; though it is received wholly by all, there is no increase; a thousand receive as much as one, and one as much as a thousand. The whole Christ is present on many altars, and on each in many fragments of the host. Thy flesh, O Christ, is eaten indeed and Thy blood is truly drunk. And Thou art priest and victim; and there are present the holy angels there, praising Thy greatness and Thy incomparable majesty. This is the work of Thy power, Lord, Who dost do great and wonderful works of Thyself, Who dost transcend sense and intellect, human conception and reason and fancy. Thou it was Who didst institute this sacrament and commit it to Thy disciples.

Let none, then, approach this awful Table without reverent devotion and fervent love, without true penitence, or without recalling his redemption. For it is the Lamb without spot, without taint or smirch of sin, that is eaten in the unleavened bread. Approach not before the cleansing waters have poured over thy soul; approach not without firm faith, burning charity, the vinegar of suffering, and the proving of trial. So approach, child of faith, the Supper of the Lord, the Table of plenitude and holiness, that at the last thou mayest attain to the wedding feast of the Lamb: there we shall be inebriated with the plenty of the house of God; then we shall see the King of Glory and the Lord of Hosts in His beauty, and shall taste bread in the kingdom of our Father; and our host shall be our Lord Jesus Christ, Whose power and empire are without end for ever. Amen.

# PETER TAYLOR FORSYTH

**PETER TAYLOR FORSYTH** (1848–1921) Though he was born in Aberdeen, Scotland, and graduated from the University of Aberdeen, Peter Taylor Forsyth is known as a great English Congregationalist. For twenty-five years he was a pastor in several Congregational churches in England, and in 1901 he became Principal of Hackney Theological College in Hampstead (London). In 1905, he was elected chairman of the Congregational Union of England and Wales. It was chiefly as a teacher, writer, and preacher that he became influential upon so many people in the Church during his lifetime; especially was he admired by clergy and theological students. A son of Karl Barth's was asked why he thought England had not been caught up in the theology of his father as had the Continent; his reply was that England had not needed Barth—it had Forsyth. After graduating from the University of Aberdeen, Forsyth studied under Albrecht Ritschl in Göttingen, whose theology had been a determining factor in bringing this young Scotsman to a liberal theological position. However, during his years as a pastor Forsyth was moved by theological unrest and began to perceive the shallowness of liberalism and humanism, which were often closely allied. As his own theology developed he found it centered in the cross; thus he recovered the meaning of the Atonement and Reconciliation as coming only through the crucifixion.

"The Fatherhood of Death," a sermon preached in the City Temple in behalf of the London Missionary Society, shows how Forsyth called his hearers to have their faith strengthened and deepened by returning to the cross. Though he was much more powerful when heard than when read, one can easily sense that he was an impressive preacher; he spoke often in staccato sentences, rapidly and with great incisiveness. One of his followers remarked that in days of theological confusion, the preaching of Forsyth was like "a bell ringing in the night."

# The Fatherhood of Death*

*Now is the judgment of this world; now shall the prince of this world be cast out. And I, if I be lifted up from the earth, will draw all men unto me.*

JOHN 12:31-32

Jesus had always felt that his earthly mission was to the Jews. His ointment was held for the time in that small alabaster-box. But you remember how the universal scope of his work was borne in upon him in contact with the Syrophenician woman. And at the same time he was forced by the attitude of the Jews to face an early death. The two convictions, universality and death, were one. There was but one way for his work to become universal. To fill the world with the healing odor, the box must be broken. The emancipation of his gospel must come by his death. Already he had seen death to be inevitable from without, from the temper of his foes. He could not escape it. Now it is carried home to him, how necessary it was from within, from his Father. He must not escape it. His work required it. It was in God's will. The will of the Pharisees becomes to him, by a sure mystery and miracle, the will of God. Both willed his death. But how different the intention! What he realized comes home anew, but with tragedy and glory.

* From *Missions in State and Church* (London: Hodder & Stoughton, Ltd., 1908). Used by permission of the publisher.

So when the disciples thought to gratify him by the news of his popularity, his reply was mixed, and it was disconcerting. He was elated, indeed, for a moment. "The hour is come for the Son of Man to be glorified." Ah, at last! they thought. But the only way to such glory filled him with melancholy. "Except a corn of wheat die." What! harping on death at such a time! They did not understand it. But he was often careless whether they understood or not. We are much too lucid for his greatness. He was not now teaching, but soliloquising. The agony struck home to him. Gethsemane had begun. The temptation was resumed. He saw the kingdoms of the world, and the glory of them. It was not their pagan splendor, but the glory they might yield to God, if Messiah put out his latent powers and became their literal King. He flushed to anticipate the scene. He saw his own puritan race keen for a lead. He saw empire wide open to such powers as his, where he might serve God on a royal scale, and make him an offering of a conquered world. Yet he saw just as surely that for him that way was barred. Swift and universal empire, even if beneficent, could be neither divine nor final. It fitted neither the true God nor the real world, neither grace nor need. And it was too vulgar for his soul. His vast powers were to be called in at a moral bidding. They were to be fixed on a task not only obscure, but bewildering, unpopular, and apparently futile. His star rose, only to be smothered by the black cloud of death. His joy suddenly sweeps round to sorrow. A world was before him, his foot was on the frontier—and he must turn away to die. How like was the Moses of the new Israel to the Moses of the old! It was bitter. If a man make his fortune just to find he has heart disease and cannot last a twelvemonth it is bitter enough. And life is full of such fates. But these are minor bitternesses compared to the misery that the prospect of death brought to him who was the fulness of life and power for good. And even that, again, was small and personal compared to another grief. It was the grief of knowing that his duty would bring not only trouble but perdition to the Israel he loved. His death must be the damnation of the race he could have imperialized. It was not the darkness of death, but the damnation in it that struck through him, and turned his sadness to his passion. It is agony for a man to do for conscience what he knows may ruin his family. How much more when he has to do what will condemn them, what will bring out all the evil in them and be death unto death to them; what will drive them to blaspheme the Holy Ghost, call his sacrifice a mere craze and his mission lunacy—yea, to protect themselves by putting him away? That, you will remember, was what Christ's own family thought when he took up his work. They went out to bring him back as mad, and put him under restraint. And it was what his whole nation were coming to think also. And so, when an occasion, however trivial, bore this swiftly and sharply in on him, it was almost more than he could bear. That was the case now: "How is my soul troubled! Father, spare me this hour." And the Father would not. Jesus well nigh lost heart at the revived sense of his tragic doom, of involving in calamity all he loved. So he did once before, when he saw the awful result of his work in family estrangement and the breaking up of homes. "It is dreadful," he said. "I have a baptism to be baptized with; and how am I crushed until it be over!" (Luke 12:50.)

But the attack only called out the resources of his solemn will. He stood still and silent. The passion had begun. He was conquering his distress by prayer. He always did. Beware of soliloquy (you poor Hamlets of an unhinged age!) if it do not turn to prayer. He recovered his spiritual self-command, which was his habitual obedience to the purpose of God. And he not only regained calm; he rose to exaltation again. Calm will not meet depression. Depression is in the nature of a passion with such souls as his, and it must be expelled by a counterpassion of faith and action. He rose to the eternal, glorious issue before Him. "I die alone. But unless I die I am more alone. If I die I bear much fruit." The prize was the world, the enemy the prince of this world; the work was judgment; the conflict the decisive battle of the immortal sinful soul; the pressure was the Father's will. So from the anguish of "Now is my soul troubled. What shall I say? Father, save me from this hour," he swept upward in spirit to the Father's side There only had he true vision of the kingdom of the world and its glory. There the end is clear from the beginning. "But for this cause came I unto this hour. Father, glorify thy Name." And as a peal of thunder broke near it coincided for him on his holy height with the inward voice of God. "Now is the judgment of this world. Now shall the prince of this world be cast out [of the earth]. And I, if I be raised from the earth, shall draw all men unto me." He meant his departure to the Father by death, and not the specific miracle of his resurrection or his ascension.

It was the Cross that catholicized Christ, and eternalized him. It rent the husk of Israel which bound his incarnate life. It broke the pot in which the tree of life was nursed, and transplanted it to the open air and the whole earth. The Cross is the point at which history is made an integral part of eternity. Christ must die to come really near mankind.

The stamp of universality in Christ's religion, then, lies not chiefly in his teaching. That was for the lost sheep of Israel, and much of it for the hour only. It lies in his work more than in his word. He was a man of action more than of speech; he said little of what he did most. Most martyrs have little to say. His word lies in his healing more than in his teaching. It lies in the Cross, which continued his healing rather than his speaking, and which crowned his deeds rather than his truths. There is more of the cross that he came for in his cures than in his doctrine. The Cross was not central to Christ's teaching as the kingdom was; but it was central to what is more than his teaching—to his healing, to his Person, work, and victory. It is more original than his teaching and more universal. It is by the Cross that he chiefly reaches the world. And Christianity spread at the first, not as a religion of truth, but as a religion of power, help, healing, resurrection, redemption. Harnack's great missionary history of the first Church has made that clear. It was not the teaching of Jesus that made and spread the Church, but the gospel of the Christ.

It was in the Cross that Christ conquered. It was there that Christianity was set up. The Church was founded there. The Resurrection and Pentecost started the Church, but it was the Cross that founded it. Its history begins with the Resurrection, but its life begins with the Cross. The Cross did what the Resurrection published.

The Cross is the gift of the Father's heart! That is a hard saying.

Yet it was the faith of Christ. "Father," he said, "glorify thy Name," as if he had said, "In my Cross reveal thine." He gave as it was given him, and what he gave was the Cross. To sit on his right hand and on his left was not his to give, but to be crucified on his right and left was. "If any man will come after me, let him take up his cross and follow me; and where I am there shall also my servant be." Cannot you hear that from the Cross itself? Do you think that is simply a promise of glory? It is so exegetically. But if it is no more than that, why is it embedded in a context of death and suffering only? For Christ, death and glory were one. It was not that the shame led to the glory. It was the glory. Paul, at least, gloried in that shame. From the Cross itself the words thrill our faith. "Where I am there shall my servant be." "Come up unto me" here. He gave the Cross, and gave as he received. He received the Cross. It was the Father's first gift and great grace to the Son; the Resurrection was but the second. What greater gift is there to us than a great trust and a great opportunity? If he gave the Son to have life, he also gave him to have death, the power divinely to die. And how could he give him what he had not in himself? The Cross came first from the Father, in whom it is eternal. It is no temporary expedient, no historic accident. The Father is the Redeemer behind all. The source of the Father's grace is not the Son, but the Father. That was Christ's own faith. "I will draw all men unto me," he said. Yes, but he also said, "No man cometh unto me, except the Father who hath sent me draw him."

It was the Father that put Christ upon the Cross. Would he have stayed there had it not been so, had it not been God's trust to him? For the Son, Fatherhood had death in it. It meant disheartenment, failure, desertion, heart-break. The revelation of the Father had to speak that tongue. The God who saves to the uttermost saves from the uttermost. He is the God of the God-forsaken, the Father of the fatherless. "My God," said Christ then, not "My Father." When our soul awoke in hell he was there. The faith of the saved may be radiant, but the faith of the Saviour, and the saving hour, had to be a darkling faith. But it is the faith that matters; it is neither the light nor the dark.

At least we may say that Fatherhood, if it is to be universal, means death. It cannot be missionary without the Cross. It might love the lovely without the Cross, but it could not redeem, and redeem the bad, black world. It was a fatherly death that Christ obeyed to gain the world. The Cross is more called for by the Fatherhood of such a world than by its sovereignty. Is it not? It is a tragic world; there is a curse on it. And Fatherhood could not come home to it, to its whole grim reality, if if did not speak its most tragic note. So much of our shallow liberalism never strikes that note. The revelation of the Father may indeed belong to the poetry of life, but to the greatest poetry. It is no idyll; it is tragedy, the tragedy of history. The world's new life begins in its dreadest hour. The kingdom's birth is the Redeemer's woe. And the joy of heaven was once in travail with a whole world. The universal Church of the Father is the firstborn of death. Death was never so solemn and great as when it became the word of the Father, and founded the Church to win the world.

The missions of a universal Father rest on a gospel of Fatherhood sovereign by death. Is it a strange thing, then, that missionaries should daily die as other men do not? They minister at that world-altar of the Father. They are specially delivered unto death. You cannot separate the mission and the Passion in a universal Christianity. There is no world crown without the Cross. The world can never conquer the world, nor civilization master the human soul. War cannot do it, nor diplomacy, nor trade. One supreme empire is a deadly dream, a national superstition, the final futility of the proud, practical man. The victory which overcomes the world is faith; and faith not only trusts the Cross, but wears it, lives it, and dies it. The Church that missions really dies with Christ, and its missionaries but show forth its death. They are priests of a sacrificial Church. You can serve, but you cannot save the democracy except by dying for it, and sometimes dying at its hands.

We are too strange to the Cross if we are shocked at such demands. Some have been afraid of taking the Cross seriously lest they should be swept back from the Father into the old orthodoxies. But the Fatherhood that does not take the Cross seriously and even sternly is sentiment and not faith. And it makes men too easy with themselves to be faithful to the world. One reason why the Church is too little missionary abroad is that it is not a missionary Church at home. It is established on good terms with its world instead of being a foreign mission from another. The Fatherhood as Christ trusted it is our joy and crown, but it is also our doom. "I am crucified unto the world, and the world unto me." It is better to die with Christ than to live with the world, to be Christ's priest than the world's prince. It is not happier, but it is better. Back let us go, not only to Christ, but to the Cross, to behind the Cross, where we see it from the other side. Let us go back from our social impatience to the effective way of faith— back from our exacting socialism, our moral rigorism, our critical severity, and the impotence of them all, to the holy, tender sacrifices of the Father's Cross and the contagious obedience of the beloved Son.

That is where missions arise and where the men are found. Success may bring money, but only the Cross brings both martyrs and heroes. We cannot stake our missionary enterprise upon results. The great thing is already done. What needs doing is all less than has been done. What has to be done for the world is already done in God. "A glorious throne set on high from the beginning is the place of our sanctuary." Is this mystical? But that is not the point. Is it real? Is it true at our real center, where we are what we are, and where we measure the world? Our missions but proclaim on the housetop what is told us in the most secret place. The world has been saved. We live in the midst of a universal salvation, even if the whole world lie in wickedness. If all men else denied that, we know it. God has a few to whom he whispers in the ear. Most of the world does deny it, and no few of the Church; but the New Testament is sure of it. Christ was sure of it. He is sure of it. And his certainty is more than all the misgivings of our experience. His faith in himself takes possession of us. We have the Holy Ghost. God has given us the reconciliation. All things are yours—life, death, and the future, thrones, policies, and Satans, all heavens, worlds, and hells. "All things are delivered unto me of the Father." "Ye are Christ's, and Christ is God's."

# FRIEDRICH DANIEL ERNST SCHLEIERMACHER

(1768–1834) A short man with slightly deformed shoulders, but with a noble and serious countenance, entered the pulpit. He was reputed to be the "most eminent Christian preacher in Germany," though the high plane of his preaching, which made many demands upon his listeners, indicated that he was certainly not the most popular preacher. He read his sermon with great care, and one sensed from his penetrating voice that there issued from his heart deep feeling, and that he found great joy in preaching. That man was Friedrich Schleiermacher, one of the most important and widely known theologians of the nineteenth century. He was ordained to the ministry in 1794 and held a preaching position in Berlin, where he became involved in the Romantic movement and which led him to write his well-known *On Religion: Speeches to Its Cultured Despisers*. He later taught theology at Halle and at Berlin and was the soul of the movement which led to the union in 1817 of the Reformed and Lutheran Churches. Though nurtured in Moravian piety, he rebelled against its narrow limitations of the Christian life. Schleiermacher had a broad spirit and penetrating intellect; he saw the Christian life as inclusive of all that was good and noble. His definition of religion as the feeling of absolute dependence expressed his belief that religion, philosophy, and art do not contradict each other, but that the spirit of religion can and does permeate the whole of life. At the same time he insisted that there was a distinct inner life of the Church in which each member participated; he considered the preacher as the representative of the common inner life who was to speak to it and awaken it to consciousness of itself and worship. Preaching was an integral part of worship, and as such it was a liturgical act. His well-defined views on preaching became very influential in the churches in Germany.

This famous sermon on "Christ's Resurrection an Image of Our New Life" mirrors his theology, which he constantly transposed into homiletical form, by reflecting his views on preaching, his own inner life, and keen insight into the meaning of Easter.

# Christ's Resurrection an Image of Our New Life*

*We were buried therefore with him by baptism into death, so that as Christ was raised from the dead by the glory of the Father, we too might walk in newness of life. For if we have been united with him in a death like his we shall certainly be united with him in a resurrection like his. We know that our old self was crucified with him so that the sinful body might be destroyed and we might no longer be enslaved to sin. For he who has died is free from sin. But if we have died with Christ, we believe that we shall also live with him.*
ROMANS 6:4–8, RSV

It is natural, my friends, that the glorious festival of our Saviour's resurrection should attract the thoughts of believers to a far remote time, and that it should make them rejoice to think of the time when they shall be with him who, after he had risen from the dead, returned to his and our Father. But the apostle, in the words of our text, recalls us from what is far off to what is close to us—to the immediate present of our life here. He takes hold of what is the most immediate concern, of what we are at once to share in and which is to form us, even here, says, unto death, that as he was raised from the dead through the glory into the likeness of Christ's resurrection. We are buried with him, he

* From Mary F. Wilson (trans.), *Selected Sermons of Schleiermacher* (New York: Funk & Wagnalls Co., n.d.). Used by permission of the publisher.

of the Father, we also might walk in newness of life. And this new life is that which, as the Lord himself says, all who believe in him possess even now as having passed through death to life. The apostle compares this with those glorious days of our Lord's resurrection; and how could we more appropriately keep this feast—a feast in which, above all others, many Christians draw renewed strength for this new life from the most intimate union with our heavenly Head—how could we better celebrate it than by endeavouring to receive this directly for ourselves from the words of the apostle? Let us then, according to the teaching of these words, consider the resurrection life of our Lord, as the apostle presents it to us, as a glorious, though it may be unattainable, model of the new life in which we are all to walk through him.

This new life is like that of our risen Saviour, first, in the manner of his resurrection. In order to appear to his disciples in that glorified form, which already bore in it the indications of the eternal and immortal glory, it was necessary that the Saviour should pass through the pains of death. It was not an easy transformation; it was necessary for Him, though not to see corruption, yet to have the shadow of death pass over him.

Thus, my friends, we know what is the new life that is to be like the resurrection life of the Lord. A previous life must die; the apostle calls it the body of sin, the law of sin in our members, and this needs no lengthened discussion. We all know and feel that this life, which Scripture calls a being dead in sins, pleasant and splendid as may be the form it often assumes, is yet nothing but what the mortal body of the Saviour also was, an expression and evidence of the power of death, because even the fairest and strongest presentation of this kind lacks the element of being imperishable. Thus with the mortal body of the Saviour, and thus also with the natural life of man, which is as yet not a life from God.

As the apostle says, the Lord was raised from the dead by the glory of the Father, and thus also, according to the words of the Saviour, no man comes to the Son except the Father draw him; that same glory of the Father, which then called forth the Saviour from the tomb, still awakens in the soul that has died to sin the new life, like the resurrection life of the Lord. Indeed, among all the proofs of the Father's glory in heaven and earth, there is none greater than this, that he has no pleasure in the death-like condition of the sinner, but that at some time or another the almighty, mysterious, life-giving call sounds in his ears —Arise and live.

II. And, secondly, this new life resembles its type and ideal, the resurrection life of Christ, not only in being risen from death, but also in its whole nature, way, and manner. First, in this respect, that though a new life, it is, nevertheless, the life of the same man, and in the closest connection with his former life. Thus, with our Saviour; he was the same, and was recognized by his disciples as the same, to their great joy. And just so it is with the new life of the Spirit. If the old man has died to sin, and we now live in Christ, and with him in God, yet we are the same persons that we were before. As the resurrection of the Lord was no new creation, but the same man, Jesus, who had gone down into the grave, come forth again from it; so in the soul before it died the death which leads to life in God, there must have lain the capability of receiving that life when the body of sin should die and perish; and that life is developed in the same human soul amidst the same outward circumstances as before, and with its other powers and faculties remaining unchanged. We are entirely the same persons, only that the fire of the higher life is kindled in us, and also that we all bear the signs of death, and that the remembrance of our former state is present with us. Yes, in manifold ways we are often reminded of what we were and what we did before the call to new life sounded in our hearts; and it is not so easy to efface the scars of the wounds, and the numberless traces of the pains under which the old man had to die that the new man might live. And as the glad faith of the disciples rested on the very fact that they recognized the Lord as being, in the glory of his resurrection, the same person that he was before; so also in us, the confidence in this new life, as a permanent and now natural state with us, rests only on this—that we recognize ourselves in it as the same persons that we were before; that there are the same faculties, lower and higher, of the human soul, which formerly served sin, but are now created anew as instruments of righteousness. Indeed, all the traces of that death, as well as of the former life, make us more vividly conscious of the great change that the life-giving call of God has produced in us, and call for the most heartfelt gratitude.

And as the Saviour was the same person in the days of his resurrection, so his life was also again of course a vigorous and active life; indeed, we might almost say it bore the traces of humanity, without which it could be no image of our new life, even in this, that it gradually grew stronger and acquired new powers. Now so it is, my friends, with our new life—that is like the resurrection life of the Lord. Oh, how very gradually it gains its faculties in us, grows and becomes strong, only bearing still more than the new life of the Lord the traces of earthly imperfection. How intermittent at first are the manifestations of this new life, and how limited the sphere of its action! But in proportion as it becomes stronger, this new life ought the less to give the impression of being a mere phantom life. If our new life in God consisted in mere states of feeling and emotions, which were not in the least capable of passing into action, or perhaps did not even aim at doing so, what would such a life be but a ghost-like apparition that would no doubt make men uneasy in their accustomed course, but without producing any improvement in it? No, it is a life of action, and ought to be ever becoming more so; not only being nourished and growing stronger and stronger through the word of the Lord and through heart-communion with him, to which he calls us, giving himself to us as the meat and drink of eternal life, but every one striving to make his new life intelligible to others about him, and to influence them by it. The life-giving Spirit, whom he has obtained for us, effects all this in each in the measure that pleases him; and if once the life of God is kindled in the human soul, if we have once, as the apostle says, become like him in his resurrection, then his powers are also more and more abundantly and gloriously manifested in us, through the efficacy of his spirit for the common good.

But along with all this activity and strength, the life of the risen Saviour was yet, in another sense, a secluded and hidden life. And thus it is also, my friends, with the new life in which we walk, even if it is, as it ought to be, strong and vigorous, and ever at work for the kingdom of God; yet it is at the same time an unknown and hidden life, unrecognized by and hidden from the world, whose eyes are holden; and he who should set himself to force the knowledge of it upon them, who should hit upon extraordinary proceedings in order to attract their attention to the difference between the life of sin and the resurrection life, would not be walking in the likeness of the Lord's resurrection. As the people in the time of Christ had opportunity enough to inquire about his resurrection, in seeing how his disciples continued to hold together, so our neighbors also see our close alliance, which has nothing to do with the affairs of this world; and if they, because of this, inquire about what unites us, the answer will not be lacking to them. But our inner history we will as little thrust upon them as the risen Christ thrust his presence on those who had slain him, and who had therefore no desire to see him. Instead of this, as he showed himself only to his own, we also will make known our inner life only to those who are just in the same way our own; who, glowing with the same love, and cheered by the same faith, can tell us in return how the Lord has revealed himself to them. Not by any means as if we followed some mysterious course, and that those only whose experiences had been entirely alike should separate themselves into little exclusive groups; for even the days of the Lord's resurrection present examples of various kinds of experience, and of one common inner fellowship connected with them all. And not only so, but even those who as yet have experienced nothing at all are not sent empty away. Only they must first become aware, by what they see without our thrusting it upon them, that here a spirit is breathing to which they are strangers, that here is manifested a life as yet unknown to them. Then will we, as was done then, lead them by the word of our testimony to the foundations of this new life; and as, when the word of preaching pierced men's hearts, when to some of them the old man began to appear as he really is, and they felt the first pangs that precede the death of the sinful man, there also sprang up faith in the resurrection of him whom they had themselves crucified; so will it always be with the knowledge of the new life proceeding from him who has risen.

And lastly, my friends, we cannot feel all these comforting and glorious things in which our new life resembles the resurrection life of our Lord, without being at the same time, on another side, moved by sorrow by this resemblance. For if we put together all that the evangelists and the apostles of the Lord have preserved for us about his resurrection life, we still cannot out of it all form an entirely consecutive history. There are separate moments and hours, separate conversations and actions, and then the risen one vanishes again from the eyes that look for him; in vain we ask where he can have tarried, we must wait till he appears again. Not that in himself there was anything of this broken or uncertain life, but as to our view of it, it is and cannot but be so; and we try in vain to penetrate into the intervals between those detached moments and hours. Well, and is it not, to our sorrow, the same with the new life that is like Christ's resurrection life? I do not mean that this life is limiited to the few hours of social worship and prayer, glorious and profitable as they are; for in that case there would be cause to fear that it was a mere pretence; nor to the services, always but small and desultory, that each of us, actively working through the gifts of the Spirit, accomplishes, as it were, visibly and tangibly according to his measure, for the kingdom of God. In manifold ways besides these we become conscious of this new life; there are many quieter and secret moments in which it is strongly felt, though only deep in our inmost heart.

But notwithstanding this, I think all without exception must confess that we are by no means conscious of this new life as an entirely continuous state; on the contrary, each of us loses sight of it only too often, not only among friends, among disturbances and cares, but amidst the commendable occupations of this world. But this experience, my dear friends, humbling as it is, ought not to make us unbelieving, as if perhaps our consciousness of being a new creature in Christ were a delusion, and what we had regarded as indications of this life were only morbid and overstrained emotions. As the Lord convinced his disciples that he had flesh and bones, so we may all convince ourselves and each other that this is an actual life; but in that case we must believe that, though in a hidden way and not always present to our consciousness, yet it is always in existence, just as the Lord was still in existence even at the times when he did not appear to his disciples; and had neither returned to the grave, nor as yet ascended to heaven. Only let us not overlook this difference. In the case of Christ we do not apprehend it as a natural and necessary thing that during those forty days he led a life apparently so interrupted; but each of us must easily understand how, as the influence of this new life on our outward ways can only gradually become perceptible, it should often and for a long time be quite hidden from us, especially when we are very busy with outward work, and our attention is taken up with it. But this is an imperfection from which as time goes on we should be always becoming more free.

Therefore always back, my friends, to him who is the only fountain of this spiritual life! If, ever and anon, we cannot find it in ourselves, we always find it in him, and it is always pouring forth afresh from him the Head to us his members. If every moment in which we do not perceive it is a moment of longing, as soon as we become conscious of the void; then it is also a moment in which the risen one appears to our spirit, and breathes on us anew with his life-giving power. And thus drawing only from him, we shall attain to having his heavenly gifts becoming in us more and more an inexhaustible, continually flowing fountain of spiritual and eternal life. For this he rose from the dead by the glory of the Father, that we should be made into the likeness of his resurrection. That was finished in his return to the Father; our new life is to become more and more his and the Father's return into the depths of our souls; there they desire to make their abode; and the life of God is to be ever assuming a more continuous, active and powerful form in us, that our life in the service of righteousness may become, and continue even here, according to the Lord's promise, an eternal life.

## Prayer

Oh, for this end, thou exalted Saviour, help us more and more by the contemplation of thy glory! As thou art exalted from the earth, draw us more and more towards thee! As thou didst walk in the days of thy resurrection, so let us more and more live and walk in the bond of love and faith which thou didst form among thy people, and be ever receiving more abundantly from thee nourishment and strength for our spiritual life! And as thy resurrection was blessed to thy disciples for the establishing of thy kingdom on earth, for the encouraging of the faint-hearted, for banishing despondenecy from men's hearts, and for making known the deepest mysteries of the Scriptures; oh, thus may our new life be more and more, through the power of thy Spirit, a proclamation of thy word and of all the mysteries of thy grace, a loving support to all that is weak, an effectual call to life for all that is still dead, a quiet, undisturbed enjoyment of thy love and of the blessed fellowship with thee in which thy people stand. Amen.

# GEOFFREY ANKETELL STUDDERT-KENNEDY (1883–

1929) With a cigarette dangling from his lips, an unpretentious Anglican cleric strode onto a makeshift platform to address British troops during the First World War. Here was no ordinary parson; "Woodbine Willie," as he had been tabbed by the troops, spoke to them in straightforward and often colloquial terms which held their attention and had earned their respect. G. A. Studdert-Kennedy was a popular chaplain, a man's man, fearless, independent, and unconventional; and he was one of the most singular and original speakers and preachers in the Church of England during that war. In 1917, he was awarded the Military Cross for conspicuous gallantry. After the war he preached a passionate crusade against war on behalf of social justice, a crusade which he carried on valiantly until his untimely death. In an Anglo-Catholic setting of formality and splendor his sermons were direct and informal, and through them he helped to bring the Church into living touch with ordinary people, for whom often it had seemed removed and irrelevant. He was a prophet led by a vision who made religion seem a reality, and who worked constantly to make it a reality in both personal and social life. In 1922, he became rector of a parish in London; then in the Industrial Christian Fellowship he worked to Christianize industrial relations. He was widely respected as a great preacher, and as well a user of incongruous phrases; his forms of expression were natural, original, and often striking. He also had talent for writing hymns and poetry, some of which he used in his sermons. One is found in the sermon printed here.

A kind and generous person, Studdert-Kennedy was noted for his St. Francis-like recklessness of charity. His deep love combined with a steady faith enabled him to face the oppressive power of sin which had so revealed itself to him during the war. It has been said that his preaching lacked an inward sunshine; there was an undercurrent of sadness stemming from his identification with men's pain, sorrow, and guilt. Yet he had an unshakable hope arising from his faith, as is so clearly shown by this very personal sermon preached in 1920 on the ascension of Christ into heaven. Never a robust man and suffering from asthma, he contracted a serious case of influenza and died at the early age of forty-six.

# He Ascended into Heaven*

**D**id he? Where is heaven? What is it? Is it a place? Is it a spiritual condition? Can we know what it is, or where it is? God is Spirit, without body, parts, or passions. What do you mean by "sitteth at the right hand of God the Father"? You cannot mean it literally because he has not got a hand. You cannot mean that he literally sat down. Do you mean that he literally went up? Is this history or allegory? Did he really ascend? Was there ever a day or night when that small band stood with upturned faces gazing into the clouds and straining their eyes to catch a glimpse of the slowly disappearing figure with hands outstretched to bless them in his last farewell? And suppose he did go up into the heavens, suppose it was an actual case of self-levitation, what difference does it make to you or me? Granted for the moment that he did do it, what odds does it make to me now, or to anybody else? Does it matter whether I believe it as a fact or treat it as a beautiful legend? Of course, I don't deny its beauty; I think the pictures of the Ascension are amongst the most inspiring and exalting that great art has ever given us—but does it matter to me and to the world whether this actually happened or not?

Here are two distinct questions. Did it happen? and what difference does it make if it did?

* From *I Believe—Sermons on the Apostles' Creed* (New York: George H. Doran Co., 1921). Used by permission of Harper & Row, Publishers, Incorporated.

Let us get down to the first. Did it happen? did he ascend? The only evidence that we have for the picture which is so familiar and so gloriously beautiful—the picture of that dear and well-beloved figure rising slowly from the earth, with pierced hands held out in everlasting benediction—the only evidence we have for it is the testimony of St. Luke in the Acts of the Apostles. Is it true?

How can I tell for certain? How can any one tell? If one is to approach the question coldly, and in a sceptical spirit, remembering the honest man's duty of doubt, it seems to me that the only conclusion we can come to upon the evidence is that it cannot be proved. The evidence is not sufficiently strong to convince a reasonable and impartial person approaching the matter in a purely scientific spirit.

Well, does not that give the whole show away? That is what I have always felt, you say, ever since I was a child. The Christian Creed won't wash or wear. When you plunge it into the cold water of reason it shrinks until there is nothing left of it, nothing save this splendid but shadowy figure who fades away into the mists of time, and leaves us alone with wars and workhouses, factory chimneys and squalid streets—alone in a modern, mechanical, vulgar world of sordid realities. O my God, these tales of unbearable beauty that break the hearts of men because they are not true! Bother your beastly questions. If it is a dream, why need you come in with your vulgarity, and spit on your fingers to turn it over and examine it? I am sick of your book and your honesty. Do we not need our dreams? I have never asked myself these questions before, and why need I ask them at all? Better men than you have believed it without question, and who are you to doubt them? Go and say your prayers, and ask God to strengthen your faith.

That's one me. But there is another that answers, "Please, I don't want to be vulgar, and I don't want to be blatant. I don't want to ask questions, but the beastly things ask themselves. They kept on asking themselves while I was saying my prayers. Is it true? How do you know it is? Isn't it only a fool's paradise this faith of yours? You have only St. Luke for it, and it is a strange and unique occurrence. You must be honest first and religious afterwards—you know you must.

You know the horrors that come if you twist those things the wrong way round—orthodox lies for the glory of God. It's no use, you must be honest first." Of course, there are more things in heaven or earth than are dreamed of in your philosophy or any one else's, if it comes to that, but then the fact that anything may be true is no proof that any one thing is. The fact that Christ may have ascended does not prove that he did; you have no evidence that will convince an impartial intellect, and that ends it.

But does it? I doubt if intellect ever ends it. It is not big enough. You cannot take this story and cut it off from all the rest, isolate it and put it under the microscope of historical criticism, and then decide that there is nothing in it. You cannot get at the real truth of it that way, you would only get the same result as a chemist would who analyzed the Sistine Madonna and expressed it in chemical formula; it would be truth of a sort, but not the truth. A great song is not a series of atmospheric vibrations causing molecular changes in the matter of the brain, it is laughter and tears, it is joy and sorrow, it is life itself, it is a person calling to a person, a heart that seeks a heart. It is hard to put these things into words, but you understand what I mean, don't you? This Ascension picture is not merely itself—bald, isolated, historical fact; the reality of the Ascension picture is the Personality of the Ascending Christ. Before we can properly weigh and estimate the value of the evidence for its reality we must have some understanding of that Personality.

You must take up the Christian challenge in its due order, you cannot swallow it whole, it will give you indigestion, mental, moral, and spiritual stomach-ache; before you decide about the Ascension of Christ you must decide about Christ himself. Who and what was he—a myth? a magician? a man? the Perfect Man? a God? You must start where those who lived and died for their Ascended Lord started, face to face with Jesus. You must have seen Jesus before you can see the Ascending and Ascended Christ. You must have set out to follow him, and you must have found him at once inevitable, impossible, and infectious— in a word, divine. You must have found him in your own soul, crucified, continually crucified, and yet rising again, before you can grasp the meaning of his Ascension. You can only pass through Good Friday and Easter Day to your Ascensiontide. It is no mere put-off that. You must know what a man was, what his power and his character was, before you can rightly judge about the truth or falsehood of an event recorded in his life. What might quite well happen to one person might be utterly impossible for another.

There is always the factor of personality to be reckoned with in estimating historical reality. If I did not believe that Jesus Christ was like no other person that ever lived, if I did not believe that he was unique, the one and only, this story would have no reality for me; it would be as the fairy tales, shadow without substance, which is a sickening diet for working men. But if you have entered into the challenge thus far, if you have taken up the life and the struggle it demands, if you have set out on the great adventure, it makes a whole lot of difference. The reality of the story will then become more and more an absolute necessity for you. We must go back and stand before the Character and ask ourselves again, What about it? What about him? I believe in the Ascension because of Christ. I do not believe in Christ because of the Ascension.

The thing is this. Across the ages, when I take up the New Testament, I find myself talking with men who knew Some One that I know, who loved Some One that I love, and who worshipped Some One that I worship. This Person, as far as this world was concerned, was a dead failure. His earthly career fizzled out upon the Cross. He was like a Véry light shot up into the sky, dazzling the eye with its brilliance, and then dying away to leave a deeper darkness behind. They all knew that, these men. They all knew that from a worldly point of view his life was one succession of failures, that his career was as unlike that of the Messiah the people expected as it well could be— he could not even get twelve entirely faithful followers. Yet I find these men calmly confident that he was and is the One Supreme success, that in him, and in him alone, there is no failure but complete and perfect triumph. How did he succeed in producing this impression upon them? Why were they not cast down and brokenhearted when he left them? Why were they not plunged into the depths of despair as they were after the Crucifixion? The answer that they gave was that although he went away, the manner of his going was such that it convinced them that all was well, that he would come again, and that meanwhile they would not be left alone and leaderless, but that in some new way he would be with them still. The manner of his going was not like a retreat, but like an advance; it spoke of victory, and not defeat. It was not a departure, it was an ascension, it was the revelation of what he was—equal with God. They were not down-hearted, because Jesus was with God, and God was with them, and could never leave them.

That is their account of how it was they were not down-hearted, but bubbling over with excitement and expectation. Christ had fought, and Christ had won; in him was victory. That was the universal Christian impression. Whether St. Luke gives an exact and accurate account of the way in which that impression was produced, or whether he gives the traditional picture in which Christ's followers were wont to express the impression made upon them by his departure, cannot, I believe, be decided with certainty on the evidence we have. I think it is the simplest and easiest supposition to go upon, that the picture is substantially accurate, but whether it is or not, it is certain that it describes in the most vivid and compelling fashion the convictions that his departure created in the minds of those who witnessed it. He went away triumphant and to come again. It was an ascension, not a failure and farewell. That is certain, and that is the main thing. The manner in which the conviction was created is not so important, the conviction that this is the victory that overcometh the world, even our faith, that is all-important, and it is, and always has been, the essence of Christianity. But you may say, Yes, I know the impression of victory is the main thing, but was it not a false impression, were not these early Christians confident that he would come again quite soon? They were mistaken, those early Christians, they were mistaken about this. How can we be sure that they were not mistaken about his Ascension too? How can we be sure that it was not just a legend which grew up to express their early enthusiasm and buoy them up in their false hopes? To them his return to heaven was like the return of an Eastern conquerer, with sin and death as captives in his train.

That is what it meant to them. Can it mean that to us? Can we regard his task as accomplished and his triumph as complete when

> Here on the earth as years pass by,
> Centuries piled upon Calvary,
> The story of man is but one long line
> Of insults heaped on the plan Divine.
> Murder and misery, rape and war,
> Sin like an open, festering sore,
> Oozing its filth through the souls of men,
> Dragging them down to the dust again,
> Worming its way through their noblest deeds,
> Burying God in their Godless creeds.
> Priests that spit in the face of Christ,
> Cardinals decked for the traitorous tryst
> They keep with a God their souls despise,
> For the policy's sake of the worldly wise.
> Children conceived and born in sin,
> Rotten with syphilis, soaked in gin,
> Housed like pigs in their filthy stys,
> Cursed from the day they opened their eyes.

Is not this triumph of Christ a mockery? Is not this victory which was assured to the first Christians by the manner of his departure a lie? Does it not look as if the whole conception was an illusion and the New Testament merely the story of a great human hope that history has killed as it has killed a million other splendid hopes, and will probably kill a million more?

> How can it be that Christ can reign in glory,
> Calmly content with what his love has done,
> Reading unmoved the piteous, shameful story
> Of the vile deeds men do beneath the sun?

If Christ is the same yesterday, today, and for ever, then his soul must be wrung now as it was wrung in the days of his flesh, as he looks down upon the world as it is today. Once more these two thousand years must make a difference. We cannot disregard them. Once more, I say, time may be nothing to God, but if he is a reality at all, sin must be much, and these two thousand years have been two thousand years of sin—of sin and suffering beyond the power of any words to compass or express. If they change for us the Resurrection experience, they must change for us the Ascension experience too. It cannot be for us a perfect and completed thing; we are bound to see it against a different background—against the background of the two thousand years. History has done its worst, done its very damnedest, to kill the hope, to destroy the faith, and rob us of our certainty, but once again the gallant Creed rings out its note of defiance. It has not killed the hope, it cries; the hope, nay, more, the calm and confident certainty, still burns and blazes in the hearts of those who have found God in Christ. To them the final reality of life is perfectly expressed in Christ Crucified, Risen, and Ascending, with hands outstretched to bless them. That is what they see everywhere. They do not see him regnant on a great white throne, with all his work behind him, and all his sorrow done—they know he sorrows now, as he did then—but they do see him as the equal of the Highest, the expression, the very image, of what the Power behind life is. If they look into their own souls they find him there—crucified, but deathless and ascending—Christ in them the Hope of Glory, bound to triumph in the end. If they look at the history of the world with its struggle and its strife and its sin, they find him, once more crucified, but deathless and ascending, slowly but surely coming to his own, irresistibly moving to the accomplishment of his purpose. The picture of the dear and well-beloved figure with the pierced hands, slowly rising upwards into regions out of sight makes all history luminous. History is not the story of the descent of man from the apes, but the ascent of God in Man to the angels. We believe in the Risen and Ascending Christ, and we find evidence of it everywhere.

Had we clung fast to the Truth revealed in the Ascension, the Revelation of the meaning of life and history that it contains, the new knowledge of God's method of creation by evolution might have been for us a pure and unmixed blessing. We would never have allowed ourselves to look down to the beasts for the meaning of life as we did, we would have remained steadfastly gazing up into heaven. We would never have been deceived into thinking that because we were descended from the jungle, therefore the laws of the jungle must govern our lives forever. We would never have allowed the blasphemy to be spread abroad that strife, struggle, war, and remorseless competition were the laws of God. The blight of pseudo-scientific cant would never have ruined our social lives. We would have known that evolution was not a descent but an ascension, not a mechanical and determined ascension, but a moral and spiritual progress which can only take place as men are in Christ, living their life in his spirit, and basing their thought on his law—the law of love.

We have forsaken the Truth and paid the inevitable penalty, but let us return to it now.

There is in it power to heal the gaping wounds of war.

We can turn away from that picture, and with its truth as our great treasure firm and fast we can honestly face the facts of life, and stare them in the face, and defy their power to hurt or harm, in the power of the Ascending Christ.

# JOHN HENRY JOWETT (1864-1923)

When after a long inner struggle the Englishman, John Henry Jowett, finally accepted the call to become the minister of the Fifth Avenue Presbyterian Church, New York, the American newspapers played upon his coming and tabbed him "the greatest living preacher." The sensationalism of the press did not fit the man, and the American public was in for some surprises. The first came in the luxurious hotel where Dr. Jowett and his wife stayed after their ship arrived late at night. The chef had remained late in the kitchen, waiting to prepare an elegant dish; there was not a little disappointment when he received the long-awaited order: two glasses of warm milk and toast. Dr. Jowett had been born in Halifax, Yorkshire, and was educated at Edinburgh University and Oxford. He was a Congregationalist, and he had been such a good student that he was offered as his first charge an important church in Newcastle. He was a devoted pastor and an extremely fine preacher, who was also an artist of language. He was a shy and humble person and very definitely not a platform man; but nevertheless he was elected President of the Free Church Council. When he came to New York in 1911, there were large crowds to hear him, but the curious were disappointed because he was not a sensational preacher. Some of his American parishioners thought him a bit stiff, not recognizing his natural self-discipline and diffidence. He was not an ambitious man, nor a respecter of persons. After the First World War he chose to return to England, where he became minister to Westminster Chapel in London until his death. He stood straight in the pulpit, clad in conservative attire; he was a slight man and spoke in even, almost conversational tones. He preached primarily to those who had intellectually accepted Christianity, but who needed their faith warmed and stirred. What a warming the congregation of the Fifth Avenue church received when he delivered this sermon!

# The Soldier's Fire*

*He shall baptize you with the Holy Ghost and with fire.*   MATTHEW 3:11

Such is the divine promise. Let me read the story of its fulfilment. "And when the day of Pentecost was fully come they were all with one accord in one place. And suddenly there came a sound from heaven as of a rushing mighty wind, and it filled all the house where they were sitting. And there appeared unto them cloven tongues, like as of fire, and it sat upon each of them."

Here then are men and women who are about to receive the promised gift of the Spirit of God. They have been waiting as their master directed, waiting in prayer, and in prayer incalculably strengthened by community of desire, waiting in trembling watchfulness and expectation. Then the much-hoped for day arrives and their spirits receive the infinite reinforcement of the gift of the Holy Spirit.

What happens to the human spirit is suggested to us under the familiar symbols of wind and fire. "Like unto a rushing mighty wind"; "like unto fire." Do not let us be enslaved by any hampering details in the figures. Let us seek their broad significance. And what is the characteristic of a rushing mighty wind? It dispels the fog. It freshens the atmosphere. It gives life and nimbleness to the air. It is the minister of vitality. And the breath of God's Spirit is like that; it clears the human spirit, and freshens it, and vitalizes it; it acts upon the soul

* From *The Whole Armour of God;* copyright 1916 by Fleming H. Revell Company (New Jersey). Used by permission of the publisher.

like the air of a spiritual spring. And as for the symbol of the fire; fire is the antagonist of all that is frozen; it is the antagonist of the torpid, the tepid; it is the minister of fervour, and buoyancy, and expansion. The wind changes the atmosphere, the fire changes the temperature; and the holy Spirit of God changes the atmosphere and temperature of the soul; and when you have changed the atmosphere and temperature of a soul you have accomplished a mighty transformation. It is about this change in the moral and spiritual temperature that I want to meditate, the gift of fire which we receive in the baptism of the Holy Ghost. If the spirit of man and the spirit of God come into blessed communion, and the fire of God is given, how will it reveal and express itself? For if there be a gift of fire in the soul we shall most surely know it.

First of all I think I should look for the holy fire on the common hearthstone of human love. If the fire of God does not warm up the affections I fail to recognize what its heat can be worth. The first thing to warm up is the heart. The intimate friend of the Holy Spirit is known by the ardor of his affections. He loves with a pure heart fervently. He is baptized with fire. Now I need not seek to prove the existence of cold hearts among us. I am afraid we must accept them without questions. Whether there are hearts like firegrates without a spark of fire I cannot tell. Personally, I have never met with anyone in whose soul the fire of love had gone quite out. I think that if we sought very diligently among the gray dusty ashes of any burnt-out life we should find a little love somewhere. Yes, even in Judas Iscariot, or in the dingy soul-grate of old frozen-out Scrooge. But there are surely souls so cold, and so destitute of love, that the poor fire never leaps up in dancing, cheering, welcome flames. Their temperature is zero.

There are other souls with a little fire of love burning, but it is very sad, very sodden, very sullen, very dull. There is more smoke than fire. There is more surliness than love. Their fire is not inviting and attractive. There is a little spitting, and spluttering, and crackling, but there is no fine, honest, ruddy glow. Their temperature is about ten above freezing. They are not frozen but they are not comforting.

There are other lives where the fire of affection is burning more brightly, and certainly with more attractive glow, but where it seems as if the quality of the fuel must be poor because the fire gives out comparatively little heat. The heart sends out a cheery beam across the family circle; but it does not reach beyond. There is no cordial warmth for the wider circles of fellowship. The fire burns in the home but it does not affect the office. It encompasses the child but it has no cheer for the stranger.

What awfully cold lives there are in the city, just waiting for the cheer of "the flame of sacred love!" There are souls whose fires have died down at the touch of death. There are others whose glow has been dulled by heavy sorrow. There are others whose love has been slaked by the pitiless rains of pelting defeat. There are others again whose hearts are cold in the midst of material wealth. They have richly furnished dwellings, but their hearts are like ice. They are unloved and unlovely, and they are frostbitten in the realms of luxury. Wealth can buy attention; it can never purchase love. My God! What cold souls there are in this great city!

And, therefore, what a clamant and urgent need there is for love-fires at which to kindle these souls that are heavy, and burdened, and cold. And when the Holy Spirit is given to a man, and he is baptized with fire, it must surely, first of all, be the fire of cordial, human affection. And such is the teaching of experience. When John Wesley came into the fulness of the divine blessing in a little service at Aldersgate Street, London, he said that he "felt his heart strangely warmed." He was receiving the gift of holy fire.

You find and feel the glow of that love-fire throughout the New Testament Scriptures. They who have the most of God's Spirit have the most of the fire. The truth of the matter is this, we cannot be much with the Spirit of Christ, and not take fire from his presence. In these high realms, communing is partaking, and we kindle the same affection as fills the heart of the Lord. "We love because he first loved us." His fire lights our fire, and we burn in kindred passion. So do I proclaim that when the fire of God falls upon our spirits the sacred gift kindles and inflames the soul's affections. When we are baptized with the Holy Ghost and with fire, we receive the glowing power of Christian love.

Where else shall we look for that holy fire in human life? I think I should look for the presence of the fire of the Holy Ghost in fervent enthusiasm for the cause of Christ's Kingdom. And that indeed is what I find. The New Testament instructs me in this, and it teaches me that where man is baptized with the Holy Spirit and with fire his own spirit becomes fervent. He is declared to be "fervent in spirit," and the original word means to bubble up, to boil, as in a boiling kettle; it is the emergence of the mighty power of steam. And so the significance is this: the fire of God generates steam, it creates driving power, it produces forceful and invincible enthusiasm. You will find abundant examples of this spirit miracle in the Acts of the Apostles; perhaps the book might be more truly named "The Acts of the Holy Spirit," for all the glorious activity is generated by his holy fire. Let your eyes glance over the apostolic record. Mark how the fire of God endows man with the power of magnificent initiative. Take the apostle Peter; once his strength was the strength of impulse, a spurt and then a collapse, a spasm and then a retreat, proud beginnings bereft of patience and perseverance. But see him when the Spirit of God has got hold upon him, and what a gift he has received of initial and sustained enthusiasm! "And Peter, filled with the Holy Spirit!" You should see him then, and note the strength of his drive, and the ardor of his enterprise!

The first apostles drove through tremendous obstacles. Indeed, they never had the comfort of an open and unimpeded road. Every road was thick with adversaries. What then? Through them or over them! "But, Sire," said a timid, startled officer to Napoleon, on receiving apparently impossible commands, "But, Sire, there are the Alps!" "Then there must be no Alps," replied his audacious chief. "There must be no Alps!" That was the very spirit of the first apostles. Mighty antagonisms reared themselves in their way, ecclesiastical prejudices, the prejudices of culture, social hostilities, political expediences, and all the subtle and violent contrivances of the world, the flesh and the Devil. "But, Sire, there are the Alps!" "There must be no Alps!" Through them! Over them! What that coward Peter got through when the fire of God glowed in his soul! When a man has the holy fire of God within him he has a boiling fervency of spirit, and he can drive through anything.

And that same holy fire gives the same terrific power today, the same driving enthusiasm, the same patient, dogged, invincible perseverance. If a man declares that he has received the fire of God's Holy Spirit, I will look eagerly for the impetus of his sacred enthusiasm. If he be a preacher, I will look for labor in the passion, and the unsnarable energy and patience which he will assuredly put into his work. If he be a teacher, I will examine the generated steam, and note how much he can do, how far he can travel, and how long he can hold out in the service of his Lord. If he be a man who has set himself to some piece of social reconstruction I will watch with what ardor, and ingenuity, and inevitableness he is moving towards his goal. Whatever it be, the holy fire of God will reveal its presence in the soul of man in an ardent enthusiasm which cannot be quenched. It is the promise of our God, and shall he not do it? "He maketh his ministers a flaming fire"—and that fire can never be blown out in the darkest and most tempestuous nights.

And lastly, I shall look for the signs of the presence of the Holy Spirit in the fire of sacred resentment. If a man is baptized with the Holy Ghost, and with fire, I shall expect to see the presence of that fire in the capacity of hot and sensitive indignation. I need not say that there is a mighty difference between hot temper and hot indignation. Hot temper is a firing of loose powder upon a shovel. It is just a flare, and an annoyance, and a danger. But hot indignation is powder concentrated in the muzzle of a gun, and intelligently directed to the overthrow of some stronghold of iniquity. What is this capacity of indignation? It is the opposite to frozen antipathy, to tepid curiosity, to sinful "don't care," to all immoral coldness and calculated indifference. There are many people who can be irritated, but they are never indignant. They can be offended, but they are never nobly angry. The souls who are possessed with the fire of God are the very opposite to all these. I said at the very beginning of the meditation that the breath of God is like the quickening atmosphere of the spring; but it is equally true to say that it can be like the destructive blast of the African sirocco —"The grass withereth and the flower fadeth because the Spirit of the Lord bloweth upon it." The hot breath of God is like unto a blast that scorches things in their very roots. And if we share in the breath of God's Spirit we too shall be endowed with the ministry of the destructive blast, even the power of a consuming indignation. Any form of public iniquity will make our fire blaze with purifying wrath. Corruption in civic or national government, inhumanity in the treatment of the criminal and the unfortunate, the oppression of the poor, the brutal disregard of the rights of the weak and the defenceless, any one of these will draw out our souls in the hot and aggressive indignation which is the imparted fire of the Holy Ghost. If any one claims to have been baptized with the Holy Ghost and with fire, and he is indifferent in the presence of licensed iniquity, and apathetic and lukewarm when gigantic wrongs glare and stare upon him, that man's spiritual baptism is a pathetic fiction, and his boasted fire is only a painted flame.

But if a man suffer a personal injury, if some wrong is done to him, what kind of fire shall I expect to see in his life if he is filled with the Holy Ghost? Yes, if some one has done an injury to another, and the other has been baptized with the Holy Ghost, what kind of fire will he reveal? "Then said Jesus, Father, forgive them, for they know not what they do." What kind of fire is that? It is the same holy fire which flowed from the soul of the martyr Stephen as he was being stoned to death: "Lord, lay not this sin to their charge." It is a marvellous fire, a most arresting fire; and we simply cannot withstand it. It is the very fire of grace; it is live coal from the altar of God.

So this is the sort of fire I look for when a man claims to be filled with the Holy Spirit—the glowing fire of humble affection, the glowing fire of noble enthusiasm, the glowing fire of indignation, and the marvellous fire of self-forgetting grace. "He shall baptize you with the Holy Ghost and with fire."

> He came in tongues of living flame,
> To teach, convince, subdue,
> All powerful as the wind he came,
> And viewless too.

Spirit of purity and grace,
  Our weakness, pitying see,
Oh, make our hearts thy dwelling place,
  And worthier thee.

# DONALD MACPHERSON BAILLIE (1887–1954)

Mrs. Baillie brought three sons into the world. Her eldest, John, was to become a prominent church leader and theologian; her youngest, Peter, was to die at an early age as a missionary to India. Her middle son, Donald, was to become a beloved pastor to several Scottish parishes and later a much revered teacher to theological students. Donald studied theology at New College in Edinburgh; during the summers he studied at Heidelberg and Marburg. When the First World War broke out, his volunteer work with the Y.M.C.A. in France was cut short because of his weak constitution, which plagued him throughout his life. Then in 1918 he took his own parish in the United Free Church. During the next sixteen years he served in three different churches. In 1934, he filled the newly created chair of Systematic Theology at St. Andrew's University, where he remained until his death. Students considered him an ideal lecturer, not only because of his clear, orderly presentation, but also because he was a good and trusted friend to them. Many confided in him regularly, and he became to them a kind of spiritual director. His deep devotion was an inspiration to those around him. Although he was active in numerous committees, in the Ecumenical movement, and in the Student Christian Movement, and though he traveled widely lecturing, he did not achieve the prominence attained by many of the other preachers in this volume; his greatness is reflected, not in the honors paid him, but by the high esteem in which he was held by those who knew him. He was a first-rate theologian who produced the important book, *God Was in Christ;* yet even more important was that he was a man who embodied his theology, and who was always concerned that his theology would preach. It did, and with simplicity and effectiveness.

"All Saints and All Sinners" was preached to St. Andrew's University in the university chapel on an All Saints' Day; several years later, and on the Eve of All Saints', he joined the vast invisible company of them.

# All Saints and All Sinners*

*And he turned to the woman, and said unto Simon, Seest thou this woman?*
LUKE 7:44

Today is the Festival of All Saints, and you may wonder what connection my text has with it. But I hope you will see before I have finished.

The Catholic tradition has its Calendar of Saints, but the churches of the Reformation have never made so much of that. Indeed it is sometimes maintained that Protestantism recognizes no saints in that special sense; not because it does not honor sanctity, but rather because it has rediscovered what sainthood meant in the New Testament. Who are "the saints" in the New Testament? They are not a spiritual elite —that is not how the word is used. The saints were the whole body of Christians; all Christ's people are "called to be saints." But that did not mean that all Christians are regarded as having reached a sinless perfection. In that sense there are no saints in the New Testament, for even the best of Christians on earth are far from perfect. The only saints in the New Testament are forgiven sinners, always ready to acknowledge that they are utterly dependent on the mercy and grace of God.

And now let us look at this story from St. Luke's Gospel.

There are three main figures in this domestic scene: Simon the Pharisee, who was host; Jesus the rabbi, who was guest; and the fallen woman, who was uninvited. It was her presence that started the conversation. Jesus says to the Pharisee: "Do you see this woman?" But what strikes me as I read the words is that Jesus and his host were not really seeing the same woman, because they were looking at her with such different eyes. The Pharisee saw nothing but her shame, her disreputableness, the mess she had made of her life. But Jesus saw something more: he saw the woman whom God had created, the woman that God had intended her to be, yes, and even the woman that by God's grace she might yet become. They were seeing different things as they looked: Simon the Pharisee and Jesus the friend of sinners. What do we see when we look at someone who seems to have made a mess of his life?

1. Sometimes we just see the wretched fellow as he is, in all his shame and failure, and our hearts reject him, without imagination or pity. You meet a drunken man staggering home on a Saturday night, with a mouth as foul as his hands; or you encounter an unkempt, unshaven tramp who accosts you with the unmistakable whining voice. And you look at the man (or woman) with a cold virtuous disapproval, a kind of protective self-righteousness which makes a safe hedge between you and him. He is undeserving, he has made his bed and must lie on it. And as you look at him, there is something complacent and merciless in your attitude. Isn't there? Aren't we all sometimes like that?

If so, then we can understand how that Pharisee felt. He was so like us—especially like those of us who take our religion seriously. He was very much in earnest. He was sure that he was right. It was, as it were, across a gulf that he looked at this woman. She was disreputable, she was known in the town to be a fallen woman. St. Luke makes it plain in the telling of the story that the Pharisee was genuinely surprised and shocked at Jesus letting the woman speak to him or touch his feet. He thought that surely Jesus didn't know. It was not the only time a Pharisee was shocked at Jesus. They couldn't understand his interest in such disreputable outsiders. And it was just because they were so earnest and righteous that they were so surprised. That is exactly how it was with this Pharisee in the story. He had a neat and tidy mind. In his mind all humanity were divided into two classes, the good people (of whom he was one) and the bad people. He had no use at all for the bad people, no interest in them. That woman was one of the bad people. And that was an end of it. He looked at the woman, and he said to himself, "She is a sinner," and he had nothing more to say. And so often you and I are like that.

2. But sometimes, if our hearts are at all pitiful or imaginative, we see, for a moment, something more. We see the sinner as he or she might have been. And that is more like the spirit of Jesus.

We know enough about Jesus to assure us that when he looked upon that woman, or any woman like her, he saw her as one who had been created to be a daughter of God. Perhaps his imagination travelled back through the years to a pure, happy Galilean home, and in it a cradle, and in the cradle a child—the child that this woman had once been, an innocent babe, a gift of God to this world. And then perhaps in his fancy he saw children playing in the street of a Galilean village, and among them the girl that this woman had been, playing happily among her companions, with the simplicity of nature which Jesus seems to have found, and delighted to find, in children. That was what the woman had been. If only her girlhood had been soundly guided and moulded in the love of what is good, how differently things might have turned out! But somebody led her astray (and Jesus would say: Woe be to that person!). And so the girl grew up into this ruined and disreputable woman, the girl who might have grown into a good happy wife and mother, whose children would rise up and call her blessed. That was what might have been. And it would be so like Jesus to think of that.

If we had more of his spirit, we would look on life's failures with more imagination, more compassion. And perhaps instead of building a protective wall between ourselves and the sinner, we would begin to tell ourselves that there isn't so very much difference between us. We might have been worse than he, if we had grown up in his surroundings; and if he had had our opportunities, he might have been a better man than we have ever been. Perhaps he even is!

You remember what has so often been told of Bradford, the English preacher-martyr of the sixteenth century. Once when he was preaching in the open air, a condemned criminal was led past him on his way to the gallows. Bradford stopped in his preaching and pointed and said: "There but for the grace of God, goes John Bradford."

When you look on one of life's tragic failures, do you ever tell yourself humbly that, but for the grace of God, it might have been you? And do you ever think also, with compassion, of what that sinner might have been, by God's grace—as I am sure Jesus did when he said, "Seest thou this woman?"

3. But, there is yet another thing Jesus saw when he looked on this woman, and this is by far the most important of all. He saw what she could still become, by the grace of God.

In the whole story of the ministry of Jesus, is there anything more extraordinary than the way in which he went to the most unlikely looking people, people who had made a mess of their lives, and spoke to them with a kind of supernatural hopefulness, about what they could yet become? He thought not just of what they had once been in the innocence of childhood, and what they might have been if they had not gone wrong. How falsely sentimental that can become, that dwelling on the pathos of the "might-have-been," if there is nothing more. But with Jesus there was more. He looked at those people with the indefatigable faith that they could yet be made into sons and daughters of God.

He looked at Zacchaeus, whom everybody despised, and he made up his mind that it could be done. So he stopped on the road, and called to Zacchaeus to come down from the tree and take him to his house. And salvation came to the man's house that day. How often Jesus did that kind of thing! He would say to an unpromising sinner: "Your sins are forgiven; go and sin no more." To the astonishment of the Pharisee, he says to this woman: "Your sins are forgiven, your faith has saved you; go in peace." And do you see how at the end of the story the Pharisee and the sinful woman seem to have changed place with each other unawares? The Pharisee is righteous and content, but it is not he that has the makings of sainthood. Jesus is far more hopeful about the woman, because into her life there have come the great realities of repentance and forgiveness, and that is the only way to sainthood, the only kind of sainthood there is in the Church of Christ.

That kind of thing is all over the Gospel story. And one extraordinary result of this is that throughout the rest of the New Testament the word "sinner" is used in a different way altogether. The sinners now are not a class apart, a bunch of disreputable outsiders. "Sinner" now means everybody, at least every Christian, every true member of the Christian Church, because that is what this new community is. The Church of Christ is not a society of righteous people who have a good right to be there, but a community of forgiven sinners. These are the saints of the New Testament. Calvin points out beautifully in one place how in the Creed the communion of saints is followed immediately by the forgiveness of sins. "I believe in the holy Catholic Church, the communion of saints, the forgiveness of sins."

And now at length we are no longer talking of other people, whether saints or sinners. Now we are talking of ourselves. You and I, my friends, are called to be saints in that sense—called into a life in which we every day confess our sins, and receive forgiveness, and accept the grace of a new beginning, and so, as the days go by, become more like the men and women God meant us to be.

So the Festival of All Saints becomes the festival of all sinners—all sinners who are willing to cast themselves on the grace and mercy of God. And he will "make them to be numbered with his saints in glory everlasting."

# WILLIAM RALPH INGE (1860–1954)

"The gloomy Dean" of St. Paul's was born in Yorkshire, raised in a devout "tractarian" milieu, and had great success as a student at Cambridge. For a short time a Fellow at Oxford, he was ordained a priest in the Church of England and subsequently, in his middle thirties, became a vicar. From his youth he had suffered from melancholy and fits of depression, but it is reported that these were dispelled by his happy marriage. He soon became well-known for his Bampton Lectures on mysticism, which defended it as the indestructible core of religious experience and the foundation upon which theology is built. Later he also became known as a keen student of Plotinus when he delivered the Gifford Lectures on the philosophy of Plotinus. From 1911 to 1934, he was Dean of the Anglican Cathedral of St. Paul's, London; especially great was his contribution of preaching.

The sermon given in this book represents nearly the entire text of the original. It was the next to last sermon he preached as Dean; it sets forth his firm Christian hope for the fulfillment of his faith and is therefore quite appropriate for Advent, although it was originally preached in September. Dean Inge's sermons were literary events which nevertheless spoke to the situations of his hearers; it was not only his pure style but also his keen grasp of the English mind which made him one of the best known clergymen of his generation. He never let his people forget that the Christian religion is a way of the cross, a dying that is the road to real living; he gave them no easy creed, but appealed to the heroic in men and women, yet assuring them of grace and, as in this sermon, of "those things which cannot be shaken."

# The Things That Remain*

*And this word, Yet once more, signifieth the removing of these things that are shaken, as of things that are made, that those things which cannot be shaken may remain.* HEBREWS 12:27

In my last two sermons from this puplit I propose to base my thoughts on my favorite book of the New Testament, the Epistle to the Hebrews. This writer always seems to speak to my condition, as the Quakers say, and not to mine only, but to the needs, the hopes and fears, the faith and the doubt of a generation which is going through trials not very unlike those which troubled the minds of the first readers of this epistle.

I shall therefore be speaking from my heart in trying to draw out some of the thoughts of this unknown but inspired writer.

The epistle is written with a purpose, and there can be no doubt about the circumstances which called it forth. The first generation of Christians had pinned their faith to the expected return of Christ in glory as the promised Messiah. They spoke of the return as the "kingdom of God." They saluted one another with the Aramaic words, "Maran-atha" ("Come, O Lord").

* From *The Things That Remain* (New York: Harper & Brothers, 1958; published in Great Britain under the title *Goodness and Truth* [London: A. R. Mowbray & Co., 1958]). Copyright © 1958 by A. R. Mowbray & Co. Used by permission of the publishers.

But as the years passed and the contemporaries of the apostle died off, a great disappointment fell upon the Church. Men began to ask, "Where is the promise of his coming?" The predictions on which they relied spoke so clearly of an early date that their credit could not be saved by relegating them to a dim and distant future. The writer takes up his pen mainly to deal with this disappointment, and he deals with it, not by whittling down the discredited prophecy, nor by empty commonplaces, but by giving us a profound and permanently valuable discussion of what Christian faith and hope really mean. He has done for faith and hope what St. Paul, in I Corinthians 13, has done for love; he has shown us what the essence of faith and hope is, and how the lower and imperfect form of them must be spiritualized and transmuted. He thus speaks of and overcomes not only the special difficulties which trouble the minds of his own contemporaries, but all similar trials of faith, all similar temptations to lose hope, which at other times and in other circumstances drive Christians to doubt God's providence and mistrust his promises.

But, further, the author writes as a Jew of the dispersion who is also a Platonist. The Jews were always the people of the promise, who lived in faith and hope. History had a meaning for them which it had never had for the Greeks. God reveals himself in history; history is the judgment of the world. This sense of the hand of God in history never forsook them, though they were often perplexed. Against hope they believed in hope. There were few nations prepared so much to suffer, and certainly their hopefulness has been justified, for the Jews have stood by the graves of all their oppressors in turn.

In this epistle we have one of the earliest attempts at the philosophy of history. It combines the Jewish belief in a divine education of mankind by means of historical events, and the Greek belief that all happenings in time and place are types and shadows of the eternal verities which abide for ever, pure and unchanged, in the mind and counsels of God. And this combination is profoundly Christian. For the student of thought it is one of the greatest contributions which Christianity made to the religious view of the world. We might call it the sacramental doctrine of history. The hand of Providence can be traced in history. God's purposes are being carried out, worked out in the rise and fall of nations. And yet—and yet—earth is but the shadow of heaven, and we who are citizens of the heavenly country are but strangers and pilgrims on the earth.

Those are two great truths which we must try to hold together, and it is because it is so hard to see how they are related to each other that we need the faith and hope of which so much is said in this epistle.

Like all great works, this epistle gives us universal truths under particular forms, and what we have to do is to understand the universal truths under the particular forms, and then to particularize them again under other forms to suit our need. The universal truth, the philosophy, is made clear in the epistle itself, and our particular needs are not so very unlike the problems of those for whom it was written. For we, like them, have had a great disappointment. We, like them, have had our promise of a golden age, a time of universal peace and happiness and prosperity, as some of us thought, in the near future. We had made a religion of our belief in progress, as the first Christians made a religion of their expectation that God would restore again the kingdom to Israel. Ours was a baseless dream like the other, but because we had made a kind of religion of it, our disappointment has shaken our faith. God's world no longer seems so desirable a place to live in, and so we, too, cry impatiently, "Where is the promise of his coming?"

To us, as to the Christians of A.D. 95, the inspired writer says, "Come, let us thrash out this difficulty together. You say you are losing faith and losing hope. You cannot see the hand of God in what is going on. Well, we will not talk about the destruction of the temple and the persecution of the Christians. We will not talk about revolutions, dictators, and unemployment. We will go deeper, and consider what are the great lessons of past history and what Christian faith and hope mean."

And how does he set about it? Look at the opening verses of the first chapter—the Epistle for Christmas Day—and note how eagerly he plunges into the subject, without a word of preface. Revelation has been gradual, historical, progressive, given through many channels. It has culminated in the incarnation of the Son, who was the instrument of creation, upholding, or, rather, carrying forward all things by the word of his power, as well as the Heir of all things. Then, attention is concentrated on the incarnation and the redemption of mankind, on Christ as man, and men as one with Christ are made lower than the angels that they may rise higher than they. Man can die with Christ, and rise again with Christ. The greater pain and the greater gain are his. The badge of his weakness is the secret of his power. For what, after all, is physical death?

> The great globe itself,
> Yea, all which it inherits, shall dissolve,
> And, like this insubstantial pageant faded,
> Leave not a wrack behind.

That is what the Bible also says, and our astronomers too. Only that shall abide which is the meaning and the purpose of God for men, that from which they came, and for which they came into the world. All else, all that is accidental, or meaningless, or frustrated in them shall be folded up as a garment. So Goethe speaks of the universe as a living garment of God. "But thou art the same, and thy years shall not fail." "Nothing that really is shall ever perish," so spoke the great thinker of the third century, "but that which passes before our eyes only seems to exist; it has no permanence, and therefore no reality."

Then the writer of the epistle passes on, in the second chapter, to a doctrine which he could not have found in Plato. "It became him through whom are all things to make the Captain of our salvation perfect through suffering." It became him—it was an act consonant with the character of the Father and Creator of all things, an act worthy of him who sent his co-equal Son into the world to redeem mankind through suffering. The love that condescends, the love that suffers is the divine love, and Christ is not ashamed to call us brethren. "He that sanctifieth and they that are sanctified are all of one." What Christ does for us he also does in us. His redeeming death is not only something that he must suffer, it is something that we must die. We have a spiritual death to die as well as a spiritual life to live. So only may Christ in us through death destroy him that hath the power of death. As a German mystic says, "The Cross of Golgotha cannot rescue thee from the evil one unless it be set up in thine own heart."

"Him that hath the power of death." There is, then, a death unto death, as well as a death unto life. There is a sin unto death. Personality is a possibility of opposites. There is for each of us a Prince of death as well as a Prince of life. That is why our religion must be a religion of fear as well as of love and hope. The author of this epistle will never let us forget that. We are to serve God acceptably with reverence and godly fear. Christ suffered for sin. He suffered to remove that which lies between us and our true life, which is Christ himself. "He suffered," says the author, "the contradiction of sinners against themselves"—not "against himself," as in our version. It is sin and separation and inner discredit from which we wish to be saved. He, our merciful and faithful High Priest, purifies us and reconciles us to God. We are purified through being first reconciled, and reconciled through our oneness with him who died for us. In Christ this is fact; in us it is faith. We know what we are and what we wish to be, but all that infinite distance between is bridged by faith and hope, by our earnest will and desire. "We are as holy as we truly wish to be holy," says an old writer. God does not impute to us by a legal fiction what we have not. He imparts to us what he gives us grace to desire earnestly.

"Today, if ye will hear his voice, harden not your hearts." So the author of the epistle quotes the psalm very familiar to us. Nothing hardens the heart like a sense of being unjustly treated. That sense is hardening the hearts of millions today, and perhaps, if we do not put away this bitterness from us, tomorrow it may be too late. The Hebrews, our author says, must be very particular. They were impatient, faithless, disobedient. Let us beware lest we fall into the same condemnation.

Why are we bitter? Why are we faithless? If the divine life lived on earth must be and was a life of suffering crowned with victory, so that even he, the sinless one, must be made perfect through suffering, shall not we count it a privilege if we are asked to bear a little more than our share of the world's burden for his Body's sake, the Church?

The doctrine of the Cross lies on the very heart of Christianity. But the doctrine of the offence of the Cross—for an offence it must always be to the majority—what does it mean? Not only that, as Plato says, we cannot get rid of sin without pain—not only that, but, as a German proverb says, "Without sorrows no one is ennobled, and to suffer for others is a divine thing." Not only is it an essential part of the discipline of life for the erring and the weak, but even more, it is part of the royal prerogative of life for the strong, those whom the Captain of our salvation calls to take their places in the forefront of the battle.

If we give this teaching its full weight it will alter our attitude completely towards the sorrow and pain of this world. It may be that our generation is called in a special degree to fill up that which is lacking in the afflictions of Christ—I am quoting, as you remember, a very bold phrase from St. Paul. If so, our age, just because it is an age of disillusionment and disappointment, and suffering, may be really an age of progress.

# JOHN DONNE (1573–1631)

One of the greatest poets of seventeenth-century England was John Donne; he was also one of the greatest preachers of that era. He was raised a Roman Catholic and studied both at Oxford and at Cambridge. In 1592, he began to study law at Lincoln's Inn; soon thereafter he became a member of the Church of England. He led a reckless and worldly youth; in 1601, he was secretly married, which resulted in the loss of his employment. Several years of poverty followed, during which time he privately pursued theological studies; later he produced polemical writings against Roman Catholicism, which helped to bring him royal and ecclesiastical respect. He was encouraged to take Holy Orders, but he refused on the grounds that he was unworthy; furthermore he was still hoping for some appointment in the court. However, after a long struggle with his conscience he was ordained to the priesthood in 1615 and became chaplain to King James I. Though much had been expected of him, his preaching at the court exceeded all expectations. After the tragic death of his wife in 1617, his religious fervor increased; now unquestionably his keen mind and intense passions were dedicated to "those things which are above." His piety and ascetic life were exemplary.

In 1621, John Donne became Dean of St. Paul's, London, where his hour-long sermons attracted huge crowds that were frequently enthralled by his preaching. Though many of his sermons were very complicated and were often filled with exaggerated allegorization of the Scriptures and tortuous metaphors which he enthusiastically modeled upon some of the preaching of the early Church Fathers, and though in numerous sermons he argues over trivial textual and theological matters and sometimes shows morbid fascination in the effects of death and decomposition, there are also moments when his genius for preaching which could reach the hearts of men bursts forth brilliantly. He was a preacher who spoke earnestly and shared with his hearers his doubts and fears, his joys and hopes, and his deep faith. He spoke eloquently on the great Christian themes, particularly on the dreadfulness of sin and death and the omnipotence of God. No passages of his sermons excel his portrayal of the justice and joys of heaven, which mark the fulfillment of life. Two selected passages from two different sermons combine to form this unit which sets forth a traditional Advent theme and provides a fitting conclusion to this book.

# The Justice and the Joy of Heaven*

*Justice:* As it is said of old cosmographers, that when they had said all that they knew of a country and yet much more was to be said, they said that the rest of those countries were possessed with giants or witches or spirits or wild beasts, so that they could pierce no farther into that country; so when we have travelled as far as we can with safety, that is, as far as ancient or modern expositors lead us in the discovery of these new heavens and new earth, yet we must say at last that it is a country inhabited with angels and archangels, with cherubim and seraphim, and that we can look no farther into it with these eyes. Where it is locally, we inquire not; we rest in this, that it is the habitation prepared for the blessed saints of God; heavens where the moon is more glorious than our sun, and the sun as glorious as he that made it; for it is he himself, the Son of God, the sun of glory. A new earth, where all their waters are milk and all their milk, honey; where all their grass is corn, and all their corn, manna; where all their soil, all their clods of earth are gold, and all their gold of innumerable carats; where all their minutes are ages, and all their ages, eternity; where every thing is every minute, in the highest exaltation, as good as it can be, and yet super-exalted and infinitely multiplied by every minute's addition; every minute infinitely better than ever it was before. Of these new heavens and this new earth we must say at last that we can

---

* From Logan Pearsall Smith (ed.), *Donne's Sermons: Selected Passages* (Oxford: The Clarendon Press, 1919). Used by permission of the publisher.

say nothing; for "the eye of man hath not seen, or ear heard, nor heart conceived the state of this place." We limit and determine our consideration with that horizon with which the Holy Ghost hath limited us, that it is that new heaven and new earth, "wherein dwelleth righteousness."

Here then the Holy Ghost intends the same new heavens and new earth which he does in the Apocalypse, and describes there by another name the new Jerusalem. But here the Holy Ghost does not proceed, as there, to enamor us of the place by a promise of improvement of those things which we have and love here, but by a promise of that which here we have not at all. There and elsewhere the Holy Ghost applies himself to the natural affections of men. To those that are affected with riches, he says that that new city shall be all of gold and in the foundations all manner of precious stones. To those that are affected with beauty, he promises an everlasting association with that beautiful couple, that fair pair, which spend their time in that protestation: "Behold, thou art fair, my beloved," says he, and then she replies, "Behold thou art fair, too," noting that mutual complacency between Christ and his Church there. To those which delight in music he promises continual singing, and every minute a new song. To those whose thoughts are exercised upon honor and titles, civil and ecclesiastical, he promises priesthood, and if that be not honor enough, a royal priesthood. And to those who look after military honor, triumph after their victory in the militant Church. And to those that are carried with sumptuous and magnificent feasts, a marriage supper of the Lamb, wherein not only all the rarities of the whole world but the whole world itself shall be served; the whole world shall be brought to that fire and served at that table. But here the Holy Ghost proceeds not that way, by improvement of things which we have and love here: riches or beauty or music or honor or feasts, but by an everlasting possession of that which we hunger and thirst and pant after here and cannot compass, that is, justice and righteousness; for both these we want here and shall have both for ever in these new heavens and new earth.

What would a worn and macerated suitor, oppressed by the bribery of the rich or by the might of a potent adversary, give or do or suffer that he might have justice? What would a dejected spirit, a disconsolate soul, oppressed with the weight of heavy and habitual sin, that stands naked in a frosty winter of desperation and cannot compass one fig leaf, one color, one excuse for any circumstance of any sin, give for the garment of righteousness? Here there is none that does right, none that executes justice, not for justice' sake. He that does justice, does it not at first; and Christ does not thank that judge, that did justice upon the woman's importunity. Justice is no justice, that is done for fear of an appeal or a commission. There may be found, that may do justice at first; at their first entrance into a place, to make good impressions, to establish good opinions, they may do some acts of justice; but after, either an uxoriousness towards the wife or a solicitude for children or a facility towards servants or a vastness of expense quenches and overcomes the love of justice in them; in most it is not, and it dwells not in any. In our new heavens and new earth dwelleth justice. And that's my comfort: that when I come thither, I shall have justice at God's hands.

*Joy:* If you look upon this world in a map, you find two hemispheres, two half worlds. If you crush heaven into a map, you may find two hemispheres, too, two half heavens; half will be joy and half will be glory; for in these two, the joy of heaven and the glory of heaven, is all heaven often represented unto us. And as of those two hemispheres of the world, the first hath been known long before, but the other, that of America, which is the richer treasure, God reserved for later discoveries. So though he reserve that hemisphere of heaven, which is the glory thereof, to the resurrection, yet the other hemisphere, the joy of heaven, God opens to our discovery and delivers for our habitation even whilst we dwell in this world. As God hath cast upon the unrepentant sinner two deaths, a temporal and a spiritual death, so hath he breathed into us two lives. Though our natural life were no life, but rather a continual dying, yet we have two lives besides that, an eternal life reserved for heaven, but yet a heavenly life, too, a spiritual life, even in this world. And as God doth thus inflict two deaths and infuse two lives, so doth he also pass two judgments upon man, or rather repeats the same judgment twice. For, that which Christ shall say to thy soul then at the last judgment: "Enter into thy master's joy," he says to thy conscience now: "Enter into thy master's joy." The everlastingness of the joy is the blessedness of the next life, but the entering is afforded here.

Howling is the noise of hell, singing the voice of heaven; sadness the damp of hell, rejoicing the serenity of heaven. And he that hath not this joy here lacks one of the best pieces of his evidence for the joys of heaven, and hath neglected or refused that earnest by which God uses to bind his bargain, that true joy in this world shall flow into the joy of heaven, as a river flows into the sea. This joy shall not be put out in death and a new joy kindled in me in heaven; but as my soul shall not go towards heaven, but go by heaven to heaven, to the heaven of heavens (for all the way to heaven is heaven), so the true joy of a good soul in this world is the very joy of heaven; and we go thither, not that being without joy, we might have joy infused into us, but that as Christ says, "Our joy might be full," perfected, sealed with an everlastingness; for as he promises that no man shall take our joy from us, so neither shall death itself take it away, nor so much as interrupt it or discontinue it; but as in the face of death, when he lays hold upon me, and in the face of the Devil, when he attempts me, I shall see the face of God (for, every thing shall be a glass, to reflect God upon me); so in the agonies of death, in the anguish of that dissolution, in the sorrows of valediction, in the irreversibleness of that transmigration, I shall have a joy which shall no more evaporate, a joy that shall pass up and put on a more glorious garment above, and be joy superinvested in glory. Amen.

I — The Fact
   A — The Means —
   B — The Meaning

}  Four Conditions to be met to enjoy new life in Christ

I — The New Life in Christ Must be preceded by Death

II — The new life in Christ Must be preceded by burial

III — The new life in Christ Must be preceded by resurrection

IV — The new life in Christ Must Manifest itself by a duplication of His life —

   a — Must increase in wisdom in favor with God & Man

   b — Must exercise itself in righteousness + holiness

   c — Must manifest itself in

*Format by Anne Hallowell*
*Set in Linotype Granjon*
*Composed by York Composition Co., Inc.*
*Printed and bound by The Haddon Craftsmen, Inc.*
HARPER & ROW, PUBLISHERS, INCORPORATED

The Holy Spirit in Conversion —
+ Contact of H. S. with Non Christian —

II -

III -

i